Achieving Quality Education for All

EDUCATION IN THE ASIA-PACIFIC REGION: ISSUES, CONCERNS AND PROSPECTS

Volume 20

For further volumes:
http://www.springer.com/series/5888

Phillip Hughes

Editor

Achieving Quality Education for All

Perspectives from the Asia-Pacific
Region and Beyond

 Springer

Editor
Phillip Hughes
Australian National University
Canberra, Australia

ISBN 978-94-007-5293-1   ISBN 978-94-007-5294-8 (eBook)
DOI 10.1007/978-94-007-5294-8
Springer Dordrecht Heidelberg New York London

Library of Congress Control Number: 2012951668

Printed on acid-free paper

Springer is part of Springer Science+Business Media (www.springer.com)

Foreword: Let a Hundred Flowers Blossom

The test of the morality of a society is what it does for its children.– Dietrich Bonhoeffer

It is hard to remember a time when education was not really important to me. I have written elsewhere in detail about the three teachers who inspired me and significantly shaped the course of my life. Alison Smith taught me for six years of primary school, in a model small school where she taught 36 pupils – six in each of six years. She knew me intimately; she knew exactly what I was capable of and never accepted anything but my best. Her words to me as a 10-year-old "*Is that your best, Phil?*" still ring in my ears and motivate me.

Doris Brown, my high school English teacher, brought the classics alive for me and related their themes to contemporary life in the lead up to and during the Second World War. Finally, when I went as a Rhodes Scholar to Oxford, CS Lewis was the academic, prolific author and Christian apologist whose classes altered my direction in life. I audited his lectures on Milton, for one term. His capacity to communicate with his listeners and bring major issues to life convinced me that I should become a teacher rather than the nuclear physicist I had intended to be.

I later came to realise that not everyone enjoyed the same opportunities to access quality education that I had. A broadening sequence opened my eyes to the inequities of education provision:

- Being part of a three-government Mission on Higher Education to find ways to provide higher education to 12 island countries of the South Pacific – countries scattered across 33 million square kilometres of ocean, an area more than three times the size of Europe with a total land mass equal to Denmark, no large islands and a total population of 1.3 million varying from Tokelau with 1600 to Fiji with 800,000. Isolation and lack of resources meant that few students were able to progress past secondary school, impacting on the countries' ability to train their own professionals and affecting the capacity of their schools to provide the educated people needed. The final solution was to establish the University of the South Pacific located in Fiji to serve all 12 countries.

- In the early 1970s at the University of Canberra, realising that many mature women of substantial ability lacked the formal entry requirements for our teacher education course. They were in competition with bright young candidates from schools who had high entrance scores but lacked experience. I had to advocate strongly to the Academic Board for a quota of entry for them. Many of them went on to have highly successful careers in education not only as classroom teachers but leaders in the profession.
- During the 1970s, spending time in Papua New Guinea to understand better the needs of the schools and their teachers and education leaders, in preparation for bringing some to train with us in Australia. The issues confronting them were not only the physical problems of a developing society but the myriad language groups.
- Around the same time, preparing teachers for indigenous students in remote communities in the Northern Territory of Australia. The small number of students in isolated locations combined with the indigenous people's itinerant lifestyle and lack of a written form of their language all posed enormous challenges for educators – and still do.
- Befriending refugees from Kosovo and hearing their stories of how civil war disrupted their schooling and how lack of formal qualifications limits their employment opportunities.
- In 2001, working in the Middle East and dealing with the fact that more than half the students' time in school was taken up by Islamic studies and the implications of that for time spent on the rest of the curriculum. The girls, even in relatively enlightened Islamic countries, were taught apart from the boys with an even more reduced curriculum, preparing them to be wives and mothers and little else. Interestingly, the elite in those countries, even the education leaders, often sent their children, including their daughters, abroad to Western countries for a broad, balanced education.
- When the OECD published the results of its first PISA study in 2000, realising that while Australia's best students were performing as well as the best in the world, a long tail of underachieving students indicated that equity was a big issue for Australian educators.
- Reading a report from the Business Council of Australia which said that around 35,000 students leave Australian schools every year without the education foundation for employment, further education or skills and knowledge to fully engage in our society. We know that such students are overrepresented in jail, on the dole and in personal and domestic crises of various kinds.

Over the years, I have done what I could to bring these issues and possible remediation to the attention of anyone who would listen. Now that my time is limited, I want one last shot at pleading the case for all those young people across the world who deserve the chance of a high-quality education that will give them the best chance of reaching their full potential. My voice will soon be silent, but I hope all who read this book will be inspired to take up the challenge of doing whatever they can to make sure every child and young person has the chance to learn and take their place in civil society. Thank you to all who have contributed to this book – I could never have done this without you. If Michael Jones, at 24 years of age, the youngest contributor to this book, is representative of his generation, I am very hopeful for the future.

21st June 2012   Phillip Hughes

Contents

Introduction: Kelli Hughes

On February 26, 2011, I sent this email to about 50 colleagues with whom my husband, Phillip Hughes, had worked in a whole range of education-related activities during a lifetime in the field of education.

On January 28, after a couple of weeks of feeling unwell, my husband, Phil, was diagnosed with cancer of the bile duct. Just 2 weeks later we were told that it was malignant. Phil along with his family has considered the full range of possible interventions and he has decided only to accept palliative care. We are currently in St George Private Hospital, Sydney and Phil wants to publish a book in the months he has left – he is keen to make a final contribution towards what he sees as a major issue in education. I am contacting you as one of a number of people he would like to contribute to that book.

This is the idea. As the seventh child of a working class family from a tiny town in Tasmania, Australia, an effective education in Tasmania and later Oxford, provided opportunities for Phil that most children from his background would never dream of. You will know that he has been passionate about an effective education for all, for the whole of his adult life. So Phil is inviting you to write a concise paper, up to around 2,000 words, expressing your own views as to what you think is necessary to provide an effective, relevant, high quality education for all children. What, for example, should be the priorities and best approaches to adopt to achieve such an education. Alternatively, you might want to write about valuable ways that already exist to provide high quality and effective education for all but are not being fully utilised; or else your ideas about future directions and activities to reach that goal.

The next step is for you to tell me whether or not you will be able to write a piece along the lines suggested and confirm the date when it would be available.

Within an hour or two, emails, phone calls and text messages came bouncing back – the first from Paris. Phil was elated. Not only were people responding to his request but they were also reminiscing about their experiences with Phil and encouraging him during a really tough time of life. Here are just a few.

Having known what these times are like, my thoughts and best wishes go out to you both. Yes, I would be touched and honoured to make a contribution. Please let Phil know of my admiration for his never failing advocacy for education. He will be living the profession's moral purpose for as long as he draws breath, I know.

It goes without saying that I would be honoured and delighted to contribute to Phil's last project. He is an educator and academic I have always admired and a person of great goodness and grace. I am not surprised that he and the family have decided to approach his final journey as one of palliative treatment, and I'm not surprised that he wishes to be productive to the end!

I would be very pleased to write something for inclusion in the book. In fact, there's something I've been meaning to write for a while, but haven't had a reason to start. I would also like to do this for Phil whom I admire so very much. Thanks for inviting me to be part of the project and give Phil my best wishes. You are both in my thoughts and prayers.

Phil has been very kind to me and my career was very much shaped by his vision and philosophy when he supervised my doctoral thesis at the University of Tasmania. He always had time for me to guide me in the right direction.

Around 40 colleagues agreed to write a paper for this book, and most of them were able to deliver, often in spite of the heavy workloads they were already carrying.

Just a couple of weeks after inviting colleagues to contribute to Phil's book, he had his 85th birthday. Not only colleagues but many family members, friends and former students sent him greetings.

Under your leadership of the School of Teacher Education at that dynamic time the course of my professional life was forever changed for which I am most thankful and deeply appreciative. (A student from the University of Canberra in the 1970s while Phil was the head of School of Education)

If there is one impression that stands out in my experience it has been your general acceptance of people irrespective of race, achievement or status. You fostered the development of persons who wanted to serve their community with their particular gifts within a variety of equally important roles. (A staff member from the University of Tasmania where Phil was head of the School of Education during the 1980s)

I love his passion for education. But even more I love the fact that he truly values and respects the experiences of the children being educated. As a child, it is incredibly empowering to have someone truly value your perspective and to view you as the central agent in your own education. It certainly helped me to take control of my education and for that I will always be grateful. (A granddaughter who is about to submit her PhD)

It was typical of Phil that at a time when many others would have coiled up and shut the world out, he was eager to make one final contribution to the passion that absorbed much of the 85 years of his life – making quality education accessible to all. At the core of Phil's passion was the One whom he regarded as the greatest teacher of all, Jesus Christ, whose life and spirit were the example Phil sought to follow and who continued to sustain him during difficult days and nights.

My thanks go to all of those who have contributed to this book, but especially to Phil's colleague of many years and close friend Rupert Maclean who has made the publication of this possible. I must also thank family, friends and the host of doctors and nurses who made Phil's days enjoyable and as comfortable as possible.

Canberra   Kelli Hughes
June 2012

Achieving Quality Education for All: Perspectives from the Asia-Pacific Region and Beyond

Phillip Hughes (Editor)

Series Editors Introduction

This is an important book on an important subject. It is edited by one of Australia's most eminent and widely respected and influential educators, Professor Phillip Hughes. In editing this volume, Professor Hughes draws on his extensive experience, both within Australia and worldwide, with government education authorities, particularly in the Australian Capital Territory and in Tasmania, and with education for development agencies such as AusAID, UNESCO and UNICEF. I have written elsewhere in detail about the important contributions of Phil Hughes to education and schooling in Australia and internationally and refer interested readers to a book devoted to celebrating the work of Phil Hughes: Rupert Maclean. (Ed.), (2007), *Learning and Teaching for the Twenty-first Century*, Springer, Netherlands.

In essence, this book addresses the question: what role can education and schooling play in contributing to a more just, equitable and peaceful world, where there is sustainable economic and social development for all and poverty reduction? Although current action to achieve high-quality and relevant education for all, Education for Sustainable Development and the United Nations' Millennium Development Goals provide a useful foundation for action, the authors in this book clearly demonstrate that this is insufficient. They argue that it is also important to pay greater attention to devising concrete, action-orientated ways of promoting social justice and peace building, through means such as lifelong learning, skills development for employability, values/ethics education and high-quality, relevant educational research.

The authors of the chapters present powerful and coherent arguments concerning the importance of strengthening the public sector in education, examine the vexed issue of how to promote quality in teaching and make equity work, scope progress achieved to date in international education movements such as Education for All and Education for Sustainable Development and examine the importance of educational research. In various ways, the contributors refer to the importance of adopting a holistic approach to learning. That is, while formal education, through institutions such as schools and colleges, is an important way in which individuals learn, there is an increasing need to stress the importance of 'lifelong learning'. Lifelong learning involves three types of learning: *formal learning*, which occurs within a teacher-student relationship, in an academic environment such as a school system; *nonformal* learning, which is organised learning that occurs outside the formal learning system, such as in a training workshop where people can learn by coming together with people of similar interests and exchanging viewpoints; and *informal learning,* which refers to the experience of day-to-day situations, such as learning from everyday life, from friends and from the mass media.

We believe that this book will reach a wide audience of education policymakers, researchers and practitioners who admire and respect the significant work of Phil Hughes in education. Sadly, Phil passed away towards the end of 2011, before the publication of this interesting and important volume. We would like to thank all of those who have contributed to bringing this project to fruition under what were very difficult circumstances due to the death of Professor Hughes. In particular, we thank Phil's wife, Kelli Hughes, and KWOK Sin Yan (Ada), research assistant in the Centre for Lifelong Learning Research and Development, the Hong Kong Institute of Education, without whose great efforts and care, this project would not have been completed in such a timely way.

Hong Kong   Rupert Maclean
Tokyo   Ryo Watanabe
7 June 2012

Part I
Prelude: The Public Sector in Education

The eight papers in this section present powerful and coherent arguments for the strengthening of the public sector in education. The context of their thinking is the recognition that education for all is not a distant hope but an achievable reality.

Geoff Masters emphasises the dangers of stereotyping, where students are assigned to low-achieving groups and, predictably, typically perform to match the stereotype. He makes an important point: *'there is a question as to whether emphasising group membership is counterproductive. A preoccupation with demographic distinctions may serve only to highlight existing differences and cement future expectations'*.

Denise Bradley points out sharply the inequity which is the basis of many education systems, making a powerful argument for social justice. As she points out, countries with such inequalities are perpetuating harmful and expensive divisions. *'All Australian schools receive some public funds but schools in the poorest and most socially deprived areas of our country, schools which educate the children most in need of a rich and nurturing educational experience, languish'*.

Don Anderson takes these arguments further, stressing the need for a more equitable approach to education. *'I see the divide between public and private schooling as the single greatest structural impediment to advancing the quality of education in Australia'*.

Deborah Meier has been one of the leading figures in the USA seeking major reform in schools. She founded a network of small public schools in East Harlem and later in Boston. The schools she has helped create serve predominantly low-income African-American and Latino students. She is a passionate advocate of an effective education for all, despite their background. *'At the very least, school should be a place where children are not treated as though they are data or numbers in someone else's policy war, or as only "future" members of society.' 'Each school community needs to think through what important achievements look and sound like—set their standards and defend them even as they revise and edit'*.

Michael Fullan, surely the epitome of the universal educator given his wide involvement with so many countries, draws a powerful conclusion. His role in his own country in achieving an effective education for all gives extra weight to his words. *'In all of this what we are learning is that you have to pay close attention to personalizing education experiences for students, valuing them as individuals, building the instructional capacity of teachers both individually, and especially collectively to enable them to work in professional learning communities, and to building connections with parents, communities and business'.*

Lyndsay Connors, one of Australia's most experienced observers of education, also sees the danger from a possible decline in the quality of public education: *'It would be tragic if the "democratic right to accessible, affordable, quality education" that is embodied in the concept of a socially representative, free and secular public school system were to be lightly brushed aside'.*

Malcolm Skilbeck and Helen Connell turn to the vital question of the content of the necessary education for all. *'A task on which we have barely begun is the extension of personal and citizenship education throughout the lifecycle. If lifelong learning for all is to rise above the level of a slogan, new policies, new structures, new personnel, new content, new approaches to teaching and learning, and new ways of financing the whole educational enterprise are called for'.*

Kerry Kennedy from his vantage point in Hong Kong appeals for education to achieve its potential in transforming life chances: *'But it is education that has the potential to move individuals into a different space from where they can see life in a new way and indeed can create a new life for themselves. Education, unlike other areas of social service, can be transformational; yet it is not so for everyone'.*

Chapter 1
The Power of Belief

Geoff N. Masters

'Nobody rises to low expectations'. **Calvin Lloyd**

This essay has been written to honour Professor Phillip Hughes, an extraordinary Australian and one of the most outstanding educational thinkers this country has produced. Through his unswerving belief in the capacity of education not only to transform individual lives, but also to create a more just and harmonious society, Phil has challenged all of us to set and pursue higher expectations. These include higher expectations of the school curriculum to develop capacities for reflection, curiosity and creative thinking as well as personal values; higher expectations for the equitable distribution of educational opportunities; and higher expectations of education's contribution to ameliorating global tensions and challenges. One of Phil's early teachers, Alison Smith, encouraged him to set high expectations by asking, 'Is it your best?' Throughout his career Phil has set exceptionally high expectations of himself while promoting self-belief in others. In his own words, 'for all of us as teachers, the final victory is to retain our faith in people, in their capacity to grow' Maclean (2007).

Success in most fields of endeavour depends on an ability to visualise success. It has long been known that elite athletes mentally rehearse each performance prior to its execution. Advances in neuroscience show why this may be so important: the neurological processes involved in visualising a performance are almost identical to those involved in the performance itself. Indeed, simply watching somebody else perform activates 'mirror' neurons in the observer paralleling neuronal activity in the performer Rizzolatti and Fabbri-Destro (2010). The ability to visualise success and an accompanying belief that success is possible appear to be prerequisites for most forms of human achievement.

G.N. Masters (✉)
Australian Council for Educational Research,
19 Prospect Hill Rd, Camberwell, VIC 3124, Australia
e-mail: ceo@acer.edu.au

P. Hughes (ed.), *Achieving Quality Education for All*, Education in the Asia-Pacific Region: Issues, Concerns and Prospects 20, DOI 10.1007/978-94-007-5294-8_1,
© Springer Science+Business Media Dordrecht 2013

It also is clear that the development of self-efficacy is strongly influenced by the attitudes and beliefs of others. In schools, high achievement tends to be correlated with high parental and cultural expectations. Parents, in particular, are powerful inculcators of values and aspirations. Highly influential teachers also are commonly described as individuals who communicate a 'belief' in their students and who build self-confidence through high expectations. However, just as some students live up to high expectations, so others live down to the low expectations held for them. In education, low expectations are the equivalent of bone pointing; all too often they become self-fulfilling prophecies.

Not surprisingly, students develop differing beliefs about their own abilities to learn. Some students appear to view ability as 'fixed' and something over which they have little control. Students who believe they have low fixed abilities tend to believe that effort will make no difference. Those who believe they have high abilities often underestimate the importance of effort. On the other hand, students with an 'incremental' view of ability have a deep belief that success is related to effort. Rather than interpreting past failures as indicators of a lack of ability, these students are more likely to explain failure in terms of a lack of effort Dweck (2000). Interestingly, research has identified cultural differences in these beliefs. East Asian students tend to have more incremental views of their abilities than students of European origin.

Given its importance to ongoing learning and achievement, few outcomes of schooling are more important than the development of a belief in one's own capacity to learn. Because teachers and schools are in powerful positions to shape this belief – both positively and negatively – vigilance is required to ensure that educational practices do not unintentionally communicate and institutionalise low expectations of some learners.

One way in which educational practices can institutionalise low expectations is by *treating excellence as a limited resource*. There is general acceptance in society that not everybody can excel. Not everybody can be an Olympic athlete, just as not everybody can be tall. Indeed, if to 'excel' means to stand out from the crowd, then by definition, only some can excel. By analogy, it is argued, not everybody can (or even should) achieve excellence in the learning of mathematics or languages or science. Excellence in school achievement is a scarce resource available to only a few.

It seems likely that this deeply seated belief is driven in part by notions of intelligence. Beginning with Francis Galton in the mid-nineteenth century, it became common to identify and label varying levels of human intelligence, with each level representing an IQ range and a percentage of the population under the normal (bell) curve. A small percentage of 'geniuses' were at one extreme, and small percentages of 'imbeciles' and 'idiots' were at the other. It was a small step from concluding that high intelligence was scarce to expecting excellence in school achievement also to be scarce.

One of the clearest illustrations of the rationing of excellence is the process known as 'grading on the curve'. Under this approach, the percentage of students achieving each available performance grade is predetermined. For example, a decision might be made ahead of time to award the top ten per cent of students an 'A' and the next 15 per cent of students a 'B', regardless of their absolute levels of achievement. This practice, common in some higher education institutions, is intended to counter the possibility of 'grade inflation' (i.e. an increasing percentage of students being awarded high grades with no accompanying increase in absolute levels of achievement). The rationing of top grades to fixed percentages of students sends a clear message that excellence in educational achievement is expected of only a few. There are many other, more subtle, ways in which educational institutions communicate the same message.

However, educational achievement is not predetermined in the way that attributes such as height are predetermined. Achievement is strongly influenced by the quality of teaching, parental support and expectations and student effort. Educational achievement also is not a competition with limited spoils for the winners. Just as levels of health, wealth and educational participation have increased in the general population over time, there is no reason why the percentage of students achieving excellence also should not increase. In reality, there appears to have been a decline in absolute levels of performance in subjects such as mathematics and science in Australia over the past two decades Brown (2009).

The possibility of significantly larger numbers of students achieving excellence is made clear in international studies such as the International Evaluation of Achievement's Trends in International Mathematics and Science Study (TIMSS) and the Organisation for Economic Cooperation and Development's Programme for International Student Assessment (PISA). In reading, mathematics and science, between 10 and 15% of Australian students perform at 'advanced' international levels. Under the belief that excellence is a scarce resource, this percentage of advanced performers may seem about right. However, in East Asian countries between 35 and 50% of students perform at the same 'advanced' levels.

A second way in which low expectations can be institutionalised in educational practice is by *placing ceilings on learning*. It is well known that students are more likely to learn successfully when engaged and motivated and when provided with learning opportunities appropriate to their current levels of achievement and learning needs. Students are less likely to learn when given work that is much too easy or much too difficult for them, meaning that 'differentiated' teaching is important when students are at widely varying levels of achievement. However, expectations are lowered for students when they are assigned to classes or streams that place a ceiling on what they are able to learn or how far they are able to progress. In an effort to provide 'relevant' learning experiences appropriate to students' abilities and interests, educational courses often protect participants from intellectual rigour and limit what they are able to learn.

For example, in mathematics – which often labours under the belief that it is inherently difficult, obscure and of limited relevance for many students – it is common to create easier streams for less able students. But these easier streams, with their focus on low-level, applied learning, often have low expectations of the quality and quantity of mathematics learning and deny students access to the essence and beauty of this subject. Recent growth in secondary school completion rates in Australia has been accompanied by increases in the numbers of students taking lower-level courses of this kind. Since the mid-1990s, the percentage of year 12 students taking elementary mathematics has grown by 30 per cent, while the percentages taking intermediate and advanced mathematics have declined by 22 and 27%, respectively Rubinstein (2009).

A third way in which low expectations can be institutionalised is through the *prejudging of students' capabilities based on their group membership*. When students are grouped according to demographic characteristics, it is clear that some student groups have higher average levels of achievement than others. For example, students living in rural and remote areas tend to have lower average achievement levels than students living in urban areas. Girls tend to outperform boys, particularly in language-rich subjects. Non-indigenous students outperform indigenous students, and students from high socioeconomic backgrounds outperform students from low socioeconomic backgrounds. In some cases, these gaps are the equivalent of two or more years of school. The problem arises when expectations of individuals are then lowered on the basis of the group/s to which they belong.

In educational practice, there is often a small step from observing a correlation – for example, between socioeconomic background and achievement – to treating this observation as an 'explanation'. Low socioeconomic status is regularly invoked as an explanation for low achievement, despite the fact that some students from low socioeconomic backgrounds can be found among the highest achievers in our schools and universities, and some students from high socioeconomic backgrounds can be found among our lowest achievers. And from 'explanation', it is another small step to 'expectation' and beyond that to 'excuse'. School principals who have led significant improvements in low socioeconomic areas often report that their first challenge was to confront low staff expectations. In these schools, teachers had come to expect low achievement on the basis of students' backgrounds.

And there are other, more subtle, ways in which observed correlations can lead to lowered expectations. For example, it is a small step from comparing schools with similar student intakes to concluding that students in a particular school are performing well 'given their socioeconomic backgrounds' or 'given the proportion of indigenous students in the school'. Conclusions of this kind border on what is sometimes referred to as the 'soft bigotry' of low expectations. Prejudging and 'prejudice' have identical etymological origins: both can be the result of ignoring individuality and assigning individuals the presumed characteristics of a group.

There is a long history in school education of observing differences in average group performances and then designing programmes and initiatives to address the needs of specific student groups (e.g. the needs of boys, indigenous students or students from low socioeconomic backgrounds). However, there is little evidence that the achievement gaps such programmes and initiatives were designed to address have closed significantly in recent decades. More generally, there is a question as to whether emphasising group membership is counterproductive. A preoccupation with demographic distinctions may serve only to highlight existing differences and cement future expectations.

A fourth way in which low expectations can be institutionalised is by *prejudging students' capabilities on the basis of their age or grade*. Schools continue to be organised on traditional lines with students grouped and taught in grades based on age. Under this 'assembly-line' model, students move in a lockstep fashion from 1 year to the next, with teachers at each stage delivering the curriculum for that grade Darling-Hammond (2004). This model has been strengthened in recent years with the development of explicit grade-based curricula with accompanying assessments to establish how much of the curriculum for their grade students have mastered. This practice is another example of the use of group membership to set expectations for student learning.

The reality in learning areas such as mathematics and reading is that, despite this lockstep model, students in the same grade currently vary in their achievement levels by as much as 5 or 6 years of school. As Dylan Wiliam has observed, in practice there is only a loose relationship between educational achievement and age Wiliam (2007). If teachers treat all students of the same age as equally ready for the same grade-based curriculum and teach to the middle of the grade, then some lower-achieving students are likely to be left behind. There is evidence that many lower-achieving students fall further behind with each year of school. At the same time, expectations are lowered for higher-achieving students when learning is limited to the completion of classwork targeted at the middle of the grade. It is not uncommon to hear of classes in which more able students, rather than being challenged and extended, are given 'free time' once they have completed set classwork.

In spite of limiting beliefs and practices of this kind, many teachers, school leaders and parents share powerful alternative beliefs about student learning. These include beliefs that every individual is capable of learning, with no natural limits on what most individuals can learn; that at any given time, students are at different points in their learning and may be progressing at different rates, but that all are capable of further progress if motivated and if provided with learning opportunities appropriate to their readiness and needs; that individual differences in ability to learn are readily compensated for by effective teaching; that starting points for teaching are best established individually rather than inferred from group membership; and that excellent, ongoing progress is a more appropriate expectation of every learner than the expectation that all students of the same age/grade will be at the same point in their learning at the same time. In situations where teachers, school leaders and parents share beliefs of this kind, expectations are raised and students perform beyond the limits imposed by the rationing of excellence, low-level courses that deny access to high achievement, reduced expectations of particular demographic groups and grade-based assembly lines.

References

Brown, G. (2009). *Review of education in mathematics, data science and quantitative disciplines.* Report to the Group of Eight Universities, Canberra, Australia.
Darling-Hammond, L. (2004). Standards, accountability, and school reform. *Teachers College Record, 106*(6), 1047–1085.
Dweck, C. S. (2000). *Self-theories: Their role in motivation, personality and development.* Philadelphia: Psychology Press.

Maclean, R. (2007). *Learning and teaching for the twenty-first century: Festschrift for Professor Phillip Hughes*. Bonn: Springer.

Rizzolatti, G., & Fabbri-Destro, M. (2010). Mirror neurons: From discovery to autism. *Experimental Brain Research, 200*((3–4), 223–237.

Rubinstein, H. (2009). *A National Strategy for Mathematical Sciences in Australia*. Report prepared in consultation with the Australian Council of Heads of Mathematical Sciences, Melbourne, Australia.

Wiliam, D. (2007). Once you know what they've learned, what do you do next? Designing curriculum and assessment for growth. In R. Lissitz (Ed.), *Assessing and modeling cognitive development in school*. Maple Grove, MN: JAM Press.

Chapter 2
If Wishes Were Horses...

Denise Bradley

Wishes must be tempered by reality. I could wax lyrical about the kind of schools I would like to see, but I must accept that the kind of schools I am likely to get will be profoundly influenced by the prosperity of my country, its social cohesion and its aspirations.

Australia is unprecedentedly wealthy but more profoundly unequal in the distribution of that wealth than at any time in the last 100 years. That, combined with a growing fear of outsiders and rapid changes in global circumstances, has left us with a fractured social consensus. Inevitably, this is having a great impact on every aspect of educational provision, in how we fund, organise and teach in schools.

Since the late nineteenth century, national governments have accepted that the state must provide funds to sustain universal compulsory education. In countries like ours over the last century, the period of compulsory attendance has increased, driven by the inexorable demands of the industrial and post-industrial economy for better educated workers. However, a series of political decisions have left us with a profoundly unequal set of arrangements to support universal compulsory education. All Australian schools receive some public funds, but schools in the poorest and most socially deprived areas of our country, schools which educate the children most in need of a rich and nurturing educational experience, languish.

In principle, it seems that no one argues against the proposition that we need enough resources going to each school to allow it to do what is necessary to ensure every child has the opportunity to succeed, whatever their social and economic circumstances. Certainly, I believe that the fundamental arrangements – the funding regime for compulsory schooling – are a major test of any society which claims to be a democracy. I believe our democracy fails on that test comprehensively at present.

D. Bradley (✉)
University of South Australia, 4407/12 Neild Avenue, Ruschcutters Bay,
NSW 2011, Australia
e-mail: denise.bradley@unisa.edu.au

P. Hughes (ed.), *Achieving Quality Education for All*, Education in the Asia-Pacific
Region: Issues, Concerns and Prospects 20, DOI 10.1007/978-94-007-5294-8_2,
© Springer Science+Business Media Dordrecht 2013

What is extraordinary is that this is happening despite the knowledge of everyone – politicians, educators and lobby groups – that, as never before, the education you gain and the qualifications you acquire will determine your future economic, social and health status. And yet, the opportunities the period of compulsory schooling now affords for the children of parents who have social and economic power are greater than at any time in our history. But for the children of those who are neither educated nor prosperous, both their educational opportunities and life chances are grim.

We now know that schooling reinforces and perpetuates poverty and disadvantage. Australia as a society seems less concerned about this than at any time I can remember. Our concerns are for those close to us – our children and grandchildren – in a competitive globalising world. We contend with each other for personal, familial and social group advantage rather than accept that we are all impoverished by a society which fails to nurture and support all its citizens through its educational arrangements.

I remain shocked by the insouciance of those leaders of independent and Catholic schools and school systems who fight without giving any quarter for the maintenance of public subsidies which lead, in some cases, to students in their schools having twice or three times the sums of money expended on their education as is spent on children in public schools. They do this even though they know as educators that it is the poorest children who need the greatest help to succeed in school. Those are not the children they teach. I realise I should be pragmatic about the political realities of this situation but I remain outraged by the behaviour of these people who would argue they run schools and school systems which are designed to inculcate moral and ethical values but argue for group advantage to the detriment of those members of our community who need more resources to succeed.

So, the school I would wish to see would, first, have the resources available to do what it needs to do.

The organisation of schools and what they teach is also critical. Phillip Hughes was part of an influential movement which led to radical rethinking about education in the 1970s. The important shift in thinking was to an understanding that the curriculum was more than the syllabus. Curriculum theorists drew our attention to the need to take account of all the arrangements entered into by a school that impinged on teaching and learning. This had two consequences: the first was a new emphasis on holistic planning for learning, and the second was the emergence of the concept of the 'hidden curriculum', what children learned as a consequence of things that happened in school but which were not part of any conscious attempt to bring about learning.

Planning is a conscious attempt to formulate what children will know, understand and be able to do as a result of teaching activity and as a consequence to identify the resources, activities and testing to ensure these intentions are realised. While the initial emphasis was behaviourist with a focus on specifying outcomes, there was quick acknowledgement of the importance of planning for process, that the kinds of activities students engaged in could be just as important as the rigorous pursuit of prespecified objectives. I still believe strongly that what happens in schools to support children's learning should be carefully planned and its outcomes rigorously evaluated. Effective education is about much more than good intentions.

But the 'hidden curriculum' was an important concept. Its acknowledgment of the power of unintended, and often undesirable, learning in formal settings is still germane. This learning is not just from the way teachers or other pupils behave. It can also come from the very arrangements within which the school operates. In South Australia, where I worked for many years, the differences in available curriculum choices in secondary schools in the wealthy eastern suburbs compared with those in the deprived northern suburbs was striking. Politicians, bureaucrats and educational theorists would argue that these were 'appropriate' arrangements, given children's interests and backgrounds. But one set of choices meant you were very likely to leave school without a tertiary entrance score in circumstances where all available evidence is that a tertiary qualification is essential for positioning you to succeed in the fast changing, globalised economy. These arrangements told the children in eastern suburbs schools they were being groomed to succeed, while those from the northern suburbs were being told they were to be part of the reserve economy – a life on welfare and with intermittent work – short, hard and difficult.

So, second, the school I would like to see would ensure children from all backgrounds gained access to the knowledge and qualifications which would support success in later life.

Schools supported by a curriculum that affords each child a chance to develop a comprehensive set of understandings and skills need good leadership, with teachers committed to fostering worthwhile learning. Leadership seems to me critical. School principals shape the ethos of a school, articulate the expectations of teachers and represent to students the nature and exercise of authority in social settings. At present, principals are under enormous pressure. In the larger systems, they have to be both local leaders and agents of a bureaucracy that has to contend with its own sets of pressures and constraints. As someone who has been involved in management of educational enterprises for much of my career, I do not understand how you can run an innovative school that affords an educationally rich environment if you have little or no say over the teachers appointed to staff it or have to deal with industrial arrangements which appear to privilege the employment conditions of an underperforming or inappropriately behaved teacher over the educational interests of students.

I would reward principals with salary packages commensurate with those of others responsible for similar numbers of professional staff, give them genuine autonomy over the hiring and termination of teachers and provide them with regular opportunities for significant career renewal. Their professional base should be in education, but their skills should also incorporate understanding of financial matters, human resource management, team building and the processes of institutional planning and organisational growth. It should be our responsibility, whether as members of the wider school community or as agents in the larger educational system, to support their acquisition and development of these important capacities. But there has to be reciprocity.

Principals owe their school communities a personal commitment to professional development, to an intelligent articulation and advocacy of the educational purposes the school is seeking to realise. They must foster through leadership and personal example a school atmosphere that values teaching as a purposeful activity, respects students as legitimate contributors to their own education, regards teachers as professionals whose expertise has a legitimate claim to recognition and acceptance and where parents are accepted as important partners in the educational process with a reasonable expectation of knowing and understanding both their own children's levels of achievement and how well the school performs in relation to comparable others.

Most importantly, I want principals to foster a culture of reflective teaching and continuous improvement. Too often, we tolerate a culture in our schools where poor teaching passes without comment, and any performance appraisal is regarded not as a professional development activity but a bureaucratic imposition that has to be complied with for form's sake. Often, teachers' professionalism is given no real respect but instead legitimates a laissez-faire approach to their supervision which essentially involves leaving them to their own devices. A good principal would have processes in place whereby teachers get informed feedback on their performance, are encouraged to reflect on how they approach their work in and outside the classroom and are provided with support for developing new approaches, acquiring new skills and furthering new understanding. And principals should be supported in doing what most of us know rarely happens – they should require and support underperforming teachers who show no interest in improving to leave the school and the profession. As a community, we should insist they have the authority to do so and require such leadership of them.

There is nothing more important than good teachers if we are to have good schools. I want teachers to engage with their colleagues with the understanding that teaching is a collaborative activity and not principally the private transactions that take place between individual teachers and their class groups. Students should be able to participate in a programme that develops sequentially over time and is directed to the progressive building of understandings, knowledge and skills. They should not be exposed to repetition other than for the legitimate purposes of reinforcement. Their studies should be stimulating, rich in supportive resources, making effective use of technologies that facilitate searching for information and collaborative endeavour, and encourage reflection and problem-solving.

Teachers need to understand the importance of feedback on student performance as one of their most critical responsibilities, as central to teaching as is being able to introduce a topic in a lively, stimulating manner. They should relish it as one of the most powerful professional tools available to them. Sadly, feedback is too often reduced to marking and becomes an unwanted chore. We see a depressing cycle of unimaginative teaching leading to poor assessment assignments which in turn produce limited student responses that involve teachers in the worst kind of marking response – the quick red pen that invokes no learning of value.

Parents should be informed, engaged and appropriately supportive of teachers and the educational purposes their school seeks to achieve. I want children to be respected regardless of their background, race, gender or any other human characteristic and taught to respect and enjoy the differences of others. But increasingly we hear that too many schools are battling with large cohorts of students who display disruptive, undisciplined and disrespectful behaviour. Parents must be partners with teachers in a shared responsibility to maintain a school environment where everyone can learn. Parents have their obligations too!

Finally, then, the school that I would like to see is one which is properly resourced to do what it has to do and organised to maximise the chances of all its students becoming fully functioning citizens of our democracy. For this to be possible in all schools rather than in some, I now believe we need to reaffirm the moral base of the state's responsibility to provide free, compulsory and secular education – a notion first adopted in the nineteenth century and now, somehow, lost in the hubbub of contending arguments for more public resources from groups which represent schools which are neither free nor secular. In a mature democracy like Australia, we owe a responsibility to all our children but especially those who are educated in the public system to ensure that public resources are fairly shared to ensure equal opportunity for all.

Chapter 3
The Great Australian Divide: Public and Private Schooling

Don Anderson

Phil: You invited me to write about what 'is necessary to provide an effective, relevant, high quality education for all children … the best approaches to adopt to achieve such an education … what should be the priorities … what is not being fully utilised … and future directions and activities to reach that goal'. These are big questions, especially if we put the emphasis on *all* children, and I can't pretend to address the totality of requirements; but I'm delighted to have a go at part of it, and am grateful to you for stimulating me to think about the issues. As a sociologist, I like to look at how institutions or structures influence behaviour, including learning. From this perspective, I see the divide between public and private schooling as the single greatest structural impediment to advancing the quality of education in Australia. And within our schools, a resource not fully being utilised are the students themselves, not in isolation but in peer groups and autonomous learning groups encouraged to work collectively and help one another. These two – the public-private divide and student groups – are connected, and I will explain the dynamics of this later.

There is also a curriculum question associated with the divide: Do we want an increasing number of schools contributing to the reproduction of social, religious and ethnic groupings in our multicultural society, or should education policies be encouraging a mix of these elements within schools on the assumption that tolerance and an understanding of differences will be promoted? This is a question of values; it is an important one but receiving little attention in the current public-private debate.

Our system is unique among developed countries; it is also unstable politically and educationally. Elsewhere core funding by government for non-government

D. Anderson (✉)
Emeritus Faculty, Australian National University, 11 Fitzgerald St,
Yarralumla, ACT 2600, Canberra, Australia
e-mail: donander@homemail.com.au

P. Hughes (ed.), *Achieving Quality Education for All*, Education in the Asia-Pacific
Region: Issues, Concerns and Prospects 20, DOI 10.1007/978-94-007-5294-8_3,
© Springer Science+Business Media Dordrecht 2013

schools is either zero, as in the USA, for example, or 100% as in New Zealand and the Netherlands. Good arguments can be made for all or for nothing, but it is difficult to find any rationale, except political expediency, for the Australian system of partial funding (calculated using a formula which purports to estimate a school's needs or, more recently, the average social class of its students measured from Census data of the social standing of region where parents lived). When formula funding commenced in the 1970s, it was intended that the wealthiest private schools would not receive grants, but pressure from lobby groups forced federal government to back down and make grants to all private schools irrespective of their wealth. And, over the years, because political leverage remained undiminished, no matter how much the grants increased, the majority of private schools now meet most of their running costs with income from government. At the same time, the public school sector has steadily declined: from educating over 80% of all children before formula funding to less than 70% today – the lowest proportion in public schools of any developed country apart from Spain.

The divide originated in the sectarian conflict of the 1870s when the Catholic bishops forbade parents to send their children to the 'godless and immoral' public schools being established by the colonial governments. Catholic parochial schools were maintained as schools of commitment, often through heroic contributions from parents and parishes, but inevitably it was difficult to maintain good standards. Most protestant schools, mainly recruiting students from families able to afford substantial tuition fees, became schools of privilege. These two sorts of school – of commitment and of privilege – characterised the private sector until the 1970s when, after a prolonged campaign for 'state aid' led by the Catholic authorities, the Whitlam Labor Government introduced needs-based funding for all schools. Without the promise to 'abolish the divisive state aid issue forever', Labor would never have been elected. This started an era of expansion of private schooling which continues unabated to the present. And schools of commitment, particularly Christian community schools, and more recently Islamic schools, are expanding much faster than the rest of the private sector.

Schools of commitment function to nurture and reproduce particular religious or other subcultures, socialising the children according to the values and beliefs of the sponsoring community. Religious schools are the most common, but ethnic minorities in Australia are increasingly using schooling as a means of preserving ethnic identity. I have visited some schools where priority is given to religion and tradition to the extent that teaching of the regular curriculum suffers. And I find it astonishing that the taxpayer supports (at the highest funding rate) the expanding school systems of the exclusive brethren and the scientologists with their extreme ideologies and socially exclusive practices.

Schools of privilege are academically or socially selective. Academic selective schools for pupils of above average intellectual attainment are found at secondary level in many countries, often in both the public and the privately managed sectors. In the public sector, opinion is divided over whether all secondary schools should be comprehensive with the full spectrum of abilities, or whether there should be a few elite schools for pupils of outstanding ability.

Socially selective schools are a distinctive part of the private sector: tuition fees, location and admissions practices helping to maintain a distinctive profile. The sociological term 'elite' can be applied to these schools because, as numerous studies have shown, they function to reproduce a sector of society with access to power and privilege. Most of the parents are well educated with good incomes and in occupations that are professional, business or senior management – high socio-economic status (SES) for short. Not unexpectedly, there is an overlap between academic and social elite. There are elite Catholic schools, but overall in the Catholic system the proportion of high-SES parents is about half that of 'other private' schools, and in the public sector, it is less than one third. There is frequently an overlap between social elite and academic elite. As we shall see, high SES correlates with cultural capital (a concept developed by French sociologist Bourdieu), and this provides the link between peer group and performance.

A full classification of schools according to their social and educational function would include education reform or alternative schools espousing a particular educational philosophy, frequently one that is child-centred. Unlike schools of commitment, the parents do not have in common membership of coherent subcultures. These schools are more likely to be in the private sector although a number, like the School Without Walls in the Australian Capital Territory, were established in the public sector in the 1970s era of radical education innovation.

In contrast to private schools, whether elite, commitment or reform, public schools are community schools, being representative of all the children in a neighbourhood irrespective of parents' class, beliefs or ethnicity. When they are well managed, the diverse mix of backgrounds is part of the curriculum, contributing to social cohesion and the maintenance of a common culture. Nearly all community schools are in the public sector. Their social composition is representative of the population at large, but with fewer students from the professional and business classes and more from homes where the father is a manual worker. From a perspective within the Catholic community, parochial schools are community schools. Roughly half of the population who tell the Census collector their religion is Catholic have attended a Catholic school; nearly all of the remainder attend public; very few went to 'other private'.

An 'iron law' of sociology connects family socio-economic status with education achievement. The association, which has been reported ever since sociologists began studying education, is found in all countries and at all levels of school education. The most recent analysis I have seen is in Australia's National Assessment Program – Literacy and Numeracy (NAPLAN) technical paper which shows SES accounting for well over half of the variation in schools' test results. Once other factors like class size and measurement error are allowed for there is little variation remaining to be explained by quality of teaching. Not that teaching is unimportant; just that, compared with family background, it doesn't vary all that much between schools, within or between sectors.

SES influences attainment in several ways: First, students benefit directly from belonging to a home possessing 'cultural capital' – books, Internet and vocabulary rich in ideas – and having successful parents as role models. A good school with adequate resources can compensate for deficiencies in cultural capital, or amplify the advantage of those already in possession of it, but the generality of the law remains. When comparing scholastic results of different schools for the purpose of making inferences about effectiveness, allowance must be made for differences in SES background of the pupils. The NAPLAN exercise constructed an SES indicator for every Australian school so that parents could compare 'like with like'.

When type of school – public, Catholic and other private – is correlated with school performance, 'other private' comes out clearly on top, followed by Catholic and then public. But when allowance is made for SES and academic selectivity in admissions, the differences disappear, or they used to. Similar results are reported in research from the USA, the most recent being a comparison of charter schools with public. But in Australia, we may be seeing a change: Recent work from the Australian Council for Educational Research (ACER) is showing a statistically significant difference in favour of private over public. Better resources for teaching and learning in private schools may be a factor, but there are other influences at work and I believe a critical one to be the student mix.

Evidence from surveys in Australia has shown that participation in autonomous learning groups improves students' scholastic performance. In statistical modelling, it is known as 'the composition effect'. It was used in Murnane's criticism of Coleman's famous longitudinal study of school performance in the USA. Coleman found private schools did better and attributed this to better teaching. When Murnane recalculated the equations, allowing for the composition effect, the difference between public and private became insignificant. I believe this would be the same in Australia, but so far as I know, the research remains to be done.

A critical mass of able, ambitious and motivated students from families rich in cultural capital can help establish a pro-learning culture, lifting the performance of a whole class or of an entire school. A class losing one such student will not be affected much but, as the numbers moving to private schools increase, there comes a point when the average performance of the remainder suddenly declines as the pro-learning culture is eroded, students being less interested in study and less inclined to help one another with schoolwork. Teachers' energy is deflected from teaching and gets absorbed in motivating and maintaining order. With the aid of government capital grants for school building, the shift of students from public to private is accelerating. These students belong disproportionately to homes with considerable cultural capital and are more likely to participate in pro-learning activities. Elite schools – social and selective – are responsible for a good part of this process, but schools of commitment and of reform also recruit from the families better placed in the social order. At the same time, government decisions to raise the school leaving age is adding to the proportion of unmotivated and reluctant students in public schools.

In an analysis made 20 years ago, I predicted that, should the unstable public/private divide continue, the public school sector would become residualised. Since then, the funding formula has caused further loss from public schools, not just of a critical core of able and motivated students who set the standard and shape the culture of a school, but also of influential and articulate parents, who, if they had not exited, would have become voices for reform. A residual public sector will, like a social safety net, have to cater for remote areas, the poor, the handicapped and children who, for one reason or another, have parents who do not or cannot contribute to their children's education. It is not just private schools: Selective academic public high schools have the same effect, diminishing that critical core of motivated students in the comprehensive schools.

The public-private divide poses a number of dilemmas for the tolerant citizen and the tolerant state. The question of public funding is one. While there is almost universal support for the right of parents who choose to school their children outside the planned sector, there is no agreement over the extent to which that right should be subsidised by the state.

The exercise of their rights by those choosing to opt out of public schooling is unwittingly diminishing the rights of those who remain. The loss of community representativeness can threaten the core of public schooling, in the extreme case changing its function from a community to a charity service. Advocates for public schooling argue that the public school has its own ethos, representing a valuing of social equality and justice, and of community and social cohesion. They point out that many parents choose public schools for their children because of these values. Students from families of diverse beliefs and social origins constitute an important part of the curriculum.

A similar dilemma is caused by socially and academically selective or elite schools. As we have seen, the right of parents to choose an elite school may conflict with the rights of public school parents who expect their children to be educated among an effective intellectual mix of students.

A fourth dilemma concerns the tolerance that should be extended to groups whose values threaten those of the dominant society. To take an extreme example, presumably a school set up by a group of political dissidents with lessons on how to booby-trap cars would be refused a licence. But, to take a non-fictitious example: What of a sect which, believing that girls have inferior intellects to boys, denies them an academic curriculum, or a religious group which includes physical punishment of children as an expression of its theological beliefs? There are such schools in Australia.

Finally, there is a dilemma for governments with a commitment to both public and private education of how to present policies for assisting the private sector without appearing to diminish the value of the public. Substantial subsidies extend choice by making it easier for parents to use private schools, but there may also be an implicit message that private is better. This occurred in England with an assisted places scheme designed to help bright but poor children attend private schools.

Your last question, Phil, asked how to achieve these reforms so that all children receive a good education. If my analysis is correct, then we need to rid ourselves of the partial funding arrangement for private schools, which for over 40 years has produced an unstable system and is resulting in diminishing standards of achievement in public schools. A case can be made for either 0 or 100% funding of private schools. As the former is clearly out of the question, the issue is how to manage full funding so that the exercise of choice by private school supporters does not diminish the rights of those who choose public. It would mean that schools receiving state aid would have to agree to free and non-discriminatory admissions, to give preference to local applicants, to retain their difficult or underperforming students, to meet teaching and curriculum standards (we would have to bring back the inspector of schools, but with a formative role) and to operate within planning parameters so that a new school would not have a negative impact on its neighbours. Private schools choosing not to meet such requirements would receive no public funding as is the case in most other countries.

When friends asked me for advice on private or public education for their children, I used to say that because there are good schools in both sectors, they forget about whether a school is public or private and choose a school on its merits, preferably one that is near home. These days I am not so sure that this is sound advice. Private interest and public policy are at odds. Freedom of choice, with thousands of parents deciding that a private school will maximise their child's life chances, is not resulting in the greatest good for the greatest number – in Australian education, it is the back of Adam Smith's invisible hand that is at work.

Chapter 4
What Is a Good School?

Deborah Meier

At the very least, school should be a place where children are not treated as though they are data or numbers in someone else's policy war, or as only "future" members of society as though their present experience is not important in and of itself. Then we need to also think about our "purposes" for insisting that young people spend so many involuntary hours—during their vibrant and restless youths—inside schools that hardly models "the good life," not to mention why we spend so much public funds on these schools. Of course, we might wonder also why those with the money to do so spend two to four times as much on the education of their own children. The best New York City (NYC) independent schools now cost nearly $40,000 a year— almost the same as Harvard and Princeton and easily two to three times what is spent on NYC public schools, not to mention what rich families pay for "after school" education, both formal and informal. In our rush to "close the achievement gap," we spend a substantial portion of the 30 hours a week inside school class-rooms prepping them for tests—which are these days the measure of achievement— as though the "haves" will not be sure to give their young the real thing and then, on the side provide explicit one-on-one tutoring for tests at hundreds of dollars an hour. All things being equal, the "gap" will remain and the real gap in terms of a good education will grow ever wider.

Because test-taking skill is not achievement—by anyone's real reckoning.

But assuming all the above is true, what can we do if we care about the true public purpose of schools—which the rich can afford to do, even if they too often enough get caught in the "race to the top" as we now call it in education policy and view their children mostly as trophies, symbols of their success.

Educating the young has always been about preserving and passing on the best of the past, the values we most care about, and the skills and habits of heart and

D. Meier (✉)
Senior Scholar and Adjunct Professor, Steinhardt School of Education, NYU,
PO Box 609 129 Bushnell Rod, Hillsdale, NY 12529, USA
e-mail: deborahmeier@me.com

P. Hughes (ed.), *Achieving Quality Education for All*, Education in the Asia-Pacific Region: Issues, Concerns and Prospects 20, DOI 10.1007/978-94-007-5294-8_4,
© Springer Science+Business Media Dordrecht 2013

mind we believe essential for both their individual futures and for the future of the larger community as well. For us, in the USA, that has to include a heavy dose of education focused on what is necessary to preserve, nourish, and improve democracy. And surely tests with right and wrong answers are not a measure of these. Nor is sitting still and listening well, or guessing successfully what "they" want as an answer, or competing with one's classmates for the limited places in this game of musical chairs. The top colleges or the top law firms cannot be the goal for all.

Schools thus need to think carefully about what is not best taught "in school" and see that all children have access to those experiences too. Since democracy, for example, is hard to experience out of school, and families are very rarely good expressions of democratic life, the schools can ask themselves what their part is in this difficult task of turning youngsters into democrats. This is an issue for pedagogy and curriculum and for school governance as well. There probably is no single right answer, but only schools free to explore and exhibit and defend their work on this basis will further our democratic project. Math is important, but we rarely require students to understand the math that democracy rests on: a sophisticated understanding of statistics and probability and an easy fluency with large numbers—those millions, billons, and trillions that trip us up. History is important, but the specific history of past attempts at democracy, and the reasoning and trade-offs involved in their differing forms, are certainly as important as the history of wars, the sequence of British royalty, etc. Reading may be important, but not primarily so one can pass reading tests—as many students have told me they thought the purpose was. Truly! The love of reading and the voracious aptitude for learning new things, for unraveling curiosities, for living other lives that widen our acquaintance with the world—these are the purposes. What better way to inculcate empathy—so essential to democracy—than entering other worlds through great fiction, for example, and on and on.

But, of course, we also know that human beings learn most naturally and efficiently, throughout history, through "apprenticeships" of a sort. We are from birth novices in the company of those more expert than we are. There are many things we learn better from peers—perhaps moral values? But we learn most by being unconditional members of an adult community. There are few such adult communities that children today can learn from, are members of, and witness on a regular basis. For some, the only ones are those on TV sitcoms or novels designed as escapes from reality.

A good school is an extension of a good childhood in which the young are surrounded by powerful, lively, and interesting experts (for children, adulthood itself qualifies as expertise). But in most schools, the adults are largely powerless, except over the students, uninteresting, and hardly lively. A few have the charisma of great actors and create adults the children can imagine wanting to be. But democracy cannot rest on our all being great actors! In most schools, teachers make few decisions among other adults, and school adults and home adults are separate and apart—often in a state of suspended enmity. Inside the classroom, young people rarely are faced with opportunities to explore options, attend to trade-offs, express opinions, argue over evidence, weigh priorities, speak persuasively, and persist in tasks and projects that require self-monitoring and collaboration. No workplace that I can think of is like the typical school classroom, and surely no democratic institution only values the skills we admire within the classroom. Regardless of how much actual democratic power students have in school, they need environments where the skills of democracy bring so little advantage.

There are such schools. It's not surprising that such schools are more likely to be found where rich children are being educated—for teachers and students and parents. But there are exceptions—hundreds of public schools in poor communities that have struggled to create such settings for all children. They seem harder to "replicate" only because replication is not what democracy rests on. And above all, not what American democracy rests on. Each school needs to be an experiment in democracy, just as America is. Each school community needs to think through what important achievements look and sound like—set their standards and defend them even as they revise and edit. Replication is an oxymoron if we are describing a self-governing community since no two such communities are replicas of each other. Nor would we want them to be. We "merely" want all children to have the opportunity to spend their time in schools that keep providing the time and place for them to learn "in the company" of interesting and interested adults.

I want to end by quoting from an essay by the late Alice Seletsky—whose work I loved to observe in action over the many years we taught in the same school building. She begins her essay "Where the Action Is?" with these words:

> *What I like best about teaching is that there are no easy answers—to anything. Even after twenty-five years, I have to keep wondering, tinkering, changing my mind, learning…. Uncertainties which are the source of such concern and frustration* (to school reforme*rs)* *are the very elements that make teaching and learning such a live business.*

And ends with*:*

> *It is a little embarrassing to talk openly of love of teaching—this difficult, demanding, exhilarating, absorbing work…But it's the best explanation I can offer…for the peculiar compulsion I have to continue doing it until some Great Pedagogic Hand flicks the lights on and off and tells me it's time to stop.*

Is it any wonder that keeping company with Alice over many years, regardless of one's age, made life better and more interesting?

Chapter 5
Realizing Moral Purpose

Michael Fullan

I feel a strong affinity for Phil Hughes. He was the seventh child from a working-class family and the first in his extended family to get a university qualification, paving the way for future generations in his own family. My father was the seventh son, and he and my mother had seven boys of which I was the first. I too was the first in a new generation to receive a university education that again signalled a new generation of postsecondary education for generations to come. I have come to call education *moral purpose realized* because it literally opened a whole new world of ideas, global exposure and the capacity to help others. I had the honour in 2005 to deliver the Phillip Hughes Oration in Canberra in the presence of the man himself.

What Phil has done in his long, illustrious and worldwide career is to demonstrate that moral purpose is not about one's personal accomplishments but rather about giving back—contributing to 'raising the bar and closing the gap' for all children. The rest of this chapter gives a flavour of what moral purpose realized means.

Literally, in the past 12 months, we have seen direct evidence that whole countries can make significant gains in raising the bar and reducing the gap in educational performance in as short as 6 years. The Organisation for Economic Cooperation and Development's (OECD) Programme for International Student Assessment (PISA) results and analyses has now become a media sensation and is leading to increased efforts to learn from front runners as all countries try to improve. Its 2009 assessments (released in 2010) show level of results as well as movement over time in reading, math and science. Front runners Singapore, Finland, Hong Kong, South Korea and Canada all reflect deliberate policies aimed at realizing greater moral purpose.

This has captured the interest of the McKinsey Group who began to investigate 'how the world's most improved systems keep getting better'. They examined closely 20 entities (regions and countries) that had made great strides over periods

M. Fullan (✉)
Professor Emeritus, Ontario Institute for Studies in Education, University of Toronto,
498 St Clair Ave East, Toronto, M4T1P7, Canada
e-mail: mfullan@me.com

P. Hughes (ed.), *Achieving Quality Education for All*, Education in the Asia-Pacific
Region: Issues, Concerns and Prospects 20, DOI 10.1007/978-94-007-5294-8_5,
© Springer Science+Business Media Dordrecht 2013

of 5 or 6 years. For the first time, developing regions (going from poor to adequate performance) as well as those at the top end (going from good to great) were studied. In both sets, the basics were the same—committed leaders, focus, capacity building of teachers and school principals, linking to results and feedback. Those at the early stages had to pay close attention to raising the basic skills of teachers. At the higher end—once teachers had reached a certain level of capacity, the strategies that worked focused on peers learning from peers within schools and across clusters of schools learning from each other.

We have had our own experience in Ontario, Canada, working on 'whole system reform' since late 2003. A new government inherited a stagnant school system that had shown flat-line performance for 5 years in the basic measures of literacy, numeracy and high school graduation across its 5,000 schools in the public education system. For the past 7 years, we have applied the core knowledge of reform to increase systematically the capacity and performance of the system: relentless, focused leaders at the top, a small number of core priorities, respect for and investment in the capacity of teachers and school/district leaders, monitoring of results (first to feedback into improved performance and secondly for public accountability) and avoiding distractions that would have taken us from one solution to another.

It works! High school graduation has climbed steadily from 68 to 81% and is still rising. Literacy and numeracy have improved by 14% across the 4,000 primary schools. The gap has been reduced in most categories: English language learners, special education, schools with poverty, boys compared to girls—although much more remains to be done.

In all of this, what we are learning is that you have to pay close attention to personalizing education experiences for students, valuing them as individuals and building the instructional capacity of teachers both individually and especially collectively to enable them to work in professional learning communities and to build connections with parents, communities and business.

Phil must be a little bit nervous about his own country, Australia, and home state Tasmania. In PISA terms, Australia has stagnated over the past decade currently placing 9th, 15th and 10th in reading, math and science, respectively. Not disastrous, but definitely worrisome, especially given the stuck nature of current performance. I recently wrote a paper called 'Choosing the Wrong Drivers for Whole System Reform' and used Australia and the USA as examples (published by the Centre for Strategic Education, Melbourne). I very much think that Phil would agree with my analysis. The wrong drivers I argued consist of choosing 'accountability over capacity', 'individualistic rather than collective' solutions, 'technology vs. pedagogy' and 'piecemeal vs. systemic' reforms.

The moral imperative realized has at its overarching mantra a relentless focus on raising the bar and closing the gap for all students, with a special focus on disadvantaged groups. But moral purpose must also have a viable strategy in order to realize it. Any large-scale strategy must end up doing at least four basic things: (1) foster greater intrinsic motivation of teachers and students, (2) engage them in continuous improvement of instruction and learning, (3) inspire collective or team work and (4) affect all teachers and students—100%.

The key to system-wide success is to situate the energy of educators as the central driving force. This means aligning the goals of reform and the intrinsic motivation of participants. Intrinsic energy derives from doing something that is important to you and to those with whom you are working. Thus, policies and strategies must generate the very conditions that make intrinsic motivation flourish. This is as basic as the human condition. What turns most people on is being effective at something that is personally meaningful and which makes a contribution to others as well as to society as a whole. Personal contributions are all the more satisfying when they are part of a team effort melding personal and social goals. Policies and strategies that do not foster such strong intrinsic motivation across the whole system cannot be a source of whole system reform.

Few people have been fortunate enough to pursue a career where personal and social goals merge. Phil Hughes is one of those people. He has been able to realize his own moral purpose, as he contributed to the success of others. He has done this as a teacher, as an academic, as a university administrator and as a public system leader. He embodies the realization of moral purpose.

Chapter 6
Public Education: Its Value Is Beyond Price

Lyndsay Connors

I first met Phillip Hughes when he was the foundation head of education at the then new Canberra College of Advanced Education. I was a young mother, returning to study. He was a fine, inspiring leader and teacher in the Diploma of Education programme. He taught me how to start to think about the nature and significance of schools and of the profession of teaching in our society. Over the years, I learned that we had in common a deep commitment to the public school systems in Australia that had given us both opportunities for learning and life chances well beyond the hopes and expectations that a sensible person might have held for us as young children.

Many of our fellow Australians share this commitment. They share Phillip's understanding that the need for all people to have a high-quality education can only be achieved where there is a high-quality public education system, 'focusing attention and effort on those values which we hold in common as a society and which constitute our basis for a democratic society'. He advanced this argument in the context of the report *A National Declaration for Education 2001*.[1] But that report also drew attention to concerns about the perception in the Australian community that public schools were being down-valued, in the context of a more general trend towards privatisation.

Since that time, we have shared with many others growing fears that the vision of a strong and socially representative system of public schooling was slipping from our grasp. The Australian Capital Territory, where Phillip was the foundation chair for the then Schools Authority which governed the public school system, provides an example of the social stratification that has occurred over the years among schools

---

[1] This was produced by the Australian College of Education and the Australian Council for Educational Administration. See *Unicorn*, Volume 27, Number 2, July 2001.

L. Connors (✉)
Australian College of Educators, 24 Bowes Avenue, Edgecliff, NSW 2027, Australia
e-mail: lyndsayconnors@bigpond.com

P. Hughes (ed.), *Achieving Quality Education for All*, Education in the Asia-Pacific Region: Issues, Concerns and Prospects 20, DOI 10.1007/978-94-007-5294-8_6, © Springer Science+Business Media Dordrecht 2013

serving higher and lower income families and communities, even in that jurisdiction characterised by relatively high socio-economic status.

As educators, we see hope and optimism as a professional obligation. So I am writing now with evidence that there is some cause for hope coming from where, I am sad to say, I had grown to least expect it.

But I have just read the following statement:

Government schools are the backbone of our education system. The place where most students' formal education begins, the crucible of the democratic right to accessible, affordable, quality education.

It is not only the content of this statement that is significant. What is significant also is that these words were spoken by the current Commonwealth minister for education.[2]

We have both been shocked, over the past decade or more, to see advocates of public schooling – recognising the primacy of free, secular, public schooling in our democracy – being dismissed as relics of a dim past.

But I think we can take heart from the recent statement by the minister that I have cited above. There are even slight echoes here of Sir Henry Parkes, (a nineteenth-century Australian politician known as the *father of federation*) through the drawing of the relationship between democracy and high-quality public schooling in the years leading to federation:

Whatever may be our form of Government, the time will come—I hope to live to see it—when we shall take our place with all the real conditions of freedom—with all the immunities of national life, among the free nations of the globe. Let us by every means in our power take care that the children of the country grow up under such a sound and enlightened system of instruction, that they will consider the dearest of all possessions the free exercise of their own judgment in the secular affairs of life, and that each man will shrink from being subservient to any other man or earthly power.[3]

It is significant that the statement by the current Commonwealth minister has been made in the context of the first comprehensive review of schools funding in years (since the interim report for the schools commission headed by the late Peter Karmel and the review undertaken in 1984 by the commission itself). I say this because the political neglect of and indifference to public schooling, particularly at the Commonwealth level, has been brought about by the pressure on politicians to play down the radical nature of our national school funding and anomalies between the public funding of government and non-government schools and the conditions that apply to that funding. Attempting to justify the effects of years of political compromises on the nation's public school systems was difficult. A convenient alternative was to airbrush away the unique obligations and characteristics of public

---

[2] Speech: *Beyond My School 2.0*, Grattan Institute, Melbourne on 17 March 2011 by Peter Garrett AM, Minister for School Education, Early Childhood and Youth.

[3] Speech of Henry Parkes, M.P., President of the Council of Education entitled *The Public Schools Act*, on opening the public school at Dundas, on Thursday, September 4, 1869.

schooling and to ignore that it is, in reality, the backbone of the school system as a whole.

As one of our education colleagues described it, '*the Australian education system, taken as a whole, is evolving into something but we don't know what*[4]'. Perhaps we were conducting a long experiment with schools funding that was producing an evolutionary change into a hybrid organism without a backbone? If that has been the case, then the current minister appears to be calling this whole venture into question.

To distinguish public, secular and free schooling from privately owned and operated, fee-for-service schooling, religious and other does not imply an attack on the legitimacy of either and does not deny the necessity for their coexistence or their potential for reciprocity.

To argue, however, that there is no difference between public and private schools is clearly nonsense, a denial of legal reality. It certainly makes no sense in relation to schools funding. How can any democratic government ask us to believe, when it distributes the public funding that now covers the salaries of teachers in around 95% of all Australian schools,[5] that the difference between public and non-government schools does not matter or that it can simply be airbrushed away for political purposes, however bipartisan? How can there be no difference between placing those publicly funded teachers in a system of public schools where their services are freely available to children without fees or religious tests and placing them in schools where their services are available only to those that meet such tests, set privately by non-government authorities?

In a climate where otherwise informed and rational leaders either failed to understand such differences, or were prepared to claim that there were none, in order to silence public debate, it is little wonder that many of us have held deep fears for the maintenance and advancement of public schooling.

These fears are not without basis, judging by some of the proposed alternatives to the current arrangements for schools funding that have been put forward in recent months as submissions to the current review of school funding. What has been striking, in my view, has been the almost mindless ease with which proponents have been prepared to ignore the history that led to the establishment of free, secular, public school systems in this country. How easy it seems to have been for some of these proponents to cast aside the concept of education as a public good, to be funded by the society as a whole. In open societies, such as ours aspires to be, this means that education must necessarily also confer private benefits, and that the public and private benefits can and should be held in balance through regulation. Now there are those who appear to have switched to the position that education is

---

[4] Max Angus in his paper 'Commonwealth-State Relations and the Funding of Australia's Schools' in a report I wrote for the NSW Public Education Alliance in 2007, *Making Federalism Work for Schools: Due Process, Transparency and Informed Consent.*

[5] Governments cover the costs of teaching in all public schools, in all Catholic systemic schools and in at least half of all independent schools. Taken together, this means that governments are providing teachers, or the public funding equivalent, in around 95% of all Australian schools.

primarily a private good, generating some contribution to the public good as a mere by-product or side effect.

There are now those who see no problem with a system where schools all receive public funding but with 'user pays' elements, so that the benefits of this public funding – the services, the opportunities and the life chances – are allocated through market forces generated by neighbourhood inequalities, consumer (parental) choice and unfair competition among schools. There are some who see no problems with the concept of fully funded public schools open to all comers with no admission fees, but being tendered out to groups (religious or other) who would have complete power to staff them with teachers conforming to their own beliefs or interests, so that a local public school could be staffed entirely by teachers drawn from one religious tradition or denomination. There are those who see no logical problem with arguing that there is no difference between public and private schools on the grounds that there are needy schools in both sectors. A school may be needy, for example, because it was established, without adequate planning, as a non-government school by a subgroup within the community for the children of its own members who are unable to afford more than a minimal private admission fee. Or a school may be needy because it is a public school which is open to the local community as a whole, which is the only school available to many members of that community and which is underfunded by governments in relation to the learning needs of the students it enrols. Both schools are needy, but it cannot be argued that they are thereby the same.

We seem to have shifted, with little or no public debate, from the position that schools in receipt of public funding are accountable for providing governments with the data and information that those governments need to be able to account, in turn, to the public for the value received on its investment. Instead, schools are now to be primarily accountable to individual parents, who will withdraw their children from schools if they are not satisfied. It has even been proposed by some interest groups that parents with high incomes who send their children to public schools should be required to pay higher taxes, demonstrating that the radical idea that the public funding of schools is about the right of parents to a return of their taxes has become respectable in some quarters.

It would be tragic if the 'democratic right to accessible, affordable, quality education' that is embodied in the concept of a socially representative, free and secular public school system were to be lightly brushed aside in favour of concepts that have been tested and found wanting in the past, or that are untested, lacking in logic and that fail to provide the comfort of having been successfully implemented in any other comparable country.

None of us would argue that public schooling had reached its full potential or deny that there is scope for continuing reform. Growing into the true promise of public education, the vision of a school system, that is, 'of the people, for the people and by the people', has been a long and slow process, and we still have much work to do. This does not mean that the process should be abandoned, that the vision of a strong and socially representative public school system of the kind envisaged by Henry Parkes should now be dismissed as some Utopian scheme whose full benefits could never be realised.

I recall, in particular, Phillip Hughes' own great disappointment that little defence was mounted of the decision in late 1987 to abolish the Australian Capital Territory (ACT) Schools Authority. Its strength was that it brought teachers and parents into decision-making at the highest level of the system. The potential for meaningful community participation in decision-making at all levels of our public school system has never, in my view, been fully explored from an educational perspective, though we have seen sporadic and simplistic attempts to exploit the concept for political purposes. So much energy has had to go in the past decade into defending the very idea of public education that too little investment has been made in genuine reform. Demonising public school teacher unions has been one of the strategies used to attack the public school system. One reform that would be well worthwhile, in my view, would be for all Australian governments to develop an 'accord' with teacher unions in order to increase public understanding of and confidence in public education and to recognise that the conditions in which teachers work are the conditions in which students learn.

Another persisting challenge relates to demography. How do we deal constructively with issues arising from the periodic rise and fall in the overall school population and of its ongoing shifts? Our continuing inability to work out how to deal with the powerful effects of demography in the school sector has subtly undermined the stability of public schooling. We need to think about managing them better and with a view to maintaining and advancing the quality of education and equality of educational opportunity.

This challenge was never more clearly evident than in the ACT, as enrolment decline affected schools that had been built in the Canberra suburbs that sprung up in orderly succession to cater for a rapidly growing population. As new schools opened up on the frontiers, empty places appeared in schools in the older and more established suburbs, where real estate values started to climb. The effort that parents had been investing in participation to build the quality of their local schools soon began to be diverted into the less demanding exercise of choice among schools. It soon became apparent, particularly from patterns of bus travel, that parents were moving their children into schools in the suburbs where they would have preferred to live. It had become easier to try to find and move into a 'good' school community than to build one. When it came to school closures, it tended to be the schools serving the communities at the lower socio-economic end of the spectrum that were sacrificed, whereas the more influential and powerful communities could stave off closure or even attract public funding to start or expand non-government schools in areas where there was no evidence of demographic demand and where the outcome was to destabilise poorer, largely public, schools.

In the context of a policy of providing public funding for the establishment or expansion of new non-government schools largely free from demographic planning considerations, the approach taken to dealing with population shift and decline has been an inconspicuous and largely unexamined factor in the shift in the balance of enrolments away from the public school sector. The fact that the diseconomies and disruptions arising from demographic shifts have largely had to be borne by the public school sector has reduced its scope for economies of scale and for making the optimal provision for the minority of students with high support needs.

When it comes to the challenges arising from immigration, the Australian school system has generally coped well. This is not to deny the profound differences among particular ethnic groups when it comes to school participation and outcomes. It is the inability of our school system to provide for the interests, needs and aspirations of so many indigenous Australians that is its greatest failure. And, because so many of these students are dependent for any chance of a decent education on the public school system, this is an area where the gap between the vision and the reality of public schooling needs to be bridged as a matter of urgency.

Here again, we can take fresh heart from the further words of the Commonwealth minister in his recent speech at the Grattan Institute:

> Government schools are the foundation of Australian education. They must exist in every community where there are enough children to justify their establishment.
>
> They take all comers and for many are the only path out of economic or personal disadvantage.
>
> The success of Australian education is predicated on the existence of strong, vibrant, high quality public schools.
>
> Government schools teach the majority of students from poor families, the majority of students with a disability, the majority of indigenous and migrant students. And like non-government schools, government schools produce their fair share of outstanding scholars and athletes and artists.

It would be very difficult, in my view, to reconcile the above statements with the prevailing arrangements for the planning and funding of schools. Under current arrangements, the costs associated with teaching *the majority of students from poor families, the majority of students with a disability, the majority of indigenous and migrant students* are passed on as a form of windfall gain to schools outside the public system through the use of a formula for indexation purposes based on movements in average government school recurrent costs. What this amounts to is a refusal by government to acknowledge the unique obligations of public schools, while adding injury to insult by actually exploiting the financial effects of these obligations. It would be difficult to conceive of a more exploitative mechanism.

The minister's words have raised my hopes that we are hearing the beginnings of a more sensible and ethical policy narrative that does justice to our whole school system. If public schools are the backbone of our education system, as the minister has stated, then that backbone must be strong and well-nourished by those responsible – that is, by the whole Australian community through our democratically elected governments.

We may at last be seeing leadership based on an understanding that we can be free to celebrate our cultural diversity – our religious and ethnic and other social traditions and loyalties – without resorting to a class-stratified school system where choice and competition are driven by gross resource disparities among schools. Disparity is not a healthy form of diversity.

It would be wonderful if we were heading towards legislation that provides that, in all its dealings with schooling, the primary obligation of the Commonwealth is to maintain and safeguard strong and socially representative public school systems that are of the highest standard and are open, without fees or religious tests, to all children and young people.[6] This could then be further strengthened by any corresponding changes to current state and territory legislation that might be needed to ensure all governments are working within a coherent policy framework.

These are hopes that I needed to share. Time will tell whether or not they will be realised.

---

[6] As you know, this would be a slightly strengthened version of the provisions of Commonwealth legislation from the time of Whitlam until they were swept away by the Howard Government along with the advisory and consultative structures of the National Board of Employment, Education and Training.

Chapter 7
Basic Schooling for Universal Lifelong Learning: Renegotiating the Policy Agenda

Malcolm Skilbeck and Helen Connell

Introduction

A core element of the UNESCO affirmation of universal human rights more than half a century ago was access to and effective participation in basic schooling. It has yet to be achieved globally. Even in the most advanced democracies, there are still children whose participation and achievement in schooling do not meet the minimum requirements for personal fulfilment and active citizenship. Broader, more inclusive social and economic strategies will be required to ensure that the right to education becomes a practical, universal reality, not only in childhood and youth but over the whole life span.

The Right to Education: Tasks Still to Accomplish

An initial task, requiring concerted international effort as in the *Education for All* programme within the framework of the Millennium Goals, is to continue addressing the worldwide disparity between richer and poorer nations, between those able to establish universal systems of schooling and those still struggling to do so. Enormous social and economic difficulties will require decades of sustained effort to overcome. For Australia, the challenge is to play a more active, supportive and well-publicised engagement with the *Education for All* programme.

M. Skilbeck (✉)
International Education Research and Consultancy, Connell Skilbeck Pty Ltd,
2065 Portarlington Road, Drysdale, VIC 3222, Australia
e-mail: malcolm.skilbeck@deakin.edu.au

H. Connell
Connell Skilbeck Educational Consultancy,
2065 Portarlington Road, Drysdale, VIC 3222, Australia
e-mail: skilbeck.connell@deakin.edu.au

P. Hughes (ed.), *Achieving Quality Education for All*, Education in the Asia-Pacific
Region: Issues, Concerns and Prospects 20, DOI 10.1007/978-94-007-5294-8_7,
© Springer Science+Business Media Dordrecht 2013

Making our Australian systems of schooling truly educative and of real value and use to *all* who enrol in them is a direct and immediate responsibility of state, territory and federal governments, of the private sector and the community at large. Poor attitudes by students towards learning, low standards of attainment, truancy, early dropout and school violence are among the issues to address with ever more vigour. Not just renewed effort, but some quite radical changes are needed in the content and organisation of schooling, in a wider context of social and economic development.

A task on which we have barely begun is the extension of personal and citizenship education throughout the life cycle. If lifelong learning for all is to rise above the level of a slogan, new policies, new structures, new personnel, new content, new approaches to teaching and learning and new ways of financing the whole educational enterprise are called for. It will be necessary to mobilise a wide range of agencies and forces and to accept that learning takes many different forms. These include recreational, civic, occupational and interpersonal. Moreover, truly inclusive lifelong learning must directly address the needs of cultural minorities as well as the mainstream groups, the disabled and the unemployed, as well as the employed, and those with low levels of literacy and poor educational attainments, as well as those who have succeeded in school. It must therefore be responsive, flexible, affordable, accessible and creative.

Lifelong Learning for All Means School Reform

Better co-operation among stakeholders and more coherent policies focused on socio-economic conditions are required for children's success at school. Curriculum reform is necessary but it is not sufficient. Pedagogy, school governance, management and finance, assessment of need, home-school partnerships and community outreach must all be mobilised in a concerted drive to improve educational quality and effectiveness. Periodically over the past half century, there have been substantial efforts to address this broad array of issues, most notably in the creation of the Schools Commission in the 1970s and the National Board structure in the 1990s. We are overdue for a new wave of reforms – for which the national curriculum, My School website and tinkering with school funding are an inadequate substitute.

Historically speaking, the mission and overriding goal of schools has been universal participation in schooling, however rudimentary. Now, emphasis in policy making is on quality of learning and teaching, with international comparisons of countrywide performance. The basic requirement for strong foundations and lifelong learning for all, however, is not international ranking. It is the effective local delivery of policies of universal school participation for all children and systematic education for all adults who have missed out on formal schooling due to past shortcomings in provision and lack of opportunity.

Furthermore, we are now acutely aware that unacceptably large numbers of students are failing at school, underperforming, truanting, dropping out and in other ways resisting or rejecting school learning. Since there appears to be a high correlation between such phenomena and various forms of antisocial behaviour among young males, poor employment prospects and overdependency on welfare, there has been a great increase in public and political concern about educational quality and relevance and the overall well-being of children. Responsibility for this must be shared. It is undeniable that schools are part of the problem but so too are our public health policies, housing costs and availability, the underemployment realities behind employment statistics and the practices of many commercial interests, not least the food and entertainment industries. The target must be to identify, appraise and systematically improve these and other conditions that impact on learning opportunities and outcomes.

The main difficulty at the level of statements of educational goals and values is the tendency to give scant, if any, attention to these wider environmental factors. Greater attention is needed to a wide array of competencies – learning how to learn, civic consciousness and democratic participation, communicating, respect for self and others – and the forces in our society which condition student attitudes and values.

The underlying conditions in home and local environments that militate against effective school learning are too frequently ignored or treated as the responsibility of some other, quite separate domain of policy (health, housing, welfare, employment). There are some who will privately question whether the goal of universal education is really attainable, arguing that the conditions that affect school learning are such that we must simply accept chronic failure and dropout rates. Others are concerned that the increased level of public investment that might be required to overcome these conditions is so great that it cannot be sustained. The implication being that it is better to accept – tacitly if not openly – that failure is endemic in the system and that it would be better to concentrate resources where prospects of successful learning outcomes are good. Commitment to the principle of a universal right to education cuts directly across such views. The idea of a permanent underclass of the poorly educated, the unemployed and the impoverished has featured in the literature of dystopias. It is, of course, fundamentally anti-democratic. Educators, committed to the welfare of all children, cannot accept it and must continue to act on the belief that the failures and shortcomings of schooling are capable of being remedied and must become major foci of policy. A revitalised policy approach calling for coherent, whole of government strategies is needed. Instead, we have a preoccupation with administrative reform, competitive performance and international – and interstate/territory – league tables, responding to economic demand, all largely free of serious social and cultural analysis.

Rethinking the School Curriculum

Our target can be simply stated: to make schooling effective for all students and to reduce the impact on learning of those extra-school factors that are often so inhibiting. But if this is the end, how effective are the means now in place or under consideration?

At present, in Australia and many other countries, there is a drive towards the establishment of minimum national student (and teacher) standards, benchmarking, key competencies, performance indicators and measurable, internationally comparable, learning outcomes. The intent is quite clear, that is, to improve the quality of student learning and to enhance its relevance particularly to a changing employment environment and in the face of the technological revolution of our times. But it is questionable whether the results will actually meet the objective of a foundation of universal lifelong learning for all. One of the features of the standards movement is the greater use of sophisticated forms of assessment. Where these record attainments, or lack thereof, but are not accompanied by substantial well-focused efforts to overcome weaknesses, by ways of motivating students and supporting teachers, they can be both wasteful and highly divisive. Measures of student performance can have uses for policy makers and researchers, but can we expect students who have been classified by tests and examinations as weak or failing to become enthusiastic learners, ready to continue their studies and embark on a lifelong quest for knowledge and competence?

The development of testing regimes and the setting of national standards can be an effective part of well-supported, comprehensive school reform and development programmes which address student learning needs, actively engaging students in meaningful challenges. They must, however, also provide knowledge about the learning difficulties of individual students that can be used in follow-up measures specifically aimed at improving learning outcomes and setting further goals. All too often, there is a media splash, 'failing' schools are identified – and then the storm passes.

If students' performance is unsatisfactory, one part of the explanation is that inappropriate learning tasks are being set for them – the curricula are poorly connected to their interests and perceived needs. Another part of the explanation, given too little attention in policy debates, is that schooling is an integral part of the social fabric, its work profoundly affected by the life circumstances of students, teachers, families and communities. Too often, teachers are blamed, when the focus should be on the underlying socio-economic-cultural conditions of their work.

A prevailing policy assumption seems to be that there is a common, not to say universal, set of learning skills and capabilities which everyone must acquire and by a certain age. Leaving aside the arbitrariness of setting age-based standards, these learning skills are usually defined – for purposes of benchmarking, national standard setting and international comparisons – through levels or standards of literacy, numeracy, science and perhaps civic education. It is evident that while literacy and a basic level of numeracy are essential, they by no means constitute the full repertoire of tools and instruments of learning that constitute the foundations of lifelong learning.

It seems that we have adopted a kind of academic trickle-down approach. The basic skill areas are defined and set as targets for early learning, and then a variety of subject matter – covering such areas as mother tongue, elementary mathematics, basic science, history, geography, social and environmental studies, health education and physical education – is built on top as the staple of primary or elementary schooling.

Thereafter, academic subjects are cast into prescriptive syllabuses in a timetabled framework for secondary students, and specifically vocational subjects are provided, often in association with work experience. For content, approved textbooks and ancillary, teacher-chosen resources (with an overlay courtesy of Google), provide the staple of learning. In order to assess performance, there is a sequence of official assessments and tests usually leading to cumulative state examination at the end of the secondary/vocational stage. This provides (selective) entry to tertiary studies, with a test score determined pecking order of universities and courses.

The foregoing, if a simplification, does set out the main lines within which curriculum design and development, and pedagogical practices unfold. We have been unable (or unwilling) to make a serious and significant break with what has now become a highly conventional set of curriculum models which constitute the orthodoxy in teaching, examining and assessing performance. Obviously, the orthodoxy works at a certain level for many, even perhaps most, students and their teachers and is reasonably acceptable to society at large. However, on the one hand, it is a poor general introduction for all students to the mainstream of modern life, and, on the other, it does not meet the needs and expectations of very significant numbers of students who can be described as school aliens. Employers in particular have become increasingly vocal in their concern over the mismatch between what graduating students know and can do and the requirements of a rapidly changing world of work. Our social, civic, interpersonal education has certainly not produced all that we need for social cohesiveness and responsible citizenship.

Should we not, therefore, take a somewhat different view? Instead of starting with the conventional array of academic subjects and working from the inwardness of the school to the outwardness of society at large, let us adopt the opposite course of identifying the great transforming forces of contemporary life and culture. The curriculum then becomes a series of maps or charts of modern culture, and school learning the means whereby the maps can be read, used and indeed remade as the basis for lifelong engagement with education. From a systematic analysis of the ways of life of our societies, the transformations they are undergoing, the cultural values and mores, the values to which we aspire and the directions we seek – we can draw up maps which challenge and engage student interests, calling forth multiple skills and competencies. Around a core of such learnings, highly specialised skills and areas of student interest will provide for the necessary technical knowledge of our societies as well as the individual motivation of students, leading to lifelong learning.

These transforming forces are a mixture of scientific and technological change, artistic creativity, economic and political globalisation, advancing democratisation, migration and population growth, patterns of leisure, recreation and sport, environmental challenges to continued development, the information and communication revolutions and the ramifications in everyday life of the emerging knowledge-based society. As against these transforming forces, there are large areas of poverty, underdevelopment, deprivation and suffering, with critical value issues arising at the interface between what might be thought of as two world systems. Individuals who are not educated and trained to participate and indeed to contribute to the transforming processes are being increasingly marginalised. Schools and school systems that do not assist and enable students to become part of what we might call the *culture of transformation* may be described as failing schools even when on other indicators (e.g. attendance rates, examination results, observing administrative requirements, financial and management efficiency) they may claim success.

Engagement with these issues by multidisciplinary and cross-sectoral teams could lead to a reinvigoration of schooling and teacher education. The goal should be the universalisation of learning, effectively inclusive of all children and youth, and extending over the life cycle. By contrast, there is an air of complacency about the present 'settlement' of the education question. Some 150 years after the parliamentary acts establishing free, compulsory schooling along secular lines in Australia, schooling is no longer free; its compulsion is to attend not necessarily to learn, and it is increasingly fragmented along religious or perhaps more pointedly public and private lines. We have an overarching structure of targets, performance criteria and resource allocation models. What is lacking is a vision for the future, grounded in universalist, democratic principles, fundamental respect for personal values and interests, and education as itself a way of life – lifelong – for personal fulfilment and active, engaged citizenship.

Chapter 8
Education: Social Elevator or Holding Area?

Kerry J. Kennedy

Looking across the social landscape, there appear to be few public policy interventions more powerful than education. Other social services such as health care, social security benefits and policing can ensure that individuals are supported and the status quo is maintained. But it is education that has the potential to move individuals into a different space from where they can see life in a new way and indeed can create a new life for themselves. Education, unlike other areas of social service, can be transformational; yet, it is not so for everyone. I want to reflect on this apparent dichotomy and try to discern some principles and ideas that might be able to harness the transformational nature of education for all, rather than for just a few.

Can we imagine a world in which schools are not just holding areas but real social elevators for all young people? I want to explore this issue because the editor of this volume, Phil Hughes, has an abiding passion for the world's young people and their advancement. From a humble working class background, he has been able to ride that social elevator to the point where his mission became to share it with others. This is what he is seeking to do in this volume, conceived as the culmination of an active personal and professional life, much of which has been dedicated to education for all rather than just a few fortunate ones. I would like to join him in this mission and make whatever small contribution I can, conscious of my own debt to Phil who has paved the way for this important work both academically as well as by example.

I shall draw indirectly on existing research as I understand it but also my own personal experiences to try and integrate the objective and the subjective. I am conscious of my own ride on the social elevator that took me from deep inside a working class family to a new world of learning, education and leadership, and to

K.J. Kennedy (✉)
Faculty of Education and Human Development, Director of Centre for Governance
and Citizenship, The Hong Kong Institute of Education (HKIEd),
D1-1/F-54, The Hong Kong Institute of Education, 10 Lo Ping Road,
Tai Po, New Territories, Hong Kong
e-mail: kerryk@ied.edu.hk

P. Hughes (ed.), *Achieving Quality Education for All*, Education in the Asia-Pacific Region: Issues, Concerns and Prospects 20, DOI 10.1007/978-94-007-5294-8_8,
© Springer Science+Business Media Dordrecht 2013

new insights into the human condition and the planet which we all inhabit. I do not want to convey this ride as unproblematic or without some regrets. But I do want to assert its possibility, not just for me personally but for others. Having benefited from the transformational effects of education, I want to explore how those benefits become more available to others. How that might be done is the theme of what follows, just as it has been Phil Hughes' dream.

The remainder of this chapter will be divided into sections:

1. Does Social Class Matter?
2. From Rhetoric to Reality: People, Places and Priorities
3. New Values in Old Bottles

Does Social Class Matter?

Marxism and class analyses are no longer popular tools for academics. There are still some diehard neo-Marxists around, but the fast moving world of neo-liberalism and hyper-capitalism is very much in the ascendancy. Even financial crises do not seem to dent the edges of this postmodernist discourse as the concept of 'too big to fail' takes hold, forever cementing large financial institutions as the foundation of 'the big society'. But I want to take a somewhat different stance, drawing on personal experiences, to make a number of points that highlight in a personal way the lingering importance of class.

In 1964, I won two scholarships, both of which provided the possibility for me to become the first person in my family to attend university. I could only choose one, but I felt very fortunate to have such a choice. I do not believe my parents felt the same way. For them, this choice meant something quite different: delayed income, ongoing costs, further alienation and further diversion from family values. Education comes at a cost in working class families, and these costs come in different ways. It is for these reasons, I believe, that my mother encouraged me to get a job in a bank as soon as my matriculation results were known. I think she hoped this would persuade me that a steady job drawing an income might convince me of the apparent unproductive capacity of attending university. She could also see a small income stream that could support the family. She was not a mean person or an unloving mother – just a product of her life and times where money was never plentiful, tomorrow mattered more than next year and providing for the here and now was important. She knew little of Marx, but she knew what was needed for her family, and spending 4 years in university did not fit into her planning. Working class families must think of the here and now.

What can young people do in these contexts? How can schools develop resilience and resolve in students that will encourage them to learn for the future? Working class culture can only be resisted where there is a will and a purpose for doing so and where the benefits are seen to outweigh the powerful family values that seek a steady and stable here and now. In an important sense, there is nothing inherently wrong with working class culture. The truth is that these very working class values can often provide social stability in societies built on gross inequalities. It is this latter point, however, that makes resistance essential. Education is a key resource for removing these inequalities, and young people should be given every opportunity to take advantage of what society has to offer in terms of educational progression.

Schools have a special role to play in supporting working class students to think beyond the here and now. The school curriculum, the co-curricular activities and the entire ethos of the school need to support and extol the virtues of learning for the future. There may well be short-term objectives, such as examinations, and students must be supported to reach these; but at the same time, they must also become committed to learning. They must also be taught how to become resilient in the face of opposition to ongoing learning – opposition that is likely to come from their families and peers. It is very easy for working class students to be distracted from what should be their long-term goal – schools need to be alert to this and provide support and reinforcement for the learning journey.

I do not want to suggest here that working class culture is bad or its values suspect. In an important sense, these are very much determined by the unequal structures of capitalist societies. Struggling to survive is the theme of working class existence captured in the nineteenth century so well by Elizabeth Gaskell's mid-century novel, *Mary Barton*, and more recently in the film and stage play, *Billy Elliott*. This is why education is so important – it has the potential to redress these inequalities, not just for individuals but for society as a whole. Schools must be seen as agents for social progress and advancement – making the world more just, more fair and a better place to live for all and not just some people. Working class students should not be excluded from this mission but should be seen as an essential part of it. It is a great challenge for all schools and teachers.

From Rhetoric to Reality: People, Places and Priorities

How to meet this challenge is an important issue to consider so that we can move beyond rhetoric to reality. What can be done to support working class students?

People

Teachers are a school's most important resources, and for students, they are key people in their lives. Teachers may not always realize this in the day-to-day demands of a busy working life. Yet teachers are people who make a difference. I recall vividly my senior year English teacher, Norm Harris, who used to pick me up from home around 8 a.m. once a week so that I could attend his English Honours class along with two other students. I was fortunate enough to pass the Honours papers, go on to university to major in English and eventually become an English teacher.

Was this all because of Norm Harris? I cannot say for sure, but he went out of his way to support me, making the subject seem important and, in an important sense, making me feel important. He was a person who mattered in my life as a secondary school student – I think we need more Norm Harrises who can make a difference in the lives of students.

Providing support for students is a day-to-day job for teachers – it comes with the territory. The issue, however, is to provide special support for those working class students who most need it. It means teachers have to go out of their way to become special people for students – just as Norm Harris did for me. In the eyes of many students, teachers are those who have made it – through school and university to successful careers. Teachers, therefore, can be on-the-spot role models. This is important for working class students who will not have such role models at home. More often than not, teachers do not feel like role models, but it is an important part of the influence they can have on young people. It is Rudyard Kipling who is attributed with the quote:

> No printed word, nor spoken plea,
> Can teach young minds what they should be.
> Not all the books on all the shelves, but what the teachers are themselves.

Teachers as role models can be powerful supports for young people.

Places

Schools are important places for learning, but there is also a world of learning outside of schools. Theatres, art galleries, museums, historical sites, places of nature and many more can be identified as sites of learning. What is more, these are very often sites to which working class students have limited access. This is not because of an aversion of working class families to so-called high culture but simply because such activities are likely to stretch financial resources beyond the reach of such families. Schools can play an important role in filling this gap.

Excursions, interschool visits and bringing community groups into schools can all provide powerful alternative learning experiences for students. I vividly recall that my first introduction to live Shakespeare came from a drama group that was especially brought to my secondary school to give performances of the plays set for that year. It was not an experience I would ever have expected to be provided by my family. But it was so important to understanding the text and to imagining what original performances might have been like. In that first year, it had been *A Midsummer Night's Dream,* and in subsequent years, it was *Macbeth* and *The Tempest.* These performances created another 'place' for learning at relatively modest costs but with real and long-term benefits. Working class students need to be supported in gaining access to such places.

In the current environment, there are many ways to provide access to new learning places. Yet working class students might not always have access to these opportunities. Special programmes are needed, sponsored by governments, to ensure that all students have access to these new learning spaces. Technology is so important in creating access that it cannot be left to individuals or even schools to take the responsibility for ensuring access. It must be governments with a mission to create a technologically literate citizenry who take responsibility for ensuring that working class students will not be left behind in this important area of advancement in the twenty-first century.

Priorities

Education must become a priority for all students but particularly for working class students. Schools have a special responsibility for ensuring that the kind of education students experience will be a positive incentive for their future commitment to learning. Schools cannot afford to turn students off learning – this can only ensure their status as 'holding areas' rather than 'social elevators'. Ensuring that education is engaging must be an institutional priority for schools so that it can become a personal priority for students.

In saying this, I do not want to set schools up for almost certain failure or suggest that schools are already failing. But I do want to say that engagement is not always at the top of schooling's agenda. This may be a reflection of the difficulties occasioned by mass education and the complexities of work of teachers in the twenty-first century. Yet without engagement, it is unlikely that working class students can be 'hooked' on learning. Often the curriculum is alienating to such students – far removed from their experience. Teaching strategies are often focussed on classroom management and control rather than learning. Assessment can also become a burden rather than a means of engaging with new learning. Deliberate efforts have to be made to take all of these elements – curriculum, teaching and assessment – and turn them into engaging experiences for students. This is the way to win working class students to embrace learning for the future.

New Values in Old Bottles

Education is above all about values. In the twenty-first century, it has to be primarily about the value of learning. In some senses, this is not new at all – Confucius, Buddha and Jesus were amongst the greatest exponents of learning. Confucius' teachings, for example, were gathered together under the title of *The Great Learning* (大學). We cannot disregard this historical connection to our own time when once again learning is at the forefront of our thinking. But there is something new that we have to add to promote learning in our own time.

In the past, learning has been largely about 'what' – a specific body of knowledge. *The Great Learning* referred to above is a good example. It contained everything aspiring Chinese scholars needed to know to pass the civic service examination.

Today, however, learning is more concerned with 'how' – skills that equip young people with the capacity to learn irrespective of the content. This means the focus of learning needs to be on problem solving, innovation, creativity and critical thinking, amongst other things. Students need to be equipped to confront and solve new problems that will arise throughout the breadth of a working life. They must be able to create new knowledge rather than simply regurgitate existing knowledge.

Does this mean there are no longer things that are worth knowing? There are always things worth knowing – our histories, our cultures, our religions, our social practices, etc. But even these are not immune from interrogation. Equipped with skills that help them to 'learn how to learn', students can be in a commanding position to ask the right questions at the right time. They can maintain a questioning attitude to the world around them, including its previously received wisdom. Knowing 'how' to learn is an important prerequisite for knowing 'what' to learn. It means young people can take an inquiring attitude to their learning and will be less likely to take things for granted. This is exactly the kind of learning required in these complex times.

Conclusion

Schools can be social elevators for working class students when schools accept their mission to promote engaging experiences that support future learning. Teachers can contribute to this mission by being role models for their students and realizing that working class students will need extra support to reach the same goals as other students. Governments can also contribute by providing the kind of resources that will enable schools to create technology-rich environments from which all students can benefit. This virtuous circle of governments, schools and teachers, all with a special brief for working class students, can be influential in creating a fair and just society from which all can benefit and in which all can give. Such a society is inclusive rather than exclusive, socially just rather than discriminatory committed to the development of all citizens and not just some. Such a society should not be just a dream – survival in the twenty-first century may well depend on its becoming a reality.

Part II
Prelude: Quality in Teaching

The focus in Part II papers is broadly on teaching itself and the views we bring to it. This is a vexed issue, worldwide, where quite varied approaches are taken to the selection and preparation of teachers and the same variations apply to their conditions of working.

Carol Nicoll, one of Australia's most broadly experienced educators, puts forwards four maxims, number four being: '*Teacher capability and teaching quality are at the heart of effective student learning. A lifelong lust for learning and opportunities to learn through community service can be made realities by consciously engaged and committed teachers. These people exist in all schools and should be treasured and supported*'.

Brian Caldwell speaks with the background of one who has worked in many countries. He raises concerns with the major movement in Australia to set standards across the curriculum. '*I wrestle with the fact that no nation that performs at or above Australia on international tests of student achievement has adopted, let alone successfully implemented, a standards movement like that which now "sweeps across Australian education"*'.

Colin Power has had unparalleled education experience on the world stage mainly through his 12 years heading up the education section at UNESCO in Paris, but it is significant that he sees the teacher-learner partnership still as the key. This leads him to recommend ways of strengthening this relationship. '*The powerful relationship between teacher and learner is central to the task of improving the quality and effectiveness of education. The research confirms that in any education system, it is, in the end, teachers that make the difference*'.

Ian Hill speaks from a similarly wide background from his experience in the International Baccalaureate Organisation in Geneva. He comments on one shortcoming of his own education. '*Transdisciplinarity was not something I experienced; the subjects stayed in separate boxes*'. This is a pattern which he finds inadequate. He contrasts this with the IB pattern. '*IB learners are enquirers, knowledgeable, thinkers, communicators, principled, open-minded, caring, risk takers, balanced, and reflective*'. But he still sees the need for teachers who are committed to their task. '*It was the caring, committed, inspiring teachers who spurred me on – these are personal, attitudinal qualities which make the difference*'.

Joan Abbott-Chapman has a wide background in research on school performance. She is particularly concerned to identify why some students from a deprived background succeed at school in spite of the predominant pattern of failure for such students. She identified a personal quality of persistence which she called 'stickability' as one of two decisive factors. '*Analysis of qualitative and quantitative data showed that the individual's qualities of engagement and "stickability" were deciding factors in study persistence, along with the encouragement of an inspirational teacher*'.

Max Walsh has been working in the Philippines in recent years, during which time he has acted as a consultant in a number of Asian and Pacific countries. His is a reflective piece drawn from his personal experience in those settings. His particular concern is for the loss of motivation which often accompanies poor conditions in the classroom, '*…where severe overcrowding occurs then the systems foster, perhaps unwittingly, a mind-set in students that education is something to be endured until the end-point is reached and a qualification is collected*'.

Nancy Faust Sizer is maintaining an active role in American schools, a role she first undertook in company with her husband Ted Sizer in their groundbreaking initiative, the Coalition of Essential Schools. In her contribution she reflects on the role of the teacher and the strong interrelationship between the expectations of the teacher and those of the students. '*All jobs are complicated, but it seems to me that a teacher's job is more complicated than most. If you have eighty students, and most teachers in the United States have more than that, then you have eighty people whom you must know well, judge where they are in their learning, and use your time together to add value to what they know and can do. Furthermore, you must make the experience engaging to them, one they will deem worthwhile, both at the present and as they look back on it in the future*'.

Susan Pascoe writes from her broad experience, in a variety of roles, as CEO of the Catholic Education Commission in Victoria, then chief executive of the Victorian Curriculum and Assessment Authority and then commissioner in Victoria's State Services Authority. Susan has also had an active role with UNESCO, including chair of the Australian National Commission. To all her roles she brings a deep commitment to students and to quality teaching. '*Maintaining a focus on teacher preparation, induction, professional learning and support should always be a central consideration in workforce planning for school education*'.

Francoise Caillods has seen education for a variety of viewpoints and has a vast experience arising from over four decades at the International Institute of Educational Planning, UNESCO, Paris. She looks beyond the immediate benefits of investment in high-quality education, not just as an extra, but as a vital part of the purpose. '*Other benefits are also expected from such an investment such as improved health, reduced crime, social cohesion, greater equity and justice*'.

Barry McGaw points out very clearly how powerful teachers' expectations are when it comes to either providing or inhibiting the learning of individual. Teachers' expectations also have an impact on important matters such as equity in education.

Chapter 9
Teaching for Learning, Living and Serving

Carol Nicoll

I offer four eclectic maxims for schooling. They do not represent a cohesive philosophy of schooling or education, but they are a sampling of my views which I hope reflect and honour the great life's work of Phil Hughes.

Maxim 1: Educational policy should be driven by broadly researched and well-founded evidence of current trends, research and practice, which may be informed by, but should never be replaced by personal experience

One of the great unrecognized flaws in public policy development, particularly in education, is the tendency to base policy responses on personal experience. Politicians do it. Public servants do it. Journalists and social commentators do it. In a policy domain which is unlike any other (except perhaps the health system, which it is not nearly as like as is frequently suggested), everyone in the Australian community has some experience of schooling. The vast majority of us have been to school, and many of us are parents with children in schooling.

So we possess and freely share what we believe to be well-founded views on schools, teachers and education. It matters not that these views may be based on experiences which occurred many decades ago nor that those experiences may have been particular to our own situation and context rather than 'generalizable' to all Australians. It matters not that many, if not most, teachers and schools today offer students a very different schooling to that which policy makers themselves experienced.

The personal is political and whilst that can be empowering and powerful, it can also be a distraction and problematic.

Undoubtedly my views on education and schooling are influenced by my personal experiences, and I will demonstrate this in this chapter. My goal as a policymaker and educator, however, has been to make contributions, which are coloured by the

C. Nicoll (✉)
Tertiary Education Quality and Standards Agency,
Level 14 530 Collins Street, Melbourne, VIC 3001, Australia
e-mail: Carol.nicoll@teqsa.gov.au

P. Hughes (ed.), *Achieving Quality Education for All*, Education in the Asia-Pacific Region: Issues, Concerns and Prospects 20, DOI 10.1007/978-94-007-5294-8_9,
© Springer Science+Business Media Dordrecht 2013

personal but grounded in the empirical and the contemporary, and articulate something that is more than the self-evident. My hope for the broader enterprise of policymaking is that there is a real awareness of the personal and a conscious utilization of it rather than an unconscious promotion of it as the reality for all.

Maxim 2: Learning through service should be facilitated for all students

In the first of my references to my own life experience, I will share an anecdote from 1985, when I headed off overseas for a year after my first year of teaching. One of my first destinations was Vancouver Island in Canada, where I met some young people on a bus who were participants in a national programme called Katimavik (meaning 'meeting place'). I was invited to stay the night in their group house and had the opportunity to interact with a diverse range of young people from all over Canada, who were working on the building of a new child-care centre in a disadvantaged area.

At that time, the Katimavik programme involved volunteers (17–21 years) being posted for a year to live with nine others and participate in a community-based project. Participants were paid living expenses and an incentive lump sum at the conclusion of the programme. The programme has evolved considerably since it began in 1977, but it continues to involve up to 1,000 young Canadians each year in community-based projects across the nation.

Katimavik volunteers are given opportunities to learn in authentic contexts, with minimal supervision. They develop a broad range of skills, including how to live with others, teamwork, problem-solving, language skills (postings are often to language communities other than the first language of the participant), environmental awareness and civic responsibility.

This accidental encounter made a very strong impression on me, and it has reinforced a conviction that 'service learning', as I came to know it many years later, has much potential in the school context. It is part of a long tradition of experiential and active learning, originally articulated and developed in schools in the United States in the 1960s. It has been defined as 'a teaching and learning strategy that integrates meaningful community service with instruction and reflection to enrich the learning experience, teach civic responsibility, and strengthen communities' (National Service Learning Clearing House, 2011).

Volunteering and community service have been long present in many Australian schools through formal programmes such as Duke of Edinburgh Awards or less formal school-based volunteer activities and through engagement by some children in organizations such as the Girl Guides or Scouts. An increasing number of schools are now offering their students involvement in local, national or international community initiatives, which include environmental projects, charities or international aid work. They see the value for students in providing community-based opportunities to address and solve complex problems in context, rather than in isolation in the classroom, and to do so in cooperation, rather than in competition, with others.

Service learning is, however, much more than community service. It is a deliberate and conscious mode of learning which teachers need to scaffold and structure with appropriate analysis and reflection. Whilst the Katimavik programme focuses on learning experiences for young adults, I believe that community-based learning opportunities are suitable for students of most ages if tailored to their readiness and capacity for meaningful and safe engagement.

I believe that the integration and promotion of 'service learning' should be part of the educational offering in all schools, to all Australian students.

Maxim 3: The opportunity to develop a love of and commitment to learning should be an entitlement for all students.

I would like to see all children learning in safe environments, exposed to positive experiences that develop life skills, allowing them to build the appropriate foundations for optimizing their potential to become productive, active and happy participants in civil society. Thus, I essentially subscribe to a human capital paradigm of education. I do believe that active engagement in meaningful work for all, whether it is paid or not, will bring rich returns to both the individual and our nation.

Yet beyond that, I believe that a love of learning – learning for the pure personal pleasure of learning - should have a valued, if not sacrosanct, place in our classrooms. The central driver of schooling and, consequently, educational policymaking has become enhancement of and support for learning in the interests of passing of assessment, the awarding of a credential or for securing a place in tertiary education and ultimately a job. Conceptually 'a love of learning' verges on cliché status, and it is open to derision and dismissal for being illusive, intangible and a distraction from the main game of education.

I have not yet located the research that supports the importance that a love of learning has in individual development, although perhaps work on emotional intelligence and competences or multiple learning styles would provide a framework for it. But my own experience as a teacher has shown me that where a passion for learning exists, students are motivated to struggle with content that seems impermeable and problems that seem insurmountable, and will not be defeated by concepts that are not readily comprehended.

I believe that developing or acquiring a passion for learning, a desire to further develop skills, knowledge and understanding, whatever the field of endeavour or level of attainment, will bring personal satisfaction and self-confidence and increase the potential for creative and independent thought.

Where curiosity and an openness to learning seem to have a more commonly accepted place in early childhood education, as one moves through formal schooling, particularly upper secondary school, there seems less and less time for developing, facilitating or acknowledging a love of learning as an outcome. There are so many pressures on teachers and schools to put more and more into the curriculum – a crowded curriculum allows no time for something as seemingly intangible and unproductive as a passion for learning for learning's sake.

As an end in itself, I believe that a love of learning should be a priority afforded to all children, whatever their apparent strengths, weaknesses or learning preferences.

Maxim 4: Teacher capability and teaching quality are at the heart of effective student learning.

A lifelong lust for learning and opportunities to learn through community service can be made realities by consciously engaged and committed teachers. These people exist in all schools and should be treasured and supported.

I will close with another personal anecdote and share one of the most lasting memories of my schooling. It is a memory of a school garden. When I was in Year 4, a small piece of unused space in the grounds of a Brisbane government primary school was given over to a motley group of students, including myself, to turn into a vegetable garden. I have no recollection of how we were enlisted as the gardeners, but I suspect we were conscripted by our teacher. Most of us were 'fringe dwellers', outside or on the periphery of the strong friendship circles that existed in the class – we were recent arrivals from interstate and had an intellectual or physical disability, or we were just 'different'.

Over a year, we worked as a team in the garden during our breaks – improving the soil, sewing seeds, pulling weeds and watering. I learned how to work with others, particularly those with diverse and limited capacities. I learned how to learn new skills and how to assist others to learn. I learned how to manage time and organize activities. We learned in a relatively safe environment – collectively developing strategies to deal with taunts from other children about the odd group of gardeners. We learned through active engagement towards a shared goal. We learned from each other.

On reflection, I realize that whilst we thought we were operating without any supervision, without a teacher, there was a skillful educator overseeing it all. Mrs Richardson had orchestrated a learning experience more supportive and more instructive than any of the lessons which she delivered in fairly conservative parameters within the classroom. The vegetable garden was a deliberate structured learning opportunity designed and implemented by an inspired teacher.

She was a creative, responsive and innovative teacher – and it is such teachers who make the real difference in our schools. These are the teachers who are capable of facilitating and achieving high-quality educational experiences for all students.

It is no revelation that it is teachers who make the real difference in educational outcomes for students. We know this from personal experience, but it is also borne out through research – and in this, I move from the personal to a tiny snapshot of the research evidence.

In his synthesis of the literature of school outcomes, John Hattie (2003) showed that the greatest source of variance in schooling that can make a difference is the teacher – 'excellence in teaching is the single most powerful influence on achievement' (2003, p.4). The much publicized report by McKinsey & Company (2007) compared 25 school systems and concluded that three things mattered most in the performance of the top school systems, and two of these related to the teachers – 'getting the right people to become teachers' and 'developing them into effective instructors'.

If we accept that the greatest point of in-school variance to student learning is the teacher, then a most appropriate target for public investment in education should be the facilitation and enhancement of teacher capability and teaching quality.

Effective, skilled and committed teachers make the difference in student learning. Our society needs to acknowledge their centrality to national and individual development and prosperity.

References

Hattie, J. (2003). *Teachers make a difference: What is the research evidence?* Australian Council for Educational Research Annual Conference. http://www.acer.edu.au/documents/RC2003_Hattie_TeachersMakeADifference.pdf

McKinsey & Company (2007). *How the world's best-performing school systems come out on top* (Global Education Report). http://mckinseyonsociety.com/how-the-worlds-best-performing-schools-come-out-on-top/. September 2007.

National Service Learning Clearing House (2011). http://www.servicelearning.org/what-service-learning

Chapter 10
How the Call for High Standards of Teaching May Be Hijacked

Brian J. Caldwell

The front cover of the March 2011 issue of *Professional Educator*, the journal of the Australian College of Educators, carried the statement that 'As the standards movement sweeps across Australian education, all eyes will be on its success in improving quality'. Inside the publication, an advertisement of the Australian Institute for Teaching and School Leadership (AITSL) declared that 'locally and internationally, education systems are developing professional standards for teachers as a mechanism for attracting, developing, recognising and retaining quality teachers. Now, for the first time, we have a uniform set of Standards Australia wide and agreement by every system and sector or jurisdiction to implement them'.

It is a considerable achievement to gain such an agreement on well over 100 statements that set out in detailed fashion what teachers need to know and be able to do at different stages of their career. Leaving aside the many issues of how they will be used for their intended purpose, there is the challenge of reconciling the merit of breaking down the role of the teacher in this reductionist manner with a commitment to doing whatever it takes to ensure the highest standard of teaching for all students in all settings. This is a personal concern as I wrestle with the fact that no nation that performs at or above Australia on international tests of student achievement has adopted, let alone successfully implemented, a standards movement like that which now 'sweeps across Australian education'.

In preparing this short contribution, I reread two publications of the last 4 years that celebrate the work of teachers and the personal and professional achievements of Phillip Hughes. One is *Opening the Doors to the Future*, edited by Phillip, and published in 2007 by ACER Press. It contains stories of 18 prominent Australians, including Phillip himself, about the influence of their teachers. In most instances, they refer to influence that lifted them out of their immediate often highly disadvantaged circumstances to set them on a trajectory to high accomplishment in their fields.

B.J. Caldwell (✉)
Educational Transformations Pty Ltd,
Level 1 181 Bay Street, Brighton, VIC 3186, Australia
e-mail: brian@educationaltransformations.com.au

P. Hughes (ed.), *Achieving Quality Education for All*, Education in the Asia-Pacific
Region: Issues, Concerns and Prospects 20, DOI 10.1007/978-94-007-5294-8_10,
© Springer Science+Business Media Dordrecht 2013

The second is *Learning and Teaching for the Twenty-First Century*, edited by Rupert Maclean, published by Springer in (2007) as a *festschrift* (tribute) for Phillip. In each of these publications, there are accounts of teaching of the highest standard, yet there is not a single account in nearly 500 pages of anything that approximates a 'standards movement', even though every contributor celebrates or describes teaching of the highest standard.

Phillip Hughes recognises the need for large-scale reform. As he concluded in his commentary on contributions to the *festschrift*: 'The "scaling-up" of the success of individual teachers is the concern not only of individuals and governments but of international organisations' (p. 304). Moreover, he declares, there is a sense of urgency as far as context is concerned: 'There is little time left if we are to find solutions that will work. The tide of events is running in the wrong direction' (p. 300). Michael Fullan, who is at the international forefront in describing and designing efforts at large-scale education reform, contributed to the *festschrift* and referred to the impressive improvements that had been made over the last decade in Ontario, where there is no standards movement of the kind sweeping Australia. The Ontario Institute of Teachers has formulated five standards for practice in the teaching profession, all of which are summarised on a single page.

Ruth Radford cited Phillip in her contribution to the *festschrift*, referring to a statement that immediately challenges the effort to fragment the role of the teacher. The complexity of teaching, according to Phillip, 'lies in the human relationships and the myriad interactions between people and people, between people and learning materials. The vast range of individuality for people, on every dimension of experience, of personality and of mind, means that what is appropriate for one person will be less so for another. It is not surprising, then, that our reflections on teaching, and the qualities required, do not provide easy answers' (p. 296). What Phillip described here may be accommodated in several of the AITSL standards, but to give these the same weight as each of more than 100 other standards is a futile exercise. Phillip noted in his Foreword to *Opening Doors to the Future* that 'Teaching is one of the more mysterious processes between people. . . . We know less about learning than we do about the ills of the human body or organising tax returns' (p. v).

The standards movement in Australia is gathering momentum at the same time that national testing has taken hold through the National Assessment Program – Literacy and Numeracy (NAPLAN), and unprecedented transparency of school performance has emerged in the My School website. There is a powerful argument that NAPLAN and My School will lead to a narrowing of the curriculum so that much of its richness is stripped away. There is evidence that this has occurred in England (Alexander, 2009). The issue here is whether a 'tick the boxes' reductionist approach to analysing the work of teachers ('the standards movement'), in addition to a narrow focus on literacy and numeracy and the reporting of mainly quantitative data, will, in the long run, widen rather than narrow the achievements of students in different settings and de-professionalise rather than enrich the professionalism of teachers.

At Educational Transformations, we gained a more positive view of what is possible in research commissioned by The Song Room (TSR), as published in

Bridging the Gap in School Achievement through the Arts (The Song Room, 2011), launched by Hon Peter Garrett, Australia's Minister for School Education, Early Childhood and Youth in March 2011. The findings are reported in *Transforming Education through the Arts* (Caldwell & Vaughan, 2012) along with issues for policy and practice that are summarised in this chapter.

The Song Room is a non-profit philanthropic organisation that provides free music and arts-based programmes for children in disadvantaged and other high-need settings. According to The Song Room, an astonishing 700,000 students in government primary schools in Australia have no opportunity to participate in programmes in the arts. The research reported here was funded by the Macquarie Group Foundation.

We examined the performance of students in 10 schools in highly disadvantaged settings in Western Sydney. Three schools offered a longer-term programme over 12–18 months, and three schools offered an initial short-term programme of 6 months. In each instance, the programme was conducted for Grade 5 students for 1 hour on a single day once per week. A control group of four schools did not offer The Song Room programme. The three sets of schools were a matched set. At the time of the study, they scored roughly the same on the Australian Curriculum, Assessment and Reporting Authority (ACARA) and Index of Community Socio-Educational Advantage (ICSEA), as calculated in 2009. An even closer match was evident when 2010 ICSEA scores were used. The study is a rare example of quasi-experimental design in educational research. Minister Garrett drew attention to the use of NAPLAN and My School in research in noting that 'Academics are using the site as a significant repository of research material' (Garrett, 2011).

We found important differences in favour of students that undertake The Song Room programme. The findings have national and international significance. First, related research in other countries is confirmed. Second, there appears to be a direct association between the arts and outcomes in other areas. Third, the wisdom of including the arts in Australia's national curriculum is confirmed.

Students in TSR programmes outperformed students in non-TSR schools in school achievement tests and in NAPLAN tests. Fewer students in TSR programmes failed to reach minimum standards in NAPLAN tests. The percentage of students absent on a the day when TSR programmes were offered were higher in non-TSR schools than in TSR schools, an important finding given that students who are not attending school are not engaged in learning.

Grade 5 students in each school completed the well-validated Social-Emotional Well-being (SEWB) survey designed at the Australian Council for Educational Research (ACER). It has been administered to thousands of students over the years. A higher proportion of students in TSR programmes were at the highest levels of SEWB than their counterparts in non-TSR schools. Those in TSR programmes had higher levels of reliance and lower levels of stress.

While caution must always be exercised in drawing cause-and-effect relationships, these differences in comparisons in matched sets of schools were statistically significant. Moreover, the longer the students were in TSR programmes, the greater the differences. The findings were to some extent unexpected because TSR programmes ran for just one hour on one day in the week, but they are consistent with what has been found in other nations for students in similar settings.

Literacy and numeracy are critically important, and teachers must be well-equipped to raise levels of achievement. However, a testing regime and an unprecedented high-stakes transparency mechanism that serves to narrow the curriculum may be counterproductive.

It is not too late to change direction in Australia and encourage critique that follows the lead of US scholar Diane Ravitch. Ravitch is Research Professor of Education at New York University and a senior fellow at the Brookings Institution. From 1991 to 1993, she was Assistant Secretary for Education and Counsellor to Secretary of Education Lamar Alexander in the administration of President George H. W. Bush. President Clinton appointed her to the National Assessment Governing Board, which oversees federal testing. After previously supporting testing and extensive choice, including charter schools and the engagement of the philanthropic sector, she has reversed her position on each. Her strongest criticism is levelled at the testing movement and, among other things, the way it has narrowed the curriculum, including the arts.

The title of Chapter 2 in her book *The Death and Life of the American School System* (Ravitch, 2010) is 'Hijacked! How the standards movement turned into the testing movement'. She elaborates: 'How did testing and accountability become the main levers of school reform? How did our elected officials become convinced that measurement and data would fix the schools? Somehow our nation got off the track in its efforts to improve education. What once was the standards movement was replaced by the accountability movement' (Ravitch, 2010, p.16).

At the heart of the problem, according to Ravitch, is the relationship between testing and the purposes of education:

> Not everything that matters can be quantified. What is tested may ultimately be less important than what is untested, such as a student's ability to seek alternative explanations, to raise questions, to pursue knowledge on his own, and to think differently. If we do not treasure our individualists, we will lose the spirit of innovation, inquiry, imagination, and dissent that has contributed powerfully to the success of our society in many different fields of endeavour. (Ravitch, 2010, p. 226)

Ravitch is describing here the same capacities that were nurtured in the 20 people who celebrated the contributions of their teachers in Phillip's book *Opening the Doors to the Future*. Consider the story of eminent neurosurgeon Charlie Teo, who recounted the influence of his Year 6 teacher who picked him for a lead role in a play: 'We've all got hidden talents and some teachers are very sensitive to ways of bringing out those talents' (Hughes, 2007, p. 137). Teo could not remember 'a teacher who made an academic impact on me' so that 'what remain in his mind are the lessons about life' (p. 138).

A remarkable story about life and learning in *Opening the Doors to the Future* is that of Paul Brock, one of Australia's eminent leaders in education and a great teacher in his own right. He declares that 'Great educators are those who, while conserving the best in the past, enhance and even transform themselves through creatively responding to change experienced in the present' (p. 22). He is one of the co-authors of *Imagination Innovation Creativity: Re-visioning English in Education* who set out to

> ...*Stress the importance of reconnecting and re-engaging with what teachers – and thereby, potentially, students – love about English: its unique capacity to engage the mind, the spirit and the heart; to stimulate imagination, curiosity and creative capacities through meaningful immersion in the stories of humanity, and to enrich and develop students' cognitive and affective command and understanding of language in all its expansive dimensions, contexts and purposes. (Manuel, Brock, Sawyer, & Carter, 2009, p. 7)*

They conclude, as do I, that 'at a moment in Australian history when the National Curriculum is being developed, the warnings are here about the kind of testing that would defeat any well-intentioned move for richness and depth in that curriculum' (p. 9). There is too much to lose if the call for high standards wanders off course or worse, is hijacked.

References

Alexander, R. (2009). *Children, their world, their education* (Final report and recommendations of the Cambridge Primary Review). Robin Alexander (Ed.). London: Routledge.

Caldwell, B. J., & Vaughan, T. (2012). *Transforming education through the arts*. London/New York: Routledge.

Garrett, P. (2011). Fuelling discontent about private school funding. *The Australian*. April 5.

Hughes, P. (Ed.). (2007). *Opening the doors to the future*. Melbourne, Australia: ACER Press.

Maclean, R. (Ed.). (2007). *Learning and teaching for the twenty-first century*. New York: Springer.

Manuel, J., Brock, P., Sawyer, W., & Carter D. (2009). "What is within becomes what is around": Imagination, innovation, creativity. In J. Manuel, P. Brock, D. Carter, & W. Sawyer, (Eds.), *Imagination innovation creativity: Re-visioning English in education* (Chapter 1, pp. 7–12. Putney, Australia: Phoenix Education .

Ravitch, D. (2010). *The death and life of the Great American School System*. New York: Basic Books.

The Song Room (2011). *Bridging the gap in school achievement through the arts*. Abbotsford, Australia: The Song Room,

Chapter 11
A High-Quality Education for All

Colin Power

What Do You Think Is Necessary to Provide an Effective, Relevant and High-Quality Education for All Children?

In the 1960s, the education departments of each Australian state had a tiny group of professionals responsible for educational research, planning and curriculum. It was at this time that secondary education for all was becoming a reality, and given this, major reforms were needed to meet the needs of a rapidly changing and ever more diverse student population. Phillip Hughes headed curriculum and research in the Tasmanian Education Department and played a leading role making the necessary reforms not only in Tasmania but also nationally. For my part, I joined the Research and Curriculum Branch of the Queensland Department of Education in 1964, and it has been my privilege ever since to work with, and to be inspired by, Phillip Hughes.

Our shared agenda was, and still is, that of working with governments, non-government organizations and educators throughout the world to ensure that all children are provided with an education that is effective, relevant and of high quality. But what is an effective, relevant, high-quality education? The question itself is value laden: how it is answered reflects one's values and philosophy of education. While education systems do vary in terms of approach and emphasis, there is general agreement about the overall purposes of education. These are set out in the Universal Declaration of Human Rights, the Convention on the Rights of the Child and the Convention on Discrimination in Education and are enshrined in the constitution and legislation of most nations. As Article 26 of the Universal Declaration insists, "Everyone has the right to education…" which is to be "free" and "compulsory in the elementary stages". The declaration and conventions go on to specify the

C. Power (✉)
School of Education, University of Queensland, St. Lucia Brisbane,
QLD 4072, Australia
e-mail: c.power@eidos.org.au

P. Hughes (ed.), *Achieving Quality Education for All*, Education in the Asia-Pacific Region: Issues, Concerns and Prospects 20, DOI 10.1007/978-94-007-5294-8_11,
© Springer Science+Business Media Dordrecht 2013

aims of education, thus to indicate the criteria by which the effectiveness, quality
and relevance of education are to be judged (Power, 2001, 2005).

Given the emphasis accorded in the Charter of the United Nations to "the dignity
and worth of each person", education must be seen as a basic human right. It is a
right to be respected not just because high-quality education is the "engine of development" in modern societies, but because the full development of the individual
remains the basic purpose of education, and not, as in authoritarian systems, political, economic or religious indoctrination and control. Effectiveness, relevance and
quality then should be judged in terms of the extent to which schools help every
child to reach their fullest potential in terms of their cognitive, emotional and creative capacities. In essence, a quality education is one that empowers each person to
make his or her own way in life, to think critically, to care about others and the
environment, to make informed decisions and to act responsibly. It is the task of the
school to lay the foundations that enable all children to continue to learn throughout
their lives: learning to know, learning to do, learning to live together and learning to
be (UNESCO, 1996).

Both Phil and I also share a passion for helping to ensure all children have access
to an education that is of high quality and is relevant to their needs. We are committed to creating the conditions necessary to improve the quality of teaching because
the most effective schools are those with excellent teachers and outstanding principals. At the end of the day, it is what happens in the classroom that really matters.
The effectiveness of educational policies and reforms must be judged in the end by
their impact on teachers and learners, that is, the extent to which they help teachers
and schools, especially those serving the disadvantaged, to meet the learning needs
of their students.

We have made some progress towards achieving the goals of basic education for
all. When I joined UNESCO in 1989, the number of children who had no access to
schooling was well in excess of 100 million, and an estimated 960 million adults
were illiterate. In 1990, UNESCO, together with its partners, sponsored the World
Conference on Education for All (WCEFA). For the past 20 years, UNESCO and its
partners have continued to promote and to support the efforts being made to achieve
the goals of Education for All (EFA). For the first time in history, the absolute number of children and adults whose right to basic education has been denied is falling.
Nevertheless, 72 million children have no access to schooling; hundreds of millions
more drop out early, because they live in extreme poverty, the quality is poor or what
is being taught seems to be irrelevant. Moreover, over 700 million adults are illiterate: they lack the knowledge, skills and opportunities needed to break out of the
cycle of poverty and to fight for the rights of their children (UNESCO, 2010).

In the aftermath of World War II, world leaders were convinced that providing a
quality education was the key to "building peace in the minds of men" and women
and the foundation for peace, the protection of human rights, freedom and democracy. In 2000, the heads of government met at the UN Millennium Development
Summit. They agreed that universal access to quality basic education and empowering girls and women through education are the keys to the eradication of poverty
and sustainable development. In 2011, providing quality education for all remains

the essential, but often the missing, ingredient in the struggle to create a more peaceful world, to ensure that fundamental rights and freedoms are respected and to protect our fragile planet, before it is too late.

What then is necessary to ensure that the basic educational needs of all children are met? At the 1990 World Conference, the representatives of all education systems and intergovernmental organizations worldwide agreed on what we mean by basic learning needs, while acknowledging that precisely what knowledge and skills should be given priority depend on the age and circumstances of the learner and community in which he or she lives:

> *Every person – child, youth and adult- shall be able to benefit from educational opportunities designed to meet their basis learning needs. These needs comprise both the essential learning tools (such as literacy, oral expression, numeracy, and problem solving) and the basic learning content (such as knowledge. skills, values and attitudes) required by human beings to be able to survive, to develop their full capacities, to live and work with dignity, to participate fully in development, to improve the quality of their lives, to make informed decisions, and to continue learning. The scope of basic learning needs and how they should be met varies with individual countries and cultures, and inevitably changes with the passage of time. (Article 1: World Declaration on Education for All (WDEFA), 1990)*

We also agreed on some of the measures necessary for progress to be made in providing effective, relevant, quality education for all. These included:

1. *Enhancing the environment for learning. "Learning does not take place in isolation. Societies, therefore, must ensure that children receive the nutrition, health care and general emotional and physical support they need to participate actively in, and to benefit from, their education" (WDEFA, Article 6).* The countries making least progress towards the goals of EFA are those caught in a vicious cycle of conflict and poverty – countries like Somalia, Afghanistan, Niger, Sierra Leone and Democratic Republic of Congo. But the quality of the education being provided in many of the schools of wealthy nations is under threat as well: "reforms" and policies stemming from the application of free market ideology to education, health and other social services are based on the premise that quality education is not a basic human right for all but a commodity to be traded and to be bought by those who can afford it. The gaps in quality between schools serving the affluent and those attended by the poor are widening. Urgent measures are needed to ensure that all children are equally well supported by quality teaching and that the other basic conditions necessary for them to benefit from education are met (Power, 2007; Sachs, 2005).

2. *Developing political will and commitment. "Supportive policies in the social, cultural and economic sectors are required to realize the full provision and utilization of basic education for individual and societal improvement" (WDEFA, Article 8).* In assessing progress made towards EFA, the major obstacle is the lack of political will (Power, 2007; Sen, 2007). The reality is that the governments of many poor countries either cannot afford, or are reluctant to devote, a greater share of their meagre resources to education. While pretending to help, the governments of most rich countries lack the political will to honour their promises. Moreover, much of the "aid" provided is "tied aid", serving the donor's political

and trade interests. UNESCO (2010) estimates that an extra $16 billion per year is needed to achieve EFA in the world's poorest countries but aid for basic education is less than $2.7 billion. Building political will ultimately rests on "people power". Democracy works only if all citizens are well educated and take seriously their responsibilities as citizens, fighting for what is in the "common good" and pressuring governments to meet their obligations. A well-informed public is unlikely to be swayed by the "spin doctors" and more likely to play an active role in working with the school to assure quality, relevance and effectiveness of its curriculum and teaching.

3. *Mobilizing resources. "If the basic learning needs of all are to be met…it is essential to mobilize existing and new financial and human resources, public, private and voluntary" (WDEFA, Article 9).* Governments have a particular responsibility to ensure that schools have the resources needed to ensure their teaching is effective, relevant and of high quality. Having reviewed the evidence from around the world, the International Commission Education for the twenty-first century (UNESCO, 1996) concluded public investment in education needs to be at least 6 per cent of gross national product. But globally, the average public expenditure on education is about 4.1 per cent, well below the minimum figure required to assure a quality education for all. Of course, it is critically important that funds are not wasted, that is, that investments in education actually do significantly expand access to and the quality of education. When making funding decisions, governments, communities and donors need to know what the research indicates actually will make a difference. At times, large sums are spent on equipment, facilities and programmes for political rather than educational reasons ("pork-barrelling", pandering to lobby groups), or to be seen to keeping up with the latest trends in education, for example, investing heavily in hardware but not in the software, maintenance and training required for it to be effective. While maintaining the pressure on governments to meet their responsibilities, it is also clear that the burden must be shared. Parents, communities, employers and voluntary organizations also have a vitally important role to play in mobilizing the necessary human and financial resources need to develop to the full the capabilities of all children.

4. *Building partnerships with parents and the community.* It is a mistake to leave everything to the state – to do so, is to compromise the rights and responsibilities of parents and the community. In an effective education system, there is an appropriate balance between meeting the needs of the society (and not just the state) and those of the individual. To develop, every society needs a skilled workforce and for its citizens to be equipped with the knowledge and skills needed to participate effectively in their society. Effective education systems and good schools make maximum use of the resources available to them in the community, both human and financial, and forge strong partnerships with parents, community groups, other schools and universities. The research on effective schools confirms that effective schools and good teachers devote considerable energy in forging strong and mutually supportive partnerships with parents and the community. Effective education systems similarly forge strong partnerships with community

groups, professional educational and research organizations when undertaking curriculum and assessment reforms. Such partnerships are crucial if education programmes are to be relevant, and young people are to be equipped with the knowledge, skills and values needed to tackle the challenges facing them in the foreseeable future.

5. *Supporting teachers and raising the status and quality of teaching.* The powerful relationship between teacher and learner is central to the task of improving the quality and effectiveness of education. The research confirms that in any education system, it is, in the end, teachers that make the difference (Maclean, 2007; Power, 2007). What is rarely recognized is that teaching is a highly complex and demanding professional task and that there are no quick and easy fixes when it comes to assessing and improving the quality of teaching. Urgent measures are needed to improve the attractiveness of teaching as a profession. This will not happen if the standards for entry into teacher education programmes are low, the conditions of service are poor, the professionalism of teachers is not respected, and little is done to support and retain well-qualified and effective teachers. The reality is that the status of teaching is declining in many countries, endangering the quality and effectiveness of their education system. School principals, teachers and educational researchers working with them to improve teaching and learning in their schools know much more about what it takes to improve quality than most bureaucrats, politicians, would-be reformers and spin doctors. I must add that setting targets and standards makes little difference if governments and education authorities ignore them when recruiting and training teachers and if the conditions in schools are so bad that it is difficult to retain good teachers. The data generated by national and international monitoring and assessment programmes may give a rough indication of the extent to which progress is being made at the national, regional and international level towards a limited set of goals, but in themselves, they do not provide reliable, valid or usable measures of teacher or school performance (Power, 2009; Power & Wood, 1984). What is important is that each school actively works with its community to evaluate the quality and relevance of its teaching and programmes and on the basis of the evidence gathered, takes the steps necessary to improve the quality and effectiveness of the education being provided.

6. *Ensuring equity and fairness in the provision of education, nationally and internationally.* Quality education for all, means quality for all. Quality and equality are inseparable and must go forwards together, each strengthening the other. In my experience of working with countries in conflict, discrimination, injustice and inequality in education have proven to be corrosive and the root cause of many of the conflicts and social ills of society (Power, 2009). Sadly, in many countries, rates of participation in education are considerably lower for girls, indigenous peoples, the disabled and those living in poverty and in remote areas, and one must be seriously concerned about the quality of the education being provided (Power, 2001, 2007; UNESCO, 2009, 2010). In developed countries, as Connors (2011) has noted "we hear debates about equity in relation to the dollars available to schools, but little about equity in relation to access to quality

teaching". She notes that "fairness has been swept off the agenda of many democracies by the dangerous trust in markets and competition to sort out for us the kind of societies we want to be and the way we wish to treat each other".

References

Connors, L. (2011). Putting fairness back on the agendas. *Professional Educator, 10*(2), 3–4.
Maclean, R. (Ed.). (2007). *Learning and teaching for the twenty-first century Festschift for Professor Phillip Hughes*. Dordrecht, The Netherlands: Springer.
Power, C. (2001). UNESCO's response to the challenge of creating unity in diversity. In J. Campbell (Ed.), *Creating our Common Future*. Paris: UNESCO/Berghahn Books.
Power, C. (2005). Quo vadis? Education for what purpose? *Social Alternatives, 24*(2), 13–18.
Power, C. (2009, November). *Addressing UN Millennium Development Goals*. Keynote address, ANZCIES Conference, Armidale.
Power, C. N. (2007). Achieving universal primary education and EIU. *Journal of Education for International Understanding, 3*, 106–128.
Power, C. N., & Wood, R. (1984). National assessment: A review of programs in Australia, United Kingdom and United States. *Comparative Education Review, 28*(3), 355–377.
Sachs, J. (2005). *The End of Poverty*. London: Penguin Books.
Sen, A. (2007). *Civil paths to peace*. London: Commonwealth Secretariat.
UNESCO. (1996). *Learning: The treasure within*. Paris: UNESCO.
UNESCO. (2009). *EFA Monitoring Report 2009*. Paris: UNESCO.
UNESCO. (2010). *EFA Global Monitoring Report 2010*. Paris: UNESCO.
WDEFA. (1990). *Declaration and framework for action*. Paris: UNESCO.

Chapter 12
Quality Education for All

Ian Hill

Introduction

I was born in Hobart in 1947. When I did my Diploma of Education in 1968 at the University of Tasmania, Charles Hardy was professor of education, and Phil Hughes was my lecturer for the statistics section of the course. At the same time, Phil was deputy director general in the education department. It was in the latter part of the 1980s that I came into frequent professional contact with Phil when he was professor of education at the University of Tasmania, and I was private secretary to the Minister for Education. I left Tasmania in early 1990 to become director of an international bilingual (English/French) IB (see below) school in France at Sophia Antipolis, Europe's largest technology park between Nice and Cannes.

Phil visited the school, and we spent time together during his visits to Europe and kept in touch. I moved in late 1993 to Geneva as regional director for Africa, Europe and Middle East for the International Baccalaureate (IB) organisation. We caught up with each other on several occasions, and I attended meetings with him when he was working in Paris on the Delors report (1996) for UNESCO in the late 1990s. I saw Phil the last time for dinner in October 2008 in Geneva when he received the Comenius Medal from UNESCO during the International Conference on Education for his contribution to education.

I. Hill (✉)
International Baccalaureate Organisation, Route des Morillons 15,
1218, Grand-Saconnex, Geneva, Switzerland
e-mail: ian.hill@ibo.org

P. Hughes (ed.), *Achieving Quality Education for All*, Education in the Asia-Pacific Region: Issues, Concerns and Prospects 20, DOI 10.1007/978-94-007-5294-8_12, © Springer Science+Business Media Dordrecht 2013

Lessons Learnt from My Own Schooling in Hobart, Tasmania

Like most of us, I still remember the teachers who impressed me at Elizabeth Street Primary School, New Town High School and Hobart Matriculation College from which I graduated in 1964. They were knowledgeable, focused, precise, committed, firm and caring classroom practitioners. They inspired me to live up to their expectations – and they set the bar high. They gave me an excellent grounding in the various disciplines in terms of knowledge, skills and attitudes. It enabled me to go on to successful study in higher education (including an M Ed Admin from the University of New England) and to embark on a life-long career in education, commencing as a high school teacher in Tasmania and ending soon (I will retire during 2012) as deputy director general of the IB organisation in Geneva.

The following figure represents my thoughts about educational trends by the 1960s in the USA, the UK and Australia:

Traditional	Progressive
Memorisation	Reflection, analysis
Same content for all	Student choice
Hermetic subjects	Transdisciplinarity
IQ tests	Range of skills testing
Didactic	Constructivism
Teacher-centred	Child-centred
Academic intelligence	Whole child
Machine-scored tests	"Project" method
Translation (languages)	AV & AL (languages)
Closed classrooms	Open plan rooms
Passive reception	Proactive participation

The traditional part of the continuum was commonplace, except for isolated instances of progressive education which became more prevalent from the 1960s and slowly started to influence state systems. Some countries today still deliver traditional educational fare as described above; my comments about revised educational models are principally in the context of North America, the UK and Australia.

An early example of progressive (read "better quality") education experimentation was Dewey's laboratory school at the University of Chicago in 1896 which sought to tap the natural curiosity of students. His school had class sizes of a dozen or so students from upper middle class families where the parents valued education, and forward-thinking, hand-picked teachers. In later life, Dewey admitted that what he was able to produce in that select environment was untenable in mass education systems (Flanagan, 1994). Similarly in the UK, A. S. Neill's "Summerhill" of 1921 allowed students to develop without adult authority constraints and as they wish (Neill, 2011). It's an intriguing model of progressive education, still alive today and surviving an Office of Standards in Education (OFSTED) report in 2007 (see references) which rated the spiritual, moral, cultural and social development of the 78 pupils as "outstanding" and the formal curriculum as "satisfactory".

It was the work of developmental psychologists like Piaget in the first half of the twentieth century and Bruner's focus on students as problem solvers, which began to impact on state systems: pedagogy was adapted to the new knowledge about how students learn and what motivates them.

I was at school during the late 1950s and early 1960s when the impact of educators like those above was gaining ground. Thinking back, I would place my teachers towards the left hand side of the above continuum. We didn't do IQ or machine-scored tests, but the teaching was basically didactic and teacher centred, and the classrooms were closed. The only choice I remember was between studying French or German in secondary school and between a number of musical instruments such as the trumpet, violin, flute or recorder. The language classes however provided for plenty of oral work and almost no translation from French into English or vice versa. There were practical tests in the sciences and in "woodwork" and "metal-work" as they were called; in the latter, we worked with anvils and furnaces. There were plenty of sports, but no invitation to challenge a teacher's opinion or that of any textbook. Transdisciplinarity was not something I experienced; the subjects stayed in separate boxes. Interactive dialogue with teachers did not occur very much; we were basically passive, absorbing what the teachers gave us and we enjoyed it.

So the teaching I received was fairly traditional, content heavy and "bookish" with a certain amount of rote learning, but I cannot say it was bad; on the contrary, it allowed me to evolve because my curious nature urged me to go on learning. Would the same teaching work today? No. A quality education today would have a judicious mixture of progressive ideas and didactic teaching; it is unrealistic to expect that students can undertake only a heuristic learning model – discovering can take a long time and should be part of the educational model, but not the whole of it. I solved maths and science problems, but it was application of learnt rules and formulae to known problems; I'm not sure I always really understood what I was doing, but I could reproduce it faithfully.

When I trained as a language teacher in the late 1960s and then started teaching, the audio-lingual and audiovisual methodologies from both the USA and the UK were the flavour of the day. Many schools were taking up these types of courses, and they did produce tangible results, particularly in listening and speaking skills. It was in the late 1970s that I saw the first open plan classrooms which were an attempt to break down subject boundaries and facilitate team teaching. I have seen them work very successfully in a number of international schools around the world, while other schools prefer not to venture there.

My point is that quality education has a temporal dimension to it. I had a quality education for its time; taken alone it would not satisfy all my criteria today and nor would the progressive initiatives, taken alone, in their "pure" form, as mooted and practised in "laboratory" scenarios. A quality education values the past and embraces the future. It retains what is sound from the past – from traditional and progressive models – and adapts to student needs for the future in a context where "the once reliable constants have now become galloping variables" (Bennis, 1965).

The International Baccalaureate (IB) as Quality Education

My ideal of quality education is the programmes offered by the IB organisation. The IB is a pioneering, educational, not-for-profit foundation registered in Geneva with more than 3,200 schools in 140 countries (in April 2011). The IB offers its programmes for children from 3 to 19 years in English, French or Spanish, and our Middle Years Programme is also offered in Chinese (Mandarin).

The educational philosophy which underpins all programmes is elaborated in the IB learner profile which translates the IB mission into learning outcomes (see reference section). IB learners are enquirers, knowledgeable, thinkers, communicators, principled, open-minded, caring, risk takers, balanced and reflective.

The key tenets of the IB's educational philosophy are:

– International perspective: awareness of global issues and the interdependence of nations and peoples; intercultural understanding and respect.
– Educating the whole person: community service, usually for those who are less privileged, is compulsory along with creative pursuits.
– Critical thinking skills and academic rigour: be prepared to challenge when you doubt what you see or hear; also be prepared to retreat from entrenched positions in the face of compelling evidence or opinion.
– Be aware of multiple perspectives and attempt to understand their origins.
– The most useful knowledge is holistic, not compartmentalised; the best thinking is joined up.
– Understanding leads to the creative application of knowledge and skills to solve new problems.

A quality education in national systems should be in line with this philosophy. We should also recognise that there is more than just academic intelligence. Howard Gardner's work is testimony to different types of intelligences, and they all have value.

I believe IB programmes draw on sound past practices and combine with modern pedagogical approaches which are more child-centred. Hence, we have a balance between didactic teaching and constructivist learning (students using unit planners to study transdisciplinary themes). Team work in research. Memorisation is a skill which should not be shunned; if that's the only way one learns, then it's not good, but it is a valid skill and has its place.

My final point – quality education is all about teacher education. That's my pragmatic observation beginning with my own experience as a student and visiting classrooms in countries in many parts of the world. Around 1997, I was visiting the ministry of education in South Africa and saw their "Curriculum 2000" documents. They were excellent: a blend of old and new thinking, but there was no budget allocated to train the teachers in improved techniques for the child-centred part. The value of the wonderful documents was not realised. The IB insists on teacher training before a school can be accredited, and further professional development at regular intervals is obligatory.

But it's more than professional development. It was the caring, committed, inspiring teachers who spurred me on – these are personal, attitudinal qualities which make the difference.

As I finish this chapter, I am sitting on a Saturday afternoon in April in a bilingual French/English IB diploma school in Dakar, Senegal. A young Senegalese teacher on the staff has just dropped into the office I am occupying to chat. She asked me what I am doing and I told her. She listened as I explained the content of this chapter. Then she said to me, "A blend of old and new ideas in a context of academic rigour is important, but teacher attitude is everything". That's where Phil comes in.

References

Bennis, W. (1965,July). Beyond bureaucracy: Will organization men fit the new organizations? *Society*, 2(5), 31–35.

Delors, J. (Ed.) (1996). *Learning: The treasure within*. Paris: UNESCO.

Flanagan, F. (1994). *John Dewey in "The Great Educator Series"*. Downloaded on April 17, 2011 at http://www.admin.mtu.edu/ctlfd/Ed%20Psych%20Readings/dewey.pdf

IB Learner Profile. http://www.ibo.org/programmes/profile/documents/Learnerprofileguide.pdf. Downloaded on 17 April.

Neil, A. S. (2011). *Summerhill school*. http://www.summerhillschool.co.uk/pages/asneill.html. Downloaded 17 April 2011.

OFSTED report on Summerhill (2007). http://www.ofsted.gov.uk/oxedu_reports/download/(id)/90088/(as)/124870_301621.pdf. Downloaded on 17 April 2011.

Chapter 13
Student School Engagement, Self-Efficacy and Post-compulsory Retention

Joan Abbott-Chapman

Ensuring equality of opportunity in education and more inclusive approaches to student outreach and support, curriculum and pedagogy, are matters of international concern (UNESCO, 2000). As progress is being made towards the Millennium Development Goals of Education For All (EFA), with increased participation in primary education worldwide (UNESCO, 2010), the pressure will increase for governments in economically less developed nations to provide access to, and encourage take up of, opportunities at the secondary and post-compulsory levels. This applies particularly to disadvantaged and marginalized groups such as those with lower socio-economic backgrounds, indigenous people and those living in rural and remote regions (UNICEF, 2005). Although post-compulsory participation rates overall have increased markedly in the more economically developed nations over the past 20 years, disadvantaged groups still remain under-represented, especially at university level (Centre for the Study of Higher Education [CSHE], 2008; OECD, 2008). Policies designed to address these inequalities are important for national and community development (Delors et al., 1996) The success of such policies depends not only provision of educational infrastructure, resources and finances but quality education which is relevant, useful and attractive to students and families who have no previous experience of further and higher education, and which ensures that 'children acquire the skills that shape their future life chances' (UNESCO, 2010, p.104). It is important that students want to go to school, enjoy school and are motivated to stay there. In the words of the *Dakar Framework for Action*, 'The quality of learning is and must be at the heart of Education For All (EFA). All stakeholders... should work together to develop environments conducive to learning' (UNESCO, 2000, 8.65).

J. Abbott-Chapman (✉)
Menzies Research Institute Tasmania, Private Bag 23,
Hobart, TAS 7001, Australia
e-mail: J.AbbottChapman@utas.edu.au; J.AbbottChapman@menzies.utas.edu.au

P. Hughes (ed.), *Achieving Quality Education for All*, Education in the Asia-Pacific Region: Issues, Concerns and Prospects 20, DOI 10.1007/978-94-007-5294-8_13,
© Springer Science+Business Media Dordrecht 2013

For individuals, the benefits of participation in education, especially at the post-compulsory levels, are manifold, not only in terms of improved employment and income opportunities and general standard of living, but also satisfactions of personal development and access to the global knowledge economy (Wyn, 2009). A holistic vision of the goals of education, as expressed in the Australian *Melbourne Declaration,* encompasses an 'education that will promote intellectual, physical, social, emotional, moral, spiritual and aesthetic development and wellbeing' (Ministerial Council for Education and Early Childhood Development and Youth Affairs [MCEECDYA], 2008. p.4). Health is among the life-long effects of participation in education (Hammond, 2002; Walker, 2008). A large-scale study of Australian longitudinal cohort data, which examined the health implications of educational mobility, Gall, Abbott-Chapman, Patton, Dwyer, and Venn (2010) showed that individuals who attained a higher level of education than their parents were more likely to have a healthy lifestyle, with implications for their long-term cardiovascular health. Positive educational experiences also contribute to the development of resilience, self-reliance and self-efficacy (Abbott-Chapman, 2011). These qualities enable young people to navigate their way through the labyrinth of opportunities and choices for education and employment in postmodern societies and to 'take personal responsibility for managing uncertainties and risk that derive from that situation' (Wyn, 2009, p.49). In looking for modifiable variables which encourage participation and persistence, we need to find practices within schools and classrooms which foster this kind of resilience and to examine the examples of those who are successful. In a climate of increasing 'performativity' (Lingard, 2010), McWilliam (2008) suggests that in preparing young people for creative and positive futures, we need transformative education which is 'not just about new technology' or the old style of 'command and control' schooling (p.69). She asserts that 'learner capacity-building is more productive than striving for performance above all else' and that 'teachers and parents who seek to foster a healthy balance of learning goals encourage robust learners who can stick at a task' (p.120).

'Stickability' was a quality which Abbott-Chapman, Hughes, and Wyld (1991) used to describe students whom their Model of Educational Handicap predicted would not pursue their studies beyond year 10, the end of compulsory schooling, but who did so against the odds. The model included measures of school assessed ability potential (SAAP), socio-demographic background, type of school attended at year 10 and gender. Within the longitudinal cohort study of 14,579 students in Tasmania who entered year 10 in 1981 and 1986, 16% of these students who had been predicted by the Model of Educational Handicap not to go beyond year 10 did in fact do so. The 'system breakers' differed from the 'missing high flyers' whom the model predicted to be retained but became early leavers. These 'system breakers, their characteristics and educational histories are of particular interest as we seek to find ways of overcoming the effects of disadvantage' (p.71).

Analysis of qualitative and quantitative data showed that the individual's qualities of engagement and 'stickability' were deciding factors in study persistence, along with the encouragement of an inspirational teacher. In nominating these effective teachers and describing their characteristics, students prioritized their enthusiasm for, and knowledge of, their subject, mutuality of respect between teacher and student and encouragement and support of student learning. A sense of humour was also highly regarded! The importance of the student/teacher relationship, teachers' expectations for their students and overall quality of interpersonal classroom involvement, in optimizing student engagement and achievement, has been highlighted by other researchers (Cruickshank, Jenkins, & Metcalfe, 2003; Hattie, 2009). The qualities of the student/teacher relationship valued by students are also highly valued by teachers (Hughes, Abbott-Chapman, & Williamson, 2001).

A range of studies have shown that effective teachers encourage the development of students' intrinsic rather than extrinsic motivation and satisfaction, their curiosity and preference for challenge. Teaching strategies which encourage children's motivation for reading, for example, develop 'competence and efficacy beliefs' (Wigfield, Guthrie, Tonks, & Perencevich, 2004, p.301). When students are intrinsically motivated, they complete activities because they are interested and devote much time and energy to them. These beliefs apply equally to other forms of learning. Lower levels of motivation and school engagement tend to be reflected in potentially harmful risk-taking and antisocial behaviour of students who are at risk of early leaving (Li & Lerner, 2011). Higher achieving students who lack confidence in their abilities may also participate in risk-taking activities such as binge drinking, especially before examinations, as a form of self-handicapping which will, the student hopes, excuse their poorer than expected performance (Dorman, Adams, & Ferguson, 2002.) A survey of 954 year 11 and 12 students in Tasmania examined the relationship between students' perception of risk and involvement in 26 activities that young people in focus groups had nominated as risky – such as smoking cigarettes, drinking alcohol, binge drinking, using illicit drugs and engaging in unsafe sex. Findings showed that factors which inhibited risk-taking included wide personal support networks of parents, peers and other family members rather than peer group friends alone or 'no-one'. In addition, 10% of the students said they would go to a trusted teacher for help and advice with 'personal problems', as well as the 71% who would go to a teacher with study problems (Abbott-Chapman, Denholm, & Wyld, 2008).

Recent analysis of previously unpublished data from the same survey revealed that increased levels of students' sense of self-efficacy, as measured by an index of perceived personal control in education (PPCE), were significantly correlated with lower levels of risk-taking across the 26 risk activities and with higher aspirations towards further and higher education. PPCE measured the importance of education to the respondents, their perception of the likelihood of success in achieving their education goals and how much influence they felt they had in making things happen. The importance of perceived behavioural control in the overcoming of difficulties and adversity, in order to attain personal and social goals, has been widely noted in both the psychological and sociological literature, especially with regard to self-efficacy (Ajzen, 2002). Importantly, students' levels of enjoyment of school or college were very significantly correlated with levels of PPCE. In summary, the higher levels of school enjoyment and self-efficacy were associated with aspirations for further and higher education and with lower levels of harmful risk-taking. These findings are supported by Martin's research on a multidimensional model of student motivation and engagement, in which school enjoyment, classroom participation and educational aspirations are closely linked (Martin, 2007).

It is not surprising therefore that a number of studies have shown that liking school and school engagement influence student attainment and retention, in addition to a range of other family background and in-school factors (Fullarton, 2002; Lamb, Walstab, Teese, Vickers, & Rumberger, 2004). Disengaged students are unlikely to perform well at school and are more likely to become early leavers, at risk of underemployment and unemployment (CSHE, 2008; Muir et al., 2009). Secondary school achievement and retention are prerequisites of successful post-compulsory participation and employment. Therefore, in pursuit of effective education for all, the understanding of factors which encourage greater student school engagement, attainment and retention is a priority for teachers, researchers and policymakers. The UK's *National Strategy for Primary Schools* (Department for Education, 2003) explicitly recognized the importance of students' enjoyment of learning by linking excellence in teaching and students' enjoyment of learning – especially in raising national literacy and numeracy levels. The document states 'We want schools to continue to focus on raising standards while not being afraid to combine that with making learning fun' (p.4). Research shows that making learning enjoyable, interesting and challenging so that students, whatever their backgrounds, become motivated, independent learners for life, is as high a priority for schools as a focus on narrower indicators of school attainment (Gorard & See, 2010). The ancient Chinese proverb tells us 'Teachers can open the door, but you must enter by yourself'. We must all work to make schools, colleges and universities such inviting and exciting centres of learning that students' own curiosity, enthusiasm, resilience and stickability will take them 'through the door'.

References

Abbott-Chapman, J. (2011). Making the most of the Mosaic: facilitating post-school transitions to Higher Education of disadvantaged students. *Australian Education Researcher, 38*, 57–71.

Abbott-Chapman, J., Denholm, C. J., & Wyld, C. (2008). Social support as a factor inhibiting teenage risk-taking: Views of students, parents and professionals. *Journal of Youth Studies, 11*(6), 611–627.

Abbott-Chapman, J., Hughes, P., & Wyld, C. (1991). *Improving access of disadvantaged youth to Higher Education* Department of Employment, Education and Training, Evaluations and Investigations Program, AGPS, Canberra, Australia.

Ajzen, I. (2002). Perceived behavioural control, self-efficacy, locus of control and the theory of planned behaviour. *Journal of Applied Social Psychology, 32*, 1–20.

Centre for the Study of Higher Education. (2008). *Participation and equity: A review of the participation in higher education*. Melbourne, Australia: University of Melbourne.

Cruickshank, D. R., Jenkins, J. B., & Metcalf, K. K. (2003). *The act of teaching*. New York: McGraw Hill.

Delors, J., In' Al Mufti, Amagi, I., Carneiro, R., Chung, F., Geremek, B., Gorham, W., Kornhauser, A., Manley, M., Quero, M. P., Savane, M.-A., Singh, K., Stavenhagen, R., Suhr, M.W., & Nanzhao, Z. (1996). *Learning: The treasure within. Report to UNESCO of the International Commission on Education for the twenty-first century*. Paris: UNESCO.

Department for Education, U.K. (2003). *Excellence and enjoyment: A strategy for primary schools. The national strategies*. Primary Document. Accessed 9 May 2011, on: http://nationalstrategies. standards.dcsf.gov.uk/node/85063

Dorman, J. P., Adams, J. E., & Ferguson, J. M. (2002). Psychosocial environment and student self-handicapping in secondary school mathematical classes. *Educational Psychology: An international Journal of Experimental Educational Psychology., 22*(5), 499–511.

Fullarton, S. (2002). *Student engagement with school: Individual and school level influences* (Research Report Number 27). Longitudinal Surveys of Australian Youth. Camberwell, Australia: ACER.

Gall, S. L., Abbott-Chapman, J., Patton, G. C., Dwyer, T., & Venn, A. (2010). Intergenerational educational mobility is associated with cardiovascular disease risk behaviours in a cohort of young Australian adults: The Childhood Determinants of Adult Health (CDAH) Study. *BMC Public Health, 10*(55).

Gorard, S., & See, B. H. (2010). How can we enhance enjoyment of secondary school? The student view. *British Educational Research Journal*, iFirst Article, 1–20.

Hammond, C. (2002). What is it about education that makes us healthy? Exploring the education – Health connection. *International Journal of Lifelong Education, 21*(6), 551–571.

Hattie, J. (2009). *Visible Learning: A synthesis of over 800 meta-analyses relating to achievement.* London: Routledge.

Hughes, P., Abbott-Chapman, J., & Williamson, J. (2001). Teaching competencies in the classroom: Deconstructing teacher experience *Education Research and Perspectives, 28*(1), 1–24.

Lamb, S., Walstab, A, Teese, R., Vickers, M., & Rumberger, R. (2004). *Staying on at school: Improving student retention in Australia* (Report for the Queensland Department of Education and the Arts). Centre for Post-Compulsory Education and Lifelong Learning, University of Melbourne.

Li, Y., & Lerner, R. M. (2011). Trajectories of school engagement during adolescence: Implications for grades, depression, delinquency, and substance use. *Developmental Psychology, 47*(1), 233–247.

Lingard, B. (2010). Policy borrowing, policy learning: Testing times in Australian schooling. *Critical Studies in Education, 51*(2), 129–147.

Martin, A. J. (2007). Examining a multidimensional model of student motivation and engagement, using a construct validation approach. *British Journal of Educational Psychology, 77*(2), 413–440.

McWilliam, E. (2008). *Creative workforce: How to launch young people into high flying futures.* Sydney, Australia: UNSW Press Ltd.

Ministerial Council for Education, Early Childhood Development and Youth Affairs (MCEECDYA). (2008). *Melbourne Declaration on Educational Goals for Young Australians.* Accessed 15 May 2011 on http://www.mceetya.edu.au/verve/_resources/National_Declaration_on_the_Educational_Goals_for_Young_Australians.pdf

Muir, K., Mullan, K., Powell, A., Flaxman, S., Thompson, D., & Griffiths, M. (2009). *State of Australia's Young People.* Office for Youth, Australian Government and Social Policy Research Centre, UNSW. Commonwealth of Australia.

OECD. (2008). *Education at a glance. OECD indicators.* Paris: Organisation for Economic Co-operation and Development.

UNESCO. (2000). *Education for all: Meeting our collective commitments. Text adopted by the World Education Forum. Dakar Framework for Action.* Dakar, Senegal, 26–28 April 2000. Accessed on 15 May 2011 http://www.unesco.org/education/efa/ed_for_all/dakfram_eng.shtml

UNESCO. (2010). *EFA Global Monitoring Report 2010: Reaching the Marginalised.* Paris/Oxford: UNESCO Publishing/Oxford University Press. Accessed 16 May 2011, on: http://unesdoc.unesco.org/images/0018/001866/186606E.pdf\

UNICEF. (2005). *Levels, trends and determinants of primary school participation and gender parity.* New York: United Nations Children's Fund.

Walker, M. (2008). Widening participation, widening capability. *London Review of Education, 6*(3), 267–279.

Wigfield, A., Guthrie, J. T., Tonks, S., & Perencevich, K. C. (2004). Children's Motivation for Reading: Domain Specificity and instructional Influences. *The Journal of Educational Research, 97*(6), 299–309.

Wyn, J. (2009). *Touching the future: Building skills for life and work. Australian Education Review.* Camberwell, Australia: ACER.

Chapter 14
Did I Experience a Good Education?

Max Walsh

Over the course of my teaching career at both senior secondary and university level, I was always irritated when a student would ask me the question "Sir, will this topic be on the examination?" In asking that question, the student was suggesting to me that the topic being studied, no matter how stimulating, intrinsically interesting or challenging it might be, was not worth dealing with unless it was going to be examined and so contribute to his or her gaining of a certificate, degree or diploma at the end of the programme. In other words, the student was implying that the credential was the important outcome, not the learning. Is this attitude more prevalent today? What was my own attitude to learning when I was attending primary and then secondary school in the 1950–1960s? Were we concerned with gaining credentials or were we imbued with higher ideals than that?

To address this question, it is important to know the context of the learning environment at that time.

I was a "baby boomer", part of the large group of children who were born in the 1945–1950 post-war period when the nation was recovering from the setbacks from World War 2. This large pool of students flowed through primary and then into secondary school, and the sudden increase in numbers demanded additional schools, more learning materials and an increased number of qualified teachers to deal with the burgeoning numbers of students. We had easy access to free education in this post-war period of economic expansion, and we were motivated to pursue both a secondary and a postsecondary education by a number of factors, each of which determined my decision to become an educator.

Firstly, there was the certainty of gaining employment in our chosen career provided we were able to pass all required examinations. Although we did not realize

M. Walsh (✉)
Education Consultancies, 2101 AIC Gold Tower, Emerald Avenue,
Ortigas Centre, Pasig City 1605, Philippines
e-mail: maxwalsh@hotmail.com

P. Hughes (ed.), *Achieving Quality Education for All*, Education in the Asia-Pacific
Region: Issues, Concerns and Prospects 20, DOI 10.1007/978-94-007-5294-8_14,
© Springer Science+Business Media Dordrecht 2013

it quite so explicitly at the time, we could set ourselves a goal and expect to achieve it. My mother frequently told the story about how I returned home from my very first day attending Maryborough (Victoria) High School and told her that I had decided that I would become a "high school science teacher". She especially enjoyed relating how I never deviated from this goal over the following 10 years, from that first day at high school until I graduated from the University of Tasmania and started teaching mathematics and science at Burnie High School in north-western Tasmania. Clearly, I experienced something significant on that first day of school that determined my future career as an educator. I will refer to this again later.

A second important factor at the time was the frenzy that swept us up in the major revision and enhancement of science education that gained momentum in the western world after Russia had beaten the United States of America into space by launching "Sputnik", the first satellite to circle the earth. Suddenly, there was an urgent need for the west to "catch up" with its technological research and development with the physical sciences becoming the essential subjects for study. A raft of new physics and chemistry education programmes emerged in swift succession from the USA, all with the express intention of developing a new generation of scientists. There was a shift from theoretical study to an experimentally based programme, and this greater emphasis on classroom experimentation was exciting and new. My teachers in these subjects were clearly passionate about them and also excited to be pioneering these new packaged curriculum materials complete with kits containing equipment and even chemicals to be used for experimentation. Our teachers were "learning" the new approaches along with their students in a genuine "community of learners", although we never used this label then and it would not be used until many years later to describe what we were doing. We as students were enjoying learning these exciting new concepts, and the teachers were clearly enjoying teaching these "old" concepts in exciting new ways. It was at this time, in senior secondary school, that I learned to love learning. It was also apparent to me, in hindsight, that I must have experienced one of these classes on my first day at high school and it resulted in my being "hooked" on the prospect of becoming a science teacher.

The teaching that I experienced throughout my secondary and university years remained vivid for me because I had already decided on my career to become a teacher, and so I was closely observing and absorbing many of the styles and approaches being used by my teachers, and they emerged when I started teaching my own science classes in 1970. I find it so easy to recall these experiences today. When I started teaching, new curriculum packages, some of which were revised and enhanced versions of the same packaged materials that I had used in school (PSSC Physics, CHEM Study, BSCS Biology), and others developed within Australia (JSSP, ASEP), were available for us beginning teachers to use with our classes to generate enthusiasm for science and to use active learning involving an experimental approach for all students in each class. I was now the same enthusiastic teacher replicating the same approaches to teaching and learning that my own school teachers had modelled for me.

From my experience, the significant elements of the outstanding education that I was lucky to receive were twofold: outstanding, motivated and knowledgeable teachers that became role models for my own teaching style and new approaches to teaching and learning supported by excellent resources (books and materials). Our research today highlights the importance of the teacher in formal schooling along with the provision of a variety of resource materials for the alternative learning approaches that students bring to the classroom. The curriculum materials that were available to both learners and teachers allowed us to learn in various ways and at our own pace instead of the "one-size-fits-all" model favoured by didactic whole-class teaching that had persisted in earlier times.

I now realize that my learning experiences and subsequent teaching experiences were privileged ones. Since moving out of the Australian education system and into a close involvement with many of the education systems in the developing countries of Southeast Asia, I have now come to realize that the elements of a good education that I experienced are not freely available in these systems and their absence severely handicaps the successful provision of an effective education for most of the public school population.

For the past 14 years, I have been working in the education systems in several SE Asian countries, where severe overcrowding occurs and then the systems foster, perhaps unwittingly, a mind-set in students that education is something to be endured until the end point is reached and a qualification is collected. For those students who make it through until the end of high school, education for many of them is all about rote learning or the regurgitation of memorized facts for an examiner. This is a consequence of overcrowded classes that lack the two essential elements that were identified earlier as key components of my own education. One is little or no access to quality resource materials, and the second is the almost total dependence on the teacher, often poorly trained, as the sole access point to new knowledge and skills. When the successful high school graduates enter postsecondary institutions, only a select few will be "wanting to learn" and understand the importance of "learning throughout life". Instead, many of them will simply accept that learning mathematics and science, for example, is merely a way to become more employable. This goal is worthwhile in an extrinsic sense, but sadly, students can miss experiencing the intrinsic intellectual pleasure that can be derived from exposure to particular subjects in interesting ways. An enthusiastic and competent teacher can help students feel the joy of mastering a particular problem in a subject area regardless of whether the problem has some particular application in their future career.

My work in the new development assistance programmes, supported by the Australian government that are currently being designed and implemented in the Philippines, is built on my experiences that I have described earlier here. I am striving to ensure that there is now a greater emphasis on transforming education from being a trial to be endured prior to gaining employment into "education as an enjoyable activity" that fosters learning skills that can be used beyond the stage when formal schooling has finished. The new emphases are on the provision of Alternative Learning Systems that are accessible to all students through the provision of learning materials prepared at various levels of difficulty and in simple printed form and/ or using online delivery strategies. Such practices are not new in highly developed systems such as that of Australia, but for developing countries (e.g. the Philippines), this is far-reaching and innovative and will restore access to education for a large population of people who have dropped out of the system previously for various reasons. Another emphasis is on enhanced training of teachers in significantly greater numbers at both pre- and in-service levels to allow an expansion of the formal system to target disadvantaged groups.

In summary, the significant components of the formal education that I received at primary and secondary level were *highly motivated and competent teachers* who provided me with access to *high-quality learning materials* that stimulated not only my interest in science but also love of learning new information in any area of knowledge. In my work as an education consultant providing advice and guidance to senior educators in developing countries, I stress to them that continuing professional development (CPD) of teachers through well-designed in-service programmes are essential and that accompanying this CPD must be provision of resource materials (written or internet-based) that will capture students' attention and help them engage with the required learning. Both are achievable under the terms of development assistance funding, and progress is being made.

Chapter 15
Supervising or Coaching? Thoughts on Student Teaching

Nancy Faust Sizer

When I was in high school and full of hubris, I became convinced that I could do a better job than my teacher was doing, and so, sure enough but years later, I landed in an urban high school to do a rotation in practice teaching. I was paired with an old, tired – or so he seemed to me – gentleman who met me at the door to his classroom to give me one piece of advice. "Don't be easy on them but don't be too hard on them either. If you can get this crowd to remember who George Washington was, you'll be lucky." Then he introduced me to his class, showed me the textbook, and eagerly joined his buddies in the cellar where they smoked cigarettes and, I suppose, discussed the Boston Red Sox, the ways in which the principal was messing up, and wondering how I, the wife of the dean of the Harvard Graduate School of Education, was coping with the nonacademic class upstairs. I didn't really mind the fact that I was on my own, observed only once by my "supervisor" from Harvard and never by the classroom teacher. Still confident, I was convinced that I could reach the kids, if only because I would try harder than he did. What I didn't think about enough was what to do if they acknowledged me as a real teacher. Where would I take them then? I could certainly have benefited from some conversation about that.

I spent the bulk of my career in classroom teaching, and now I find myself back in a classroom in a high school whose demographics and size are similar to the one I started with, this time as a university supervisor observing and then discussing teaching with three young colleagues who are new to teaching. Of course I have done plenty of such work in the intervening years, but now it is my chief connection with the profession, and as such it has spurred a whole new round of questions – and attempts at answers. I will consider two of them.

The first is "How important are teachers?" Everyone agrees: very. Students rail at teachers who are boring or unfair, as if their very lives hung in the balance. Parents

N.F. Sizer (✉)
Education Faculty, Tufts University, Medford,
53 Sheehan Road, Harvard, MA 01451, USA
e-mail: faustie@aol.com

P. Hughes (ed.), *Achieving Quality Education for All*, Education in the Asia-Pacific Region: Issues, Concerns and Prospects 20, DOI 10.1007/978-94-007-5294-8_15, © Springer Science+Business Media Dordrecht 2013

are determined that their children will spend time with people who are knowledgeable and interesting. Politicians remember the teacher who believed in them, the one who steered them to their later success in life.

But do they really mean it? If so, why are so many students so rude? In too many classrooms, the expectation seems to be that if it is a gathering of teenagers, it is essentially a party, with lots of side conversations, playful and flirtatious pushing, and no real attempt to get to the matter at hand. Teachers' attempts to control the conversation are ignored; they are, too often, made to feel like intruders.

Why are parents so narrow and so stingy when it comes to schools? Why do they care about their own child's teacher but no one else's? Why don't all the adults in a community – whether they are presently parents of school-aged children or not – act as guardians for their children and protectors of the institutions which helped them in earlier times and which are still needed? And why don't parents treat their allies, the teachers, in the challenging job of bringing youngsters into healthy and productive adulthood, with respect? Respect would include helping children to go to school regularly and with their work done and not just waiting for some teacher to "motivate" them. I was there recently when a student came back to school after 3 months away – and just waltzed in. Why had she been gone? It was undoubtedly a complex story, but "she had a fight with her mother," was all her teacher knew. Yet, it would be the teacher's job to help her catch up.

And what about the politicians? Their memories of schooling are often so favorable that they insist on trying to replicate the "good old days," without taking time to learn about all the factors which have changed – and complicated – the work which schools need to do to be considered successful. The young woman in the last paragraph, for example, may not have been in school at all when the politician was young. Having a larger percentage of children in schools and increasing college is considered a good thing and usually for good reason. But what if schools aren't able – or willing – to offer what the students really need?

We should give those politicians a break, I suppose. They represent a body politic which seems to be looking for quick, easy, and cheap solutions not only for schools but for all the other social problems – joblessness, poor housing, and bad health – which immeasurably add to the problems of schools. Politicians must represent this group, and therefore this point of view, or they will lose their jobs. Either that or they must become teachers themselves, changing the values of those who have hired them.

A second question, even more complicated, is "What is the best way to judge a teacher's work?" All jobs are complicated, but it seems to me that a teacher's job is more complicated than most. If you have 80 students and most teachers in the United States have more than that, then you have 80 people whom you must know well, judge where they are in their learning, and use your time together to add value to what they know and can do. Furthermore, you must make the experience engaging to them, one they will deem worthwhile, both at the present and as they look back on it in the future.

Doing all this requires different venues and different skills, but what is often stressed is classroom management and demeanor. Classroom management is often kind of a gamble: you inherit students who like school or hate it, whose parents liked school or hated it, whose previous teacher was fascinating or boring, whose health is robust or shaky, and whose lunch was delicious or inedible. You juggle all these factors in early morning (when, studies say, teenagers should be still sleeping), midmorning (pretty optimal), or in late afternoon (everyone, including the teacher, is wiped out).

Over time, you learn to read your class with more ability and learn which students can help you to change the tone. You come to class with plans which incorporate what you have learned about your students' preferences and at the same time require of them the attention and grappling which will lead them to grow intellectually.

You assign homework which you use during the class so that the second exposure to the information will reinforce it in the students' minds. Some days, however, you go beyond the homework to deepen their knowledge of the subject with contributions from you and from each other. You vary the format, making use of group work where appropriate but making sure that it is well designed to add to the material and to foster intellectual teamwork, not just a relief from your own "chalk and talk" and its need to keep their attention.

You offer explanations which are enlightening and engaging to some without becoming confusing to others. You understand the pitfalls between motivation and clarification, and how too much of one can threaten the other. Many of these skills can be observed by the students, colleagues, and principals who are responsible for "fly-by" evaluations or the more extensive and considered ones which I am trying to give.

But along with the public part of a teacher's job is the private part, and this is both important and hard to assess. Mostly it consists of correcting and of conferences. When I was the chairman of a history department, I felt it necessary to know what questions the members of my department were asking on their tests and how helpful their comments were. It was a very difficult assessment to perform, and even when I convinced my colleagues to share their work, I needed to decide how helpful their comments were when I had very little knowledge of the context. It was subjective and hard to explain, but we mostly soldiered on, and our conversations grew easier and more substantial.

"Grading papers" is the least shared part of a teacher's job, yet often the most crucial. It centers around the giving of feedback, otherwise known as criticism, then more criticism, and then still more criticism. Of course, we teachers remember to say one or two "nice" things, but we see it as our job to point out errors and tell our charges how to correct them. Otherwise, how will they know what to do and how to start? Before long, even if we avoid the red ink which is referred to by students as "bloodletting," the paper is full of our corrections and comments, such as to strike fear into the hearts of even the most sturdy students. And instead of holding back, we feel proud of our thoroughness, a little self-pitying for having spent our Sunday afternoons on such a self-sacrificing task.

The comments which a teacher writes at the bottom of the page are, at best, an earnest attempt at encouragement, enlightenment, and communication. In that space, the essential message and the tone are key. They need to be simple enough to be remembered. This is because the teacher's monologue needs to become a dialogue (at least inside the student's head) before it will effectively change a student's outlook or his performance in a revision or in the next piece of work.

It's not just how much correcting we do: it's also learning how to hand over the job to the students. In the beginning, it's showing as well as telling, but in time, its guiding them in their own revisions. It's describing the moment at which one more detail would have strengthened the argument or one fewer detail would have clarified it. It's getting them to care about spelling and grammar. And this is for 80 students, each of whom will have his or her own timetable and his or her own journey.

Often, the give-and-take which makes "correction" valuable is better accomplished if it is possible to meet in conference, something which is simply not in the schedule of most schools. The environment of the conference is very private. As a teacher, I remember especially the conference after the first draft of the term paper but before the second. The piece of work needs to be shorter or longer, the argument clearer, and the evidence more substantial or compelling. The reader (the teacher) must be persuaded. But the piece of work is not to become the teacher's; it needs to be the student's best effort but also become his or her pride and joy. The conference needs to accomplish all these agendas with efficiency and good humor. And no outside evaluator, even a flexible and good-hearted department chair, will be able to judge exactly the way it was done. Yet, in many respects, it is at the heart of good teaching.

I say these are private moments, but they don't need to be completely private. Teachers can, and in some schools do, work together to devise better assignments, then to judge their results in exercises which I called "cross-correcting." This requires procedures which take time and wisdom – and skins which are thicker than most people have developed. When I did it, both as a beginning teacher and as a leader, I came to realize that my colleagues' values and judgments were sometimes sharply different from my own. At first, I even shed some private tears about it, but I also learned a great deal.

"Mrs. Sizer is a good teacher" or a "bad" teacher. What parts of her work are we describing? The progress of her students in standardized tests? The attention of her students in her classes? The amount they talk about her class when they aren't in it? The pleasure which her students take when she turns up at their games or their plays? Or is it that they feel that she believes they are good students, but could be even better ones, and delivers her message in a way that is taken as encouragement instead of a put-down?

Have we designed the kind of school in which a teacher can flourish? How many students does our teacher have? Few enough so that she can gauge how she should deliver her messages and deliver at least some of them directly to individuals rather than to the whole class? And what kinds of students does she have? How responsive are they in the face of the criticism which she considers it her duty to offer?

Public or private? Which part of her job must we judge? And how can we do it?

In the United States these days, there is much controversy surrounding these questions because so many seem convinced that too many teachers are not capable but are being protected by their principals or their labor unions when they should be fired.

The observation which I have been making that evaluating teachers is a complex, subtle, and time-consuming (therefore expensive) undertaking is often seen as a justification for not doing it at all. But that's not the point: the point is who will design and pay for an evaluation which leads to accurate findings and is fair to all? Can teachers themselves work with each other, not to supervise but to coach, and in the process become better teachers themselves? I have been in environments where teachers worked together to improve their teaching, and I believe that it works. Can we use what we call "critical friends' groups" to help those teachers who can benefit from further coaching, adjustments, and scrutiny? And to help "good" teachers also receive the help that all professionals need from time to time?

Much has changed in the 40-plus years since I myself was a student teacher, and most of it has been for the better. Cooperating teachers and university supervisors are expected to pay more attention, and more and more, we are refining what the verb "mentor" means in professional development inside the school. We are pulling back from a hierarchic and fear-based model and trying to emphasize the coaching part of our role. Most of all, we have learned that to answer two questions like those above will inevitably require coming up with many more questions, some of them impossible to answer. So be it. Our profession requires – and prospers with – such complexity.

Chapter 16
The Power of Teaching

Susan Pascoe

I know the power of teaching from the changes in my own life

(Hughes, 2007)

Phillip Hughes has witnessed and shaped many of the significant changes to education in Australia for more than 70 years. I was honoured to deliver the Phillip Hughes Oration for the Australian Capital Territory's Chapter of the Australian College of Educators on October 2006, the year Phillip turned 80 years of age. The following year, I was similarly pleased to launch Phillip's book, *Opening Doors to the Future: Stories of Prominent Australians and the Influence of Teachers*. This paper is adapted from those presentations which provided selective insights into Phillip's professional journey against the historical and policy backdrops of the decades through which he lived. Phillip's personal story is one of the transformative powers of education and of teaching. Unlike some of his contemporaries, he was able to maximise the opportunities afforded to a working-class boy from Tasmania.

One hundred and five years ago in Launceston, a strong-willed young woman named Margaret Ruby Jones, at 16 years of age, took over the building in the rear garden of her parents' house and set up her own private school. When it was fully operational, Miss Jones' academy had 30 pupils enrolled. A few years later, Ruby Jones married a gold miner from Victoria who became a garage proprietor in Devonport. He was a gentle Welshman who liked to sing songs to his children as they sat around the hearth in the cold Tasmanian winters. His name was Francis Hughes. Ruby and Francis had seven children, and they named their baby boy Phillip.

Devonport in 1926 was a quiet little country town where everyone knew everyone else. This was not a town riven by sectarianism – the Catholic primary school named

S. Pascoe (✉)
Australian Charities and Not-for-Profits Commission,
110 Leopold St, South Yarra, VIC 3004, Australia
e-mail: Susan.Pascoe@kadisha.com.au

P. Hughes (ed.), *Achieving Quality Education for All*, Education in the Asia-Pacific Region: Issues, Concerns and Prospects 20, DOI 10.1007/978-94-007-5294-8_16, © Springer Science+Business Media Dordrecht 2013

in honour of Our Lady of Lourdes stood peacefully alongside the government primary school, a two-storey redbrick structure built to last. The Catholic teachers were all nuns, while at the government primary school the teachers had been trained to impart a secular education.

Phillip recounts his impressions of the strong women who taught him in primary school in his 2007 collection on the influence of teachers. He started primary school in 1932 and the following year was taught by Miss Alison Smith in the one-room school. In those days, female teachers forfeited their job if they married, and Miss Smith remained a single woman all her life. It is characteristic of Phillip Hughes that during his term as dean of education at the University of Tasmania, he tracked her down. He visited her in a nursing home in 1988 and met with her only weeks prior to her death. Sadly she was not well enough to reminisce on her 61 years of teaching.

Only one in three of the primary school students went on to high school. In Phillip's class at Devonport High School, another boy also became a teacher and another became a doctor. But the brightest child of all was a girl. Her parents took her out of school as soon as she turned 15 – they thought that girls did not need much in the way of education. Only about 10% of Phillip's generation went on to finish secondary school.

His own education path took him from Devonport High School, to the Universities of New England and of Tasmania and to Oxford. His career path ran from teaching at the tertiary level, to curriculum development, to senior administration and academia. During this illustrious career, Phillip was inaugural chair of the ACT Schools Authority, professor of Education, CEO of the Australian Principals' Centre, roving international expert for the Organisation for Economic Co-operation and Development (OECD) and the United Nations Education, Science and Cultural Organisation (UNESCO). The term 'retirement' never registered with Phillip.

Phillip's primary school education took place during the Great Depression in the 1930s, and his secondary schooling in the 1940s was against the backdrop of World War 1. His movement from secondary to higher education coincided roughly with the end of the war and the hope-filled establishment of the United Nations (UN) in 1945 and UNESCO in 1946. Given Phillip's involvement in and commitment to UNESCO, it is worth recollecting the belief of UNESCO's founders, 'Since wars begin in the minds of men, it in the minds of men that the defences of peace must be built'. While we might use less gendered language today, in a tension-fraught planet, this conviction retains its relevance.

Post-war migration to Australia saw classroom numbers swell and the need for rapid expansion of physical, economic and social infrastructure. With these newcomers, monocultural Australians were confronted with people whose behaviours and lifestyle preferences did not match the norm. Phillip's career was beginning in this context, although arguably, Hobart was less touched by these changes than Sydney and Melbourne. John O'Grady's 1966 depiction in *They're a Weird Mob* of the confused Nino Cullotta and his adaptation to the Australian way of life characterised the essential goodness in the Australian populace as they strove to live with their new neighbours. Phillip was now married, and his own family was growing in the 1960s. Meanwhile many Australian women were agitating for equal pay and equal employment rights.

Phillip experienced significant changes in 1970. He moved from the position of deputy director-general in Tasmania to the role of head of School of Education at the Canberra College of Advanced Education. The 1970s was the decade of the influential inquiry into education provision in Australia of the respected economist, Peter Karmel. The 1973 Karmel Report fostered a broad acceptance of values such as equality of educational opportunity and the targeting of disadvantage and to the funding of a dual system of government and non-government schools. Arguably it remains the bedrock of school education in Australia today. (The current inquiry into school funding led by businessman, David Gonski, has inherited the intended and unintended repercussions of the Karmel settlement.)

During the 1980s when Phillip was steering the ACT Schools Authority, once again Karmel made a significant impact with the 1985 Quality in Educational Review Committee Report which advocated a new emphasis on outputs and outcomes rather than inputs. This had the effect of moving educators to consider more seriously the way they assessed and the outcomes of their professional endeavours, not simply what they taught. The same report introduced a more explicit recognition of the responsibility of teachers for the outcomes of students. At the state level, reviews such the 1985 *Report into Post Compulsory Schooling* (the Blackburn Report) spawned major reforms such as the development of a new senior secondary credential, the Victorian Certificate of Education (VCE)

The 1980s also saw the first of the inter-jurisdictional agreements on the expected outcomes of schooling in Australia. The national goals for schooling in Australia (the 1989 Hobart Declaration, the 1999 Adelaide Declaration and the 2008 Melbourne Declaration) have been developed and approved by all education ministers for all students in all schools, and the goals commit to common values, expectations and outcomes. These agreements have provided the philosophical foundation for school education in Australia and an oasis of consensus when political and policy objectives collide.

The early 1990s saw a rash of reviews into post-compulsory and training provision, especially the reports of Finn, Mayer and Carmichael. This is the decade that Phillip moved from academia and administration to the glamorous life of the international expert with consultancies in Paris at both the OECD and UNESCO. He managed these hardship postings valiantly! Back in Australia, further national inquiries were underway – the Ministerial Council on Education, Employment, Training and Youth Affairs' (MCEETYA's) Taskforce to develop literacy and numeracy benchmarks and the prime minister's Civics Expert Group to investigate the adequacy of civics and citizenship education in Australia. There were a number of stop-start attempts between the commonwealth and states to work co-operatively, but politics and ministerial aspirations often got in the way.

Issues of teacher quality returned to the agenda at either end of the decade with the 1993 Ministerial Statement, *Teaching Counts* and the 1998 publication of *A Class Act: Inquiry into the Status of the Teaching Profession*. The focus on teacher quality segued into the following decade with the release of the 2003 report,

Australia's Teachers: Australia's Future. This is not surprising given the evidence in the school effectiveness literature of the critical role of the classroom teacher on education outcomes.

The establishment of the Australian Institute for Teaching and School Leadership in January 2010 continues efforts to enhance the capability and professionalism of teachers and school leaders. The release of teacher professional standards in February 2011 makes clear what effective teachers should know and be able to do. Maintaining a focus on teacher preparation, induction, professional learning and support should always be a central consideration in workforce planning for school education. The education enterprise rests on teachers, and their interventions impact significantly on student learning. They are far more important than the buildings, budgets and bureaucrats that support their endeavours.

Phillip was globetrotting as an education expert in the 1990s and into the new millennium alongside many other Australian educators who were availing themselves of the opportunity to benchmark their ideas and practice internationally. Australians have been steady contributors to research meetings such as the American Educational Research Association (AERA) conference in the United States and the annual conference of the International Congress for School Effectiveness and Improvement. And they are active contributors, not just recipients of ideas from elsewhere. Education is one of those academic and professional areas where Australians punch above their weight.

Changes of the magnitude which Phillip has witnessed give pause for reflection. Over Phillip's lifetime, mass secondary education has become the norm with completion rates to year 12 now at around 78% – dramatically up from the 10% in the 1930s. We are moving to tertiary education or training as the norm for Generation Y. The Australian Council for Educational Research (ACER) *Longitudinal Survey of Australian Youth* empirically confirms the difficulties encountered by undereducated young people in Australia's knowledge economy.

While we now take learning technologies for granted, it is worth remembering that the World Wide Web and email became commonly available in the 1990s and word processing a decade earlier. Many of us are now reliant on a range of software applications for our basic work; we communicate globally and research, shop and bank online. Similarly the first decade of the twentieth century has seen the power of social media in connecting individuals, framing social interaction and mobilising protest movements.

Phillip's personal and professional journey has been traversed against a backdrop of great social and technological change. Had his primary school teacher, Miss Smith, been born 50 years later, she would have been entitled to equal pay whatever her gender or schooling sector and been able to work whatever her marital status. And had Susan, the clever girl in his Devonport High School, not been removed at age 15, she might have had similar opportunities to Phillip. Miss Smith today would be using smart boards and organising students to work online individually or in groups while she gave additional support to special needs students. Similarly, she would be referring to research gleaned from conferences, professional journals or online to determine which approach take with her learning programmes.

School education has benefitted during Phillip's lifetime from access to broader and deeper research on all aspects of its operation, from pedagogy to administration to leadership to wellbeing to governance and so on. Phillip himself has been a lively contributor, often reflecting on ways to assist the practitioner make sense of the overwhelming wealth of material at her disposal. He has supported recent moves to improve the equity and outcomes of schooling.

Phillip has seen in his international work the difficulties for systems, schools and individuals when there is no data to document, measure and compare their learning outcomes, their income, the quality of their facilities, their physical and psychological safety record and their governance practices. Australian educators are slowly overcoming their antipathy to providing data publicly on the inputs, performance and outcomes of schools. There is great potential in sites such as the Australian Curriculum, Assessment and Reporting Authority's *My School* website to inform parents, politicians and the public on the state of our schools.

Whatever the challenges and opportunities currently facing teachers in Australia, we have the wisdom and insight of educators like Phillip Hughes as a guide. Teaching is a noble profession – educators are entrusted by parents and the community to assist in the transmission of the nation's history, culture and traditions. Few careers carry a comparable weight of intergenerational civic purpose. The exemplary career of Phillip Hughes over seven decades demonstrates that the teaching profession can grow and flourish within the community that generates it and which it serves. His own path crossed state and international boundaries, transcended the distinction between teacher and administrator and retained a passion and purity of purpose.

Few of us get the opportunity to organise our own festschrift. It is characteristic of Phillip Hughes that he would use the last few months of his life to create a collection of reflections on education – one last contribution to the field which he has sustained and which has sustained him. Those of us who have been privileged to maintain insights into his life in recent months through his wife's emails and photos are aware that he sustained to the end an active family life with his large extended family. This is an example of a life well lived, both as an educator and colleague and as a family member and friend.

References

Hughes, P. (2007). *Opening the doors to the future: Stories of prominent Australians and the influence of teachers*. Melbourne, Australia: ACER Press.
Pascoe, S. (2006). *Education's new challenges and opportunities,* Phillip Hughes Oration, 17 October, 23007.

Chapter 17
Let's Emphasise Teachers' Professionalisation

Françoise Caillods

At individual level, we all know how important it is to have received a good education and the impact it may have on someone's life. Phillip Hughes is one of the many illustrations of the case of a child born in a working-class family who made a brilliant career, thanks to good teachers who raised his interest, good schools and good systems who allowed him to learn, continue his studies and reach the highest level. Phillip Hughes is not the only one. Many children of poor immigrant families make it every year in France, in the UK, in Australia and in the USA and become university professor, doctors, rich businessmen/women or successful politicians because they have had access to good schools and a good education system.

What is true of an individual is also true for a society, and many governments invest heavily in the education of their population in the hope that an educated and skilled labour force will attract foreign investments and that increased education will reduce unemployment, boost productivity and eventually lead to high economic growth. Other benefits are also expected from such an investment such as improved health, reduced crime, social cohesion, greater equity and justice. Education is a long-term investment however, and in and of itself, it may not be enough to boost economic growth. Many developing and middle-income countries have invested large amounts in the education of their citizens without this investment translating into economic growth—and jobs—thus creating a lot of frustrations particularly amongst secondary and higher education graduates. Basically, it is not sufficient to increase the number of years of schooling and to raise knowledge and skills of youngsters if they are not given the opportunity to apply what they have learnt, or if they are not given access to jobs, to land or to credit. As we can see these days in numerous countries in the Arab world, thousands of educated young people feel disillusioned and economically marginalised. What went wrong? The problem lies at three levels: lack of political reforms, lack of economic measures and framework

F. Caillods (✉)
International Institute of Educational Planning, UNESCO,
59 Boulevard, Murat, 75016 Paris, France
e-mail: francoise.caillods@gmail.com

P. Hughes (ed.), *Achieving Quality Education for All*, Education in the Asia-Pacific Region: Issues, Concerns and Prospects 20, DOI 10.1007/978-94-007-5294-8_17,
© Springer Science+Business Media Dordrecht 2013

which liberate initiatives and favour patterns of growth capable of creating jobs and poor quality of education. In numerous countries, education expansion took place at the detriment of quality: this is evident from the lack of trained teachers and head teachers, the use of old pedagogies and of traditional models of teaching and learning. It is reflected in the high number of school drop-outs and in the poor educational outcomes. In the end, many youngsters are educated and receive paper qualification, yet their level of literacy and numeracy is low; their mastery of written and oral communication is insufficient and their capacity to reason, to solve problems and to cope with uncertainties is low. These are competencies all of which are required to live and function in a modern knowledge-based economy.

But what is a good quality of education? How do we measure quality and what is necessary to provide an effective education that can produce curious, intelligent problem-solving kids?

Numerous books have been written on what makes a good education and thousands of educational research studies exist on this theme. There is now plenty of evidence on the level of performance of pupils and students at different levels in different countries, and we pretty much know what are the variables that can contribute to fostering high levels of performance. There is fairly general agreement amongst researchers that what is important to provide quality education can be clustered around the what, where and how:

> *What* learners should know: the goals of the education system and the value statements as elaborated in the curriculum and performance standards
>
> *Where and with which resources* learning occurs: education and training of teachers; class size, safety of the learning environment, availability of resources and facilities to support learning such as classrooms, books, learning materials, etc.; the length of the school days and school year; the governance structure; and the way schools function
>
> *How* learning takes place: the characteristics of learner-teacher interactions, the role learners play in their learning, the teachers' teaching practices and the language of instruction
>
> *What* is actually learned: the outcomes of education (e.g. the knowledge, skills, competencies, attitudes and values that learners acquire) and the way these are measured: through examination, tests, etc.

Other researchers add to the above list the equity dimension: if education outcomes are highly unequal and if a high proportion of students do not reach an adequate level of performance, the system cannot be considered as providing high-quality education. Education is also to be considered as a whole: it is not sufficient to emphasise good teaching conditions or to test students regularly if some other indispensable conditions are not met. As a result, most education reforms emphasise introducing actions in different areas: revision of curriculum and introduction of more active pedagogies; professionalization of teachers, training of new teachers and continuous upgrading of existing ones; improved teaching conditions and introduction of information and communication technology; reform of governance emphasising decentralisation, the role of the schools and accountability; monitoring of learning achievements through tests and reforms of examinations. Managing such reforms is quite complex, and implementing them can be quite costly. It may be necessary to prioritise certain measures and actions. Which ones should be prioritised depends on the context, the prevailing culture and the starting point.

It is interesting to note that counties that achieve best in the OECD Programme for International Student Assessment (PISA) have very different cultures and very different practices. For many years, the country that scored highest in PISA reading literacy, mathematics and science tests was Finland. In PISA 2010, the highest performance in reading literacy was attained by students from Shanghai, China, followed by Korea; Finland; and Hong Kong, China. The philosophy and practices are however totally different between Finland (fairly representative of an egalitarian Nordic model) and China, Korea or Japan (the more elitist Asian model). To give a few examples, in Finland, pupils enter school at the age of seven; they remain for 9 years in a comprehensive school, and many of them keep the same teacher for much of their school life; they have no homework or rarely; there is no fixed curriculum; the schools have a lot of autonomy, and the school programme is decided at the school level taking into account the characteristics of the pupils; the students do not undergo any test or any examination before the end of secondary education; schools routinely provide tutoring for weak students and the keyword is cooperation and teamwork rather than competition. In China however as in Korea and Japan, students study long hours: in school, before and after school in private tutoring schools. Several selective examinations determine where, in which institution, a child will go and study. China was after all the first country that introduced examinations.

There are two common features however between the two models: one is the high importance attached to education by the families and society, and the second is the high level of professionalism of their teachers.

Returning to priorities to be set as mentioned above, it seems clear that:

The *first priority* is to be given to improving teacher education and training, making sure that some of the best graduates are recruited, supported and motivated to become teachers. Teachers increasingly have to deal with students of different backgrounds and different cultures; they are expected to be sensitive to culture and gender issues and to effectively address the need of disadvantaged children and students. All over the world, they are recruited with higher education level; they receive pedagogical training of varied duration. Some receive a relatively short training and are expected to learn on the job. When this is the case, they need to be supervised and supported at school level. Research points to the fact that there is no correlation between the level of resources and the performance of students. There cannot be good schools however without good and motivated teachers. In several countries, salaries have declined in real terms compared to that of other professions; the occupation has lost much of its prestige. The very high proportion of women teachers in primary and secondary education and the very low proportion of men is a clear indication of the fact that teaching is no longer an attractive option for graduates. While in Finland, the teachers are recruited amongst the best graduates; in many other countries, teaching is a profession that students choose for the security of employment or waiting for another job. The structure of incentives for teachers may have to be revised at country level and salaries increased. In view of the impact of such a measure on the cost of education, it may become necessary to increase the pupil teacher ratio as a trade-off. Investing in professional teachers is a must. As in any other professions, teachers will have to be encouraged to engage in continuing professional development; they will be encouraged to analyse and review their own practice and be asked to review the impact of their teaching on their own students' progress. Providing continuous professional development and retaining good teachers is one of the greatest challenges of present educational systems.

The *second priority* is to be given to revising the curriculum, the content and teaching methods making sure that the knowledge and competences provided to children and youngsters are not fragmented into unrelated slices. What is taught has to be part of an integrated body of knowledge that makes "sense" as a whole and contributes to the youngsters' understanding of the world around her/him, as a whole, not in slices. This is a condition for children and youngsters—particularly those coming from uneducated and disadvantaged families—to engage in learning. In many countries, primary education is taught by one single teacher who teaches all subjects and who relates one subject to another. Moving to secondary education often means for the child being taught 10–12 subjects by different teachers who do not know each other, do not know what the others are teaching and who do not know the children. Knowledge becomes a set of unrelated slices, some interesting, but most of them not. Some teachers see several hundred pupils in a day: they do not know them; they do not remember them. Doing things differently implies that teachers of different disciplines work as a team, develop their syllabus together and multiply linkages and study of common themes and that they meet regularly to assess the needs of the class and how things progress and that they are motivated as good professionals in obtaining good results.

A *third priority* is to focus on low achievers and low-achieving schools especially in deprived areas. This means whenever possible that there should be a mix of students of different ability and different social and economic background. Focusing on low achievers and low-achieving schools does not mean stigmatising schools or pupils. It does not mean either reducing the expected level of achievements—on the contrary, it requires raising aspiration and developing a culture of achievement—or setting some objectives for the school or the class and holding them to it. It requires providing additional tutorials to students who lag behind, encouraging mentoring of weaker students by older students and pairing students having different abilities but also varying competences. It may, in some cases, also imply diversifying the curriculum to make it more relevant to the needs of a particular community, without compromising standards on basic skills such as spoken and written language, numeracy and communication.

A *fourth priority* is to make the school a more friendly place. This is particularly necessary when dealing with young adolescents. Taking care of the affective side of education and treating each student as an individual who has personal as well as learning problems is important. Some systems ask teachers to handle all of these aspects (such as the Nordic countries or the UK) even if they may recruit additional teaching personnel, but other systems appoint specialised staff—counsellors—to deal with these issues, releasing teachers from this responsibility (France). In the former system, teachers are in charge of educating students; in the other, they are more in charge of instructing and transmitting knowledge. The relationships between students and teachers are better in the first model than in the second and contribute to developing a stronger sense of belonging at school amongst students. In the first model, teachers are expected to stay longer in the school—as long as it is open; in the other, teachers come to teach and go when their class is finished. Changing this tradition and culture is not easy particularly in systems where teachers are not well paid, but it is worth trying and should be part of the process of treating the teaching profession as a normal profession. It assumes that the teachers are better paid and have a higher status as discussed above.

Fifth priority. All the priority measures mentioned above imply that the teachers become more concerned with the improvement of the school as a whole. The literature on effective schools emphasises the need to give autonomy to schools, letting each school community define its development plan, fix the targets they want to achieve and give freedom to the school board and head teacher to hire the staff. This implies empowering school heads as dynamic leaders who can set the tone and establish a can-do culture. This also means changing the pattern of recruitment of school heads, training them for that and providing support and incentives.

With the autonomy, comes the responsibility and the need to be accountable, hence, the need to monitor school achievements. Testing students is a mean to an end, however, not an end in itself.

The most effective school systems are those where teachers are highly trained professionals, well paid and selected from amongst the best graduates. These teachers have to be supported personally and professionally. In all schools but particularly in the most difficult schools, it is essential to break the isolation of teachers and to promote teamwork and sharing of experiences. Together with certain advantages—higher salary and higher status—comes some responsibility such as being accountable for results to the parents and the community. This is part of the obligation of any professional.

Selected Bibliography

Auguste, B., Kihn, P., & Miller, M. (2010, September). *Closing the talent gap: Attracting and retraining top-third graduates to careers in teaching. An international and market research based perspective.*. New York: McKinsey & Company.

Briseid, O., & Caillods, F. (2004). *Trends in secondary education in industrialized countries.* Paris: IIEP UNESCO.

Mona M., Chijioke C., & Barber, M. (2010, September). *How the world's most improved school systems keep getting better.* McKinsey & Company. http://ssomckinsey.darbyfilms.com/reports/EducationBook_A4%20SINGLES_DEC%202.pdf

OECD. (2004). *Learning for tomorrow's world. First results from PISA 2003.* Paris: Organisation for Cooperation and Development.

OECD. (2005). *Teachers matter. Attracting developing and retaining effective teachers.* Paris: Organisation for Cooperation and Development.

OECD. (2010). *PISA 2009 results: What students know and can do. Student performance in reading, mathematics and science.* Programme for International Student Assessment. Paris: Organisation for Cooperation and Development.

Osborn, M., Broadfoot, P., McNess, E., Planel, C., Ravn, B., & Triggs, P. (2003). *A world of difference. Comparing Learners Across Europe.* Bershire, UK: Open University Press.

Chapter 18
The Expectations Have It

Barry McGaw

A great deal is expected of education. For individuals, it is to ensure that they realise their full potential, in the process ameliorating the effects of social disadvantage. For nations, it is to raise their levels of 'human and social capital' to build successful knowledge economies.

Expectations are powerful, but they can be limiting as well as liberating.

I first saw this in the 1950s as a student in a differentiated secondary school system. The schools were comprehensive but contained separate academic, industrial, commercial and home economics streams that prepared students for quite different futures, including different points of departure from formal education. Many of those consigned to nonacademic futures, however, subsequently completed higher education qualifications.

I understood more of the power of expectations when I read Rosenthal and Jacobson's (1968) study of the effect of teacher expectations for which they coined the wonderful title, the *Pygmalion effect*. They showed that randomly ascribed descriptions of students' individual potential for growth spurts, shared with teachers, became self-fulfilling prophecies.

I saw it in stark relief in a study that colleagues and I undertook for the Australian Poverty Commission. We investigated the educational and occupational aspirations and expectations of secondary school students in country towns and regional cities in Queensland as well as in advantaged and disadvantaged suburban areas in the capital city, Brisbane (McGaw, Warry, Varley, & Alcorn, 1976). Students from advantaged backgrounds not only had higher aspirations than others, and expectations that matched them but were also much more likely to aspire to occupations in which they knew no one. Their aspirations and their self-established expectations were not constrained by their direct experience of others in work.

B. McGaw (✉)
Australian Curriculum, Assessment and Reporting Authority,
Level 10, 225 Pitt Street, Sydney, NSW 2000, Australia
e-mail: barry.mcgaw@mcgawgroup.org

P. Hughes (ed.), *Achieving Quality Education for All*, Education in the Asia-Pacific Region: Issues, Concerns and Prospects 20, DOI 10.1007/978-94-007-5294-8_18, © Springer Science+Business Media Dordrecht 2013

I also saw it in applications of early work in psychology to education that I set out in my presidential address to the Australian Psychological Society (McGaw, 1992). By the 1930s, the development of intelligence tests for adults had led to a view that measured intelligence could be used to establish the minimum intelligence required for each of the major professions (Terman & Merrill, 1937). The development of intelligence tests for children, coupled with a view that intelligence was essentially immutable through life, led to the development of tracked education systems designed to prepare students for different kinds of educational futures.

This view shaped the provision of grammar, secondary technical and secondary modern schools in England and Wales in the *Education Act 1944*. It was also influential in the shape of the reforms of secondary education in New South Wales, Australia under the Wyndham scheme (Committee, 1957). The scheme provided comprehensive secondary schools but a highly differentiated curriculum, particularly in the upper secondary years, to stream students in different directions.

Extensive differentiation of courses at the level of a state does not mean much unless schools can offer the full range. I found clear evidence of this problem when I reviewed the New South Wales Higher School Certificate in the 1990s. In English, four separate courses differentiated by level of demand were offered. I examined the enrolments in them of students who had been in the top 10 per cent in the state in English in grade 10. Considering only nonselective government schools in two regions of Sydney – one relatively advantaged, the other relatively disadvantaged – I found that students from the disadvantaged region were much less likely than those from the advantaged region to be enrolled in either of the two more demanding grade 11 and 12 courses. This remarkable difference in the way expectations were managed in year 11–12 for students seen a year before to have been equally capable in English arose because many of the schools in the disadvantaged region did not offer the more demanding courses, while many of those in the more advantaged region did not offer the least demanding courses (McGaw, 1997, p.44).

A state-level policy of providing for individual differences through a highly differentiated curriculum resulted in some schools' course offerings systematically lowering expectations of students while those of other schools systematically raised expectations. These differences in turn reflected differences in the social backgrounds of students.

The effects of differences in social backgrounds on educational outcomes have been well recognised in many countries. Some have educational policies and practices that seek to ameliorate these effects. Others have institutional arrangements that, if anything, exacerbate them.

With internationally comparable data on students' social backgrounds and their educational achievements, we provided important new insights on this issue in work at the Organisation for Economic Co-operation and Development (OECD) through the Program for International Student Assessment (PISA). The PISA results confirmed that, for all countries, there was a positive relationship between social background and educational achievement but showed conclusively that it was much weaker in some countries than others.

There are two indices with which to represent the relationship between two variables such as social background and educational achievement. One is the slope of the regression line that summarises the relationship, typically called the 'social gradient'. The steeper the line, the less equitable the results in the sense that differences in social background on the horizontal axis are associated with large differences in educational achievement.

In PISA 2000, some of the countries with the least steep slopes were among the highest performers, among them Finland, Japan, Korea and Canada. These countries demonstrated that it is possible to be high in both quality and equity. The social gradient for Australia was steeper than that for the OECD as a whole so, with its high mean performance, Australia could be characterised as high quality and low equity (Organisation for Economic Co-operation and Development [OECD], 2001).

In Australian education policy debates, I had often run into claims that attempts to address the effects of social disadvantage on educational outcomes would lower expectations for all and result in what was often called 'dumbing down'. The existence of high-performing countries that were also high on equity demonstrated that it is possible to 'level up'.

The second index with which to represent the relationship between two variables such as social background and educational achievement is the correlation between the two. It expresses how well the regression line summarises the relationship. If the points are clustered tightly around the line, the correlation will be high and the regression line or social gradient can be said to summarise the situation well. If there are many points well off the line, disadvantaged students performing well and advantaged students performing poorly, the social gradient still represents the average position but with many exceptions for which it does not give a good account. On this index, Australia looks rather better. It has a relatively low correlation, though not as low as those for Finland and Canada, for example. On this index, Australia is high equity.

The PISA results for Australia, with a relatively steep social gradient and a relatively low correlation reveal a country with, on average, a considerable educational advantage for the socially advantaged but with an encouraging extent of exceptions. The international comparisons show that the effects of social background on educational achievement can be ameliorated. The relatively low correlation for Australia provides encouraging evidence that the effects are being ameliorated for considerable numbers of young Australians. What Australia needs to do is to better understand how this occurs.

The way in which the education system is organised can systematically affect the way expectations are set for students. In the Scandinavian countries, there are only small differences among schools in the average performance levels of their students. In countries like Germany, Austria and Hungary, there are very large differences in the average performances of students in different schools because the system is designed to make it so. Around the age of 11, students are directed into schools of different kinds, with academic schools catering for the students performing well at that stage and a range of vocational schools catering for the others. The countries with these highly streamed systems generally performed poorly on average in PISA and had steep social gradients. Their students were being differentiated not only on the prime measure of early educational achievement but also on social background. The academic schools generally catered for the socially advantaged and the technical schools for the less advantaged (Artelt, Baumert, McElvany, & Peschar, 2003). The education systems were reproducing the existing social arrangements.

In PISA 2000, Poland was alongside Germany, Austria and Hungary in the extent of difference among schools. In PISA 2003, Poland was alongside the Scandinavian countries because it had ceased to stream its students into schools of different kinds but instead moved them without selection into comprehensive secondary schools. What was then remarkable was that Poland was the only OECD country that improved its average performance on every PISA measure between 2000 and 2003, and it did it primarily by lifting the performances of its lowest performing students. No longer assigning them to schools where they were exclusively in the company of other poorly performing students raised the expectations that were held for them and raised their performance levels. Between 2003 and 2006, Poland continued its improvement but now throughout the full range of performances. In reading in PISA 2006, Poland was no longer significantly behind Australia.

Between the Scandinavian countries and now Poland at one end with very little difference between schools and countries like Germany, Austria and Hungary that systematically make their schools different to reduce differences among students within schools, there are others with notionally comprehensive schools but with relatively marked differences among them in their students' achievement levels. They include Australia, New Zealand, the United States and the United Kingdom. The differences between the schools in these countries reflects demographic differences in the communities they serve and, in some cases, the presence of better resourced independent schools often in receipt of public funding as well as tuition fees from parents. In the case of Australia, 70 percent of the differences between schools can be accounted for in terms of differences in the social backgrounds of their students. That is, most of the differences are not due to what the schools do but to whom they enrol.

Evidence that some countries ameliorate the influence of social background on educational achievement better than others denies countries any opportunity to claim that the steepness of their social gradient is inevitable. Evidence that some schools achieve much better results than others serving students from similar social backgrounds denies the poorly performing schools the opportunity to claim that their performance is an inevitable consequence of dealing with students such as theirs.

Simply removing excuses for poor performance is not enough to achieve improvement. Lessons need to be learned from those doing better in similar circumstances, but they need first to be identified. That is the approach that Australia is now taking. An index of community socio-educational advantage (ICSEA) has been constructed using information on the education and occupation of the students' parents. The relationship at the school level between this index and students' achievements in the National Assessment Program: Literacy and Numeracy (NAPLAN) is shown in Fig. 18.1.

ICSEA scores have been set with a mean of 1,000 and a standard deviation of 100. The scale is a little truncated in Figure 1. The overall distribution is somewhat

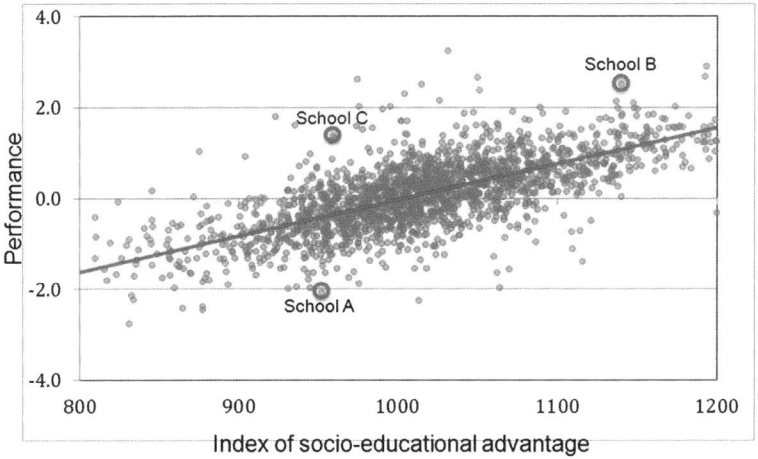

Fig. 18.1 Relationship between Index of Community Socio-economic Advantage (ICSEA) at school level and students' achievement in NAPLAN

skewed. There are 75 schools with ICSEA scores in the range below 800, down to 548. They are mostly small, remote schools for indigenous students. The truncation in the display at 1,200 excludes only 13 schools with scores from 1,201 to 1,233.

The regression line for the full data set is shown in Fig. 18.1. Schools above the regression line can be said to have NAPLAN achievements better than could have been expected on the basis of their ICSEA while those below the line could be said to have NAPLAN achievements worse than could have been expected on the basis of their ICSEA. This kind of regression analysis is often used to identify schools that have added more value (those above the regression line) and those that have added less value (those below the regression line).

It is then suggested that those adding more value could be a source of information for others on policies and practices that might help them lift their performances. From that perspective, school B could be said to be among those from which school A might learn. School C, however, would provide a more interesting and potentially helpful comparison because it has students from a similar social background.

Analyses to identify comparison schools in this way are now provided in Australia via the *My School* website (www.myschool.edu.au) which gives each school a comparison with the 30 immediately above and the 30 immediately below it on the ICSEA scale. It is too early to tell yet just how much the site has opened conversations between schools across the country, but it has certainly changed the basis on which parents can discuss school performance and school improvement with principals and teachers.

In Australia, this reform stands alongside the development of a national curriculum for the first time. It is being benchmarked against the curricula in other countries shown to be high performing in an effort to ensure that Australia does not expect less of its young people than the high-performing countries do of theirs.

All of the reform is designed to raise expectations of students and teachers. We readily expect improvements in the performances of our athletes and our enterprises so why not also our schools?

For this kind of thinking, Phil Hughes is an inspiration. His personal journey from a small primary school to Oxford as a Rhodes scholar, from nuclear physics to education with inspiration from CS Lewis and on to an extraordinary life of commitment and achievement in education in pursuit of quality and equity together is both an encouragement and a challenge to the rest of us. We are grateful for it and for Phil having remained true to himself throughout – a man of integrity without guile or arrogance.

References

Artelt, C., Baumert, J., McElvany, N., & Peschar, J. (2003). *Learners for life: Student approaches to learning. Results from PISA 2000*. Paris: OECD.

Committee Appointed to Survey Secondary Education in New South Wales (Chair: Dr H. S., Wyndham). (1957). *Report of the Committee*. Sydney, Australia: Government Printer.

McGaw, B. (1992). Testing in education. *Australian Psychologist, 27*, 1–11. [Presidential address to the Australian Psychological Society.]

McGaw, B. (1997). *Shaping their future: Recommendations for reform of the Higher School Certificate*. Sydney, Australia: Department of Training and Education Co-ordination.

McGaw, B., Warry, R. S., Varley, P. J., & Alcorn, J. (1976). Prospects for school leavers. In Australian Government Commission of Inquiry into Poverty. *School leavers: Choice and opportunity*. Canberra, Australia: Australian Government Publishing Service, pp. 33–116.

Organisation for Economic Co-operation and Development. (2001). *Knowledge and skills for life: First results from PISA 2000*. Paris: OECD.

Rosenthal, R., & Jacobson, L. (1968). *Pygmalion in the classroom*. New York: Holt, Rinehart & Winston.

Terman, L. M., & Merrill, M. A. (1937). *Measuring intelligence: a guide to the administration of the new revised Stanford-Binet tests of intelligence*. London: Harrap.

Part III
Prelude: Making Equity Work

Many of these papers are especially concerned with the issues of indigenous and disadvantaged people and the importance of providing an effective education.

Geoff Beeson begins with a broad approach, speaking about his own experiences in visiting schools in deprived areas. '*My experiences in these schools always prompted the question as to whether the students had the opportunity to gain an effective, relevant, high quality education – an opportunity equal to that of other children in the state and the nation, and appropriate for the children of a wealthy first world country*'.

The question he raises is fundamental to this book: do some students have a real chance to succeed in life, given the quality of their schools?

Michael Jones brings a unique insight and experience. At 24, he is the youngest contributor in this book. A very successful student at the Australian National University, Michael will take up a Rhodes Scholarship in Oxford in September 2011. His encounter during 2006 with some indigenous children in a remote town in northern Australia made him aware of their very limited opportunities. He began to organise for some of them to complete their secondary education to year 12, thus opening tertiary education and employment opportunities. This work will continue while he is in Oxford through the Wadjularbinna Foundation which he has established. While many people are prepared to speak out, Michael acted on his observations. '*Certainly, at a macro level, Indigenous education in a post-colonial society presents policy issues of almost Byzantine complexity. However, my experience at the individual level suggests that it also presents many opportunities for ordinary Indigenous and non-Indigenous Australians to connect and help each other overcome these challenges. The inspiring friendships I have formed in Doomadgee are a rare privilege and they remain an important part of my education as a young Australian*'.

John Grant brings to his paper a wealth of experience both in the Northern Territory of Australia and more widely. He remembers particularly the description about the children John was to teach from George Lee himself, an indigenous school teacher. '*–some children were hard of hearing, some had poor eyesight, school* *attendance was intermittent and those who had been at the school for a few years had had more teachers than they could remember'*.

This was a reality then in the 1960s. Too often, it is a reality now.

Margaret Clark also focuses on the Northern Territory and the needs of indigenous students, looking particularly at the functioning in education of the NT government. *'I argue that in the NT there are no votes in addressing indigenous disadvantage. This means there is an urgent need to develop strategies to make transparent what is happening for indigenous citizens who live in remote NT'*.

Sylvia Schmelkes is a distinguished educator from Mexico. Her work was recognised by UNESCO with the award of a Comenius Medal in Geneva in 2008. She writes bluntly about the situation in her home country. *'Mine is a third world country, Mexico. Over 50% of the population lives in poverty…. We are neighbors to the largest drug-consuming country in the world, the US, and have lately become victims of drug-related violence. The country's average schooling is 8.4 years'*. Rather than bemoan this fact, Sylvia and her husband, also a professor, work closely with the most disadvantaged people in their country, indigenous Mexicans, to address their disadvantage.

Chapter 19
Students with Additional Needs

Geoffrey W. Beeson

Schools Facing Challenging Circumstances

Not long ago, I had the opportunity of visiting several Victorian government schools that had been identified by the state education department as having student outcomes below expected levels[1]. The schools included both primary and secondary and covered metropolitan and country areas. Many features of these schools were similar to those I had seen in other struggling primary and secondary schools I had visited over previous years in my role as an external reviewer for Victorian schools, or as a part of other school-based projects with which I had been involved. Although such schools were relatively few in number, their situations left a lasting impression. My experiences in these schools always prompted the question as to whether the students had the opportunity to gain an effective, relevant and high-quality education – an opportunity equal to that of other children in the state and the nation and appropriate for the children of a wealthy First World country.

All the schools faced very challenging circumstances. They were typically located in low socio-economic areas, in some cases with high levels of unemployment and high numbers of single-parent families. In these cases, schools frequently found that many families faced financial difficulties and welfare issues. They were generally not able to find the money to pay for necessities and extras, for example, for calculators needed for higher level maths or for excursions, and schools had to take this into account in their planning. Many of the schools conducted or were developing strong welfare programmes, including offerings, such as breakfast programmes to meet the

---

[1] This was a part of an examination by the Victorian Auditor-General of how effectively that state's education department was supporting schools performing below expected levels (VAGO, 2007).

G.W. Beeson (✉)
Geoff Beeson & Associates, PO Box 22, Central Park, VIC 3145, Australia
e-mail: gwbeeson@vicnet.net.au

P. Hughes (ed.), *Achieving Quality Education for All*, Education in the Asia-Pacific Region: Issues, Concerns and Prospects 20, DOI 10.1007/978-94-007-5294-8_19, © Springer Science+Business Media Dordrecht 2013

needs of students who had little or no breakfast at home, and a clothing pool for students who could not afford a school uniform.

There was often a significant lack of parental involvement in the school, and student absence was frequently a critical contributor to lower performance levels of students. In some cases, school staff reported that they spent substantial time on tasks such as following up absences with families and contacting a student's home to "get them out of bed". It was not uncommon to find families where there was a lack of interest in and support for the school, and student attendance was not necessarily a high priority. Many students and their parents had low aspirations, and teachers' expectations of students were also often low. In some areas, many parents did not speak English, and the problem of parental lack of involvement in school was exacerbated by the existence of cultural or other inhibitions. Principals talked of the "constant battle" to get parents involved.

A common feature was that many students started primary and secondary school well behind their peers in language, social and motor skills and levels of knowledge. In addition, some schools had high proportions of students with learning or developmental difficulties in one or more of the areas of emotional maturity, cognitive skills and health and wellbeing. For such students, access to support services was crucial for improving their learning. Reflecting this situation, "students with additional needs" were rated by half of the principals responding to a questionnaire as extremely important in contributing to the school's performance difficulties. The questionnaire was sent from the Victorian Auditor-General's Office to the principals of 123 schools (105 responded) that currently or recently had student outcomes below expected levels (VAGO, 2007, p. 37).

Some of the school communities were culturally and linguistically diverse. In such situations, schools faced the challenge of finding ways of working with the diverse families. These schools recognised that children gain self-esteem when they feel their families are valued and respected. Newly arrived non-English-speaking migrant students, especially refugees with little or no schooling from developing countries that have been experiencing upheaval, placed additional demands on some schools.

Schools were often frustrated in their attempts to improve their situations by a lack of or ageing infrastructure and resources. Further, many of the schools were suffering declining enrolments, lack of strong and stable leadership and uncertainty about the future. Moreover, for the secondary schools, their most able students were often poached by other public or private schools. The combination of many of these factors led to difficulty in recruiting and retaining good teachers.

Meeting the Needs of Students

Responding to these additional, complex needs was a challenge for the schools, and they employed a variety of means to meet the challenge. Where possible, they made use of specialist staff available through the education department's regional offices, for example, psychologists, guidance officers, speech pathologists and specialist literacy or numeracy teachers. The appointment of a welfare officer in some schools helped alleviate some problems. Unfortunately, schools frequently experienced long delays in gaining access to these specialist services and were forced to look for other solutions. One school established a special space for students who were shy, autistic or disabled. Another set up an oral language centre and employed a part-time speech pathologist in conjunction with a neighbouring school, and another appointed two volunteer multicultural aides. However, most found it difficult to find sufficient funds to employ the specialist staff they needed where such staff were not available through their regional office. There were also cases where some form of needed intervention from the regional office was too slow in arriving.

Despite the difficulties, all the schools had clear and identifiable strengths, and all were committed to improving the education of their students. Typically, there were dedicated, conscientious and willing teachers who worked together and supported each other. There was often a friendly and open atmosphere, and students were happy at school. Teachers in more than one school reported that for many students, school was the most stable part of their lives. Police visited one school seeking information on the whereabouts of a 15-year-old who had left home. It transpired he was attending school as normal, sleeping where he could. Amongst other strengths in evidence were a strong focus on caring for their students, celebration of diversity, effective or improving student welfare management, productive partnerships with outside agencies and introduction of innovative programmes to meet student needs.

Central Office Initiatives

In addressing school improvement, including for schools where student outcomes are below expected levels, the education department in Victoria has adopted a more strategic approach in recent years following the launch of the Blueprint for Government Schools (DET, 2003).

The school review and improvement process, steadily enhanced over more than a decade, provides an underpinning and coherent framework for school improvement (DEECD, 2011). The department has adopted a research-based effective schools model (OSE, 2007), which incorporates eight factors correlated with improved school outcomes. Furthermore, there have been curriculum improvements and special programmes aimed at specific areas, such as the Targeted School Improvement initiative, the Reading Recovery programme and the Early Years Coordinator Training programme. Unfortunately, some special programmes have not been funded for a sufficient period for their actions to take full effect.

There have also been important initiatives at national level designed to improve the quality of education and the outcomes for students, including the Australian Government Quality Teaching Program (AGQTP, 2011), the Australian Institute for Teaching and School Leadership (AITSL, 2011) and the Australian Curriculum, Assessment and Reporting Authority (ACARA, 2011).

Despite such initiatives, and the efforts of the individual schools, not all students in these schools receive an effective, relevant and high-quality education. This is essentially because the schools are unable to access the crucial specialised support and resources they need for their students, an issue highlighted in the report of the Victorian Auditor-General Office (VAGO, 2007). For them, the resources they so urgently need are too often not available, as the demand outweighs the supply. As a result, students at these schools remain at a disadvantage compared with other Victorian – and Australian – students. While the examples and commentary above have focused on Victorian schools, there is no reason to believe the situation is significantly better or worse in other parts of Australia.

Providing Opportunities for *All* Students

There are two ways in which these deficiencies could be overcome. The first is via the application of additional funds. Unfortunately, it appears that these needed extra funds are not available. Given this situation, it is indefensible for governments to be providing funds to already wealthy private schools, while substantial numbers of needy government schools in all parts of Australia are unable to provide the necessary support services and resources for their students. Bypassing the basic needs of so many public schools in this way condemns the affected students to a second class education and denies them the opportunity to fully develop their abilities. This is a loss to the community as well as to the individual. A sound education provides a way for a young person to escape from an environment of poverty, unemployment or dysfunction to a life that is satisfying at a personal level and also valuable as a contributing and productive member of the community. It is unquestionable that extra money spent on struggling schools will produce a greater dividend in social and economic as well as educational terms than the equivalent spent on well-resourced private schools.

The lack of essential funding for students in these schools not only makes it impossible to provide the kind of education available to students elsewhere, it also tends to keep them isolated as a disadvantaged group in the community, denying in a major way the unifying role education can play. Ironically, government policies that ensure provision of funds to already wealthy private schools, and to the establishment of large numbers of faith-based schools, have a similar effect of further dividing the community or entrenching already existing divisions. Social cohesion is threatened by this approach to the funding of education.

Amongst Organisation for Economic Co-operation and Development (OECD) countries, Australia is a provider of relatively high-quality education. However, we are also a low-equity country, based on OECD data (OECD, 2010) and the exclusionary policies – in respect of entry, practices and employment – of private schools. This is not appropriate for a country that prides itself on its egalitarianism. We spend a much greater proportion of public funds on private education than the OECD average (16.9% cf. 9.7% in 2007) and vastly more than the USA and Canada

(0.2 and 2%). Countries that consistently achieve the best results in terms of literacy and numeracy – Finland and Canada – have inclusive education systems where public and private faith-based schools are complementary. It does not make sense to provide large quantities of money to minority private and often exclusionary primary and secondary schools while starving needy schools in the public sector.

The second way in which the deficiencies outlined above could be overcome is through ensuring that, not only are all schools adequately supported to meet the needs of their students, but that they and their teachers are allowed sufficient professional freedom to make decisions concerning what actions to take in the best interests of their students in the contexts in which they work and live. There appears to be a view in some sectors of the community at present that the quality of education in Australia's public schools can be manipulated by "pulling levers" at the central offices – national and state. These "levers" include national testing, setting targets, mandating certain actions and introducing new programme requirements. While these initiatives are important and potentially very beneficial, it is crucial that their numbers and the demands they make on schools are not so large as to overwhelm schools and distract teachers from their central work with students in the classroom or that they become regarded as the sole drivers of improvements in the quality of school education. There are examples where this has occurred in recent years, with harmful effects on teacher morale and performance.

Summary

As argued, there are substantial numbers of schools where students are not getting the opportunity for the effective, relevant, high-quality education that is their right and the country's need in modern Australia. At present, the levels of additional support required for them to achieve at the expected levels or better is not available. A more equitable funding system for education and an appropriate balance between demands and support from central offices on the one hand, and space for schools and teachers to exercise their professional judgement in the interests of the students in their care on the other, would go a long way towards rectifying this situation.

References

ACARA. (2011). Australian Curriculum, Assessment and Reporting Authority. www.acara.edu.au
AGQTP. (2011). Australian Government Quality Teaching Program. www.deewr.gov.au/schooling/qualityteaching/AGQTP/
AITSL. (2011). Australian Institute for Teaching and School Leadership. www.aitsl.edu.au
DEECD. (2011). *Accountability and improvement framework for Victorian schools*. Melbourne, Australia: Department of Education and Early Childhood Development Victoria.
DET. (2003). *Blueprint for government schools*. Melbourne, Australia: Department of Education & Training, Victoria.

OECD. (2010). *Education at a glance.* Directorate of Education: OECD Indicators. www.oecd. org/eag2010

OSE. (2007). *School improvement: A theory of action.* Melbourne, Australia: Office of School Education, Department of Education Victoria.

VAGO. (2007). *Improving our schools: Monitoring and support.* Melbourne, Australia: Victorian Auditor-General's Office, Victorian Government Printer.

Chapter 20
Reflections on Education in Remote Indigenous Australia

Michael Jones

In September of 2006, I was kicking a football around with a 12-year-old boy; he was the son of some friends with whom I was staying. Out of nowhere, he announced – as small boys sometimes do – that when he grew up, he hoped to be a sailor in the navy. I replied that he would have to work hard at school and practise being very well behaved if he wanted to join the navy. My small friend nodded thoughtfully, passing the ball from hand to hand before he spoke: 'Dad says I'll have to finish high school…Do you reckon I'll be able to finish high school?'

At the time, I didn't even think before responding. High school graduation seemed such a safe thing to promise in Australia, particularly to this bright young man. I'm sure I probably added another qualifier about working hard and behaving, but I'm equally sure my tone would have left little room for doubt. I can vividly remember kicking the ball back to a wide grin and bright, excited eyes. In most backyards in Australia, this conversation would have probably gone no further. But in September of 2006, I was in Doomadgee, a remote Aboriginal community on the Gulf of Carpentaria. The Doomadgee school only taught up to year 10. Whilst I didn't know it, making good on my glib promise was about to become the biggest challenge of my life.

I met Phillip Hughes at the ACT Rhodes Scholarship dinner in December 2010. We soon fell into discussion about our mutual interest in the state of educational opportunities in Australia's remote Aboriginal communities. I am the first to admit that my experience in the field of education is limited; it is far less, I am sure, than that of others who have contributed to this volume. Prior to 2006 my only involvement with education in Australia was as a fairly unreflective recipient of some excellent opportunities. Following 2006 I worked with some friends in the community of Doomadgee, in North West Queensland, to organise better educational opportunities for their children. In 2009 this cooperative endeavour was formalised through the incorporation of the Wadjularbinna Foundation.

M. Jones (✉)
Magdalen College, University of Oxford, High Street,
Oxford, OX1 4AU, UK
e-mail: michael.jones@magd.ox.ac.uk

The failings of Australian education policy in remote Aboriginal communities are widely acknowledged. This acknowledgement has been explicit since 2008, with the significant gap between the percentages of indigenous and non-indigenous students who attain a year-12 qualification becoming a central concern of the Commonwealth Government's 'Closing the Gap' initiatives.[1] The education gap in indigenous communities is a complex issue to which I certainly do not profess to have an adequate answer; indeed, experience has taught me that as a non-indigenous Australian, I will never totally understand some of the issues facing young indigenous people. What I offer in this chapter are reflections derived from my experiences in Doomadgee in the hope they might be useful to an audience interested in Australian education. These are divided into three broad lessons I have learned: (1) that the importance of a broad and inclusive understanding of 'education', (2) that self-belief is the first step to education and (3) that non-indigenous ignorance remains a significant barrier.

A Broad and Inclusive Understanding of 'Education'

When I first arrived in Doomadgee, I considered myself to be pretty well educated; I had 'done well' at a 'good school' and was now studying law at the Australian National University. If pressed, I probably would have justified my claim with reference to a fairly classical definition of education, as the transmission of society's accumulated knowledge from one generation to another. However, I soon discovered that my education had not prepared me at all for life in a remote Aboriginal community. Indeed, were it not for the patience of the locals and the generous tutelage of their elders, I suspect my learning curve would have been impossibly steep. This led me to do some rethinking.

Whilst all Australians would agree that Australian children should be educated, defining the content of this education is quite complicated in a post-colonial context. Certainly it is more complicated than the formal attainment of a year-12 certificate. From the indigenous perspective, often the institutions and processes of formal education have been complicit in the erosion of indigenous culture since colonisation.[2] Moreover, a definition centred upon the transmission of accumulated, communal social knowledge seems inadequate when indigenous and non-indigenous communities regularly misunderstand each other. In Doomadgee, members of the community powerfully associated the school with the recent mission past; this

---

[1] In 2006, 47.4% of indigenous Australians aged between 20 and 24 achieved a year-12 qualification as compared to 83.8% of non-indigenous. In remote communities, such as Doomadgee, this gap is far wider still. See, *Closing the Gap: Prime Minister's Report 2011* (Canberra: Department of Families, Housing, Community Services and indigenous Affairs).

[2] May, S., & Aikman, S. (2003). Indigenous education: Addressing current issues and developments. *Comparative Education, 39*(2), 139–145.

meant different things to each family, depending upon their treatment on the mission. Moreover, children were to varying degrees undergoing an education in traditional culture; this varied according to tribal heritage and family. Whilst some children were keen to finish year 10 in Doomadgee and then progress on to boarding school, others had different aspirations which could equally be described as 'education'.

In this context, I quickly learned my first lesson: a broader and more inclusive understanding of an 'adequate' education was required. To my mind the opposite of education is ignorance. If we understand an adequate education to provide what is necessary for a person to live a rich life, contribute usefully to society and pursue their aspirations, then the process of education must – at its most basic level – eliminate sufficient ignorance for this to occur. Unfortunately, this basic standard of 'adequate' education was not widely evident in Doomadgee. With some very notable and inspiring exceptions, ignorance made indigenous and non-indigenous people fearful of each other; it often prevented both groups from engaging socially, and it thwarted many of their aspirations. I cannot avoid the conclusion that with a broader under-standing of education, particularly among the non-indigenous population, this situation might have been avoided.

Self-Belief Is the First Step

During my visits to Doomadgee, I met some remarkable young people who displayed great courage and determination in successfully pursuing their education, often moving thousands of kilometres away from their homes. In my opinion, what distinguished these young people from the many negative statistics I had read about was a firm sense of self-belief.

Recent research in the United Kingdom suggests that there is a correlation between negative self-perception among working-class students and their failure to progress to higher education.[3] Among students of equal ability, research has shown those from working-class backgrounds consistently perceived that other students of similar ability had outperformed them in literacy and numeracy testing; this then affected the students' subsequent choices.[4] My experiences in Doomadgee suggest that a similar dynamic to this class-based behaviourist obstacle prevents some indigenous students from continuing their studies. Although, I would suggest that the obstacle for indigenous students is even more severe.

Non-indigenous Australians are often unaware of the many ways in which daily experience can undermine the self-belief of an Aboriginal student and reinforce a nega-tive self-perception of their education. The litany of examples I witnessed in Doomadgee

---

[3] Thorpe, A., Snell, M., Hoskins, S., & Bryant, J. (2007). False uniqueness: The self-perception of new entrants to higher education in the UK and its implications for access – A pilot study. *Higher Education Quarterly, 61*(1), 3–22.

[4] *Ibid*, 15–6.

are too many to list here, but I will describe two that were both obvious and significant. The first example is the structure of the community school. My conversations continually reinforced how damaging it was that the community school did not teach students beyond year 10. Certainly, there were some understandable reasons for this, given the remoteness of the community. However, there can be no doubt that it sent a powerful message to students that years 11 and 12 were not for them. Quite simply, the average student in Doomadgee was aware that under such an arrangement only very exceptional students would make it to boarding school. Consequently, the self-belief for most students faltered at this hurdle. The second example I would like to give is the experience of racism. The extent to which racism remains a common part of indigenous experience in Australia should not be underestimated. Obviously, this is damaging to an individual student's self-esteem, to an extent that no non-indigenous Australian can fully understand. However, racism is perhaps particularly significant for students in remote communities; this is because it can often leave them unwilling to make the necessary move away into a predominately non-indigenous environment, be it a boarding school or university.

The students who I observed overcome these barriers all possessed great fortitude of character. They also usually had the benefit of committed and inspiring parents. However, it is important to understand that often even these two vital assets were not enough.

Non-indigenous Ignorance

The third lesson I learned in Doomadgee was that effective education usually requires a dialectic exchange between a student and teacher or mentor. Importantly, this makes it impossible to teach or mentor a student effectively from a position of ignorance. It is for this reason that I believe one of the most significant barriers to adequate education in remote Aboriginal communities remains non-indigenous ignorance.

The most obvious manifestation of this problem should be in the classroom. To my mind there is no doubt that a high level of cultural competency is required of school teachers in remote Aboriginal communities. To the credit of the individuals who teach in Doomadgee, my experience was that cultural faux pas were rare. This said, these individual teachers were often labouring heroically in the absence of proper resources. Genuine investment in cultural training would almost certainly improve outcomes. It would also probably prevent these young teachers burning out so quickly.

In my view, it is the continuing ignorance of broader non-indigenous society which is most damaging to the education of remote Aboriginal students. It is often easy for non-indigenous Australians, particularly in urban settings, to forget that schools do not educate children in a social vacuum. Successful education occurs within a matrix of support; beyond family and friends, this is provided by community groups, prospective employers, social and professional networks, school alumni, religious groups and a myriad of other organisations. It is through this matrix of support that most students place their lessons in context and develop their ambitions for a career beyond school. In my experience, this network of support is under-developed in remote indigenous communities and sometimes completely absent. Remoteness is certainly a factor in this failing, but there are persuasive examples of it being successfully overcome.

During my times in Doomadgee, it was quite evident, even as an outsider, that some organisations within the non-indigenous community had invested time and effort in cultural competency and were successfully reaching out to indigenous youth. Notable among these were sporting codes (particularly the NRL and AFL), mining and agricultural companies, the armed forces (particularly the Army Regional Force Surveillance Units) and to a lesser extent arts and cultural organisations. Certainly, some of these organisations were motivated by commercial ends. However, the relative ease with which they were able to overcome the tyranny of remoteness and establish a presence in the mind of local students was nonetheless impressive. In my opinion, the success with which these culturally savvy organisations achieved their ends demonstrates two things: first, that non-indigenous ignorance as much as remoteness is what prevents indigenous students engaging with institutions important to their academic future, and second, that there is a possible path forwards in this area if non-indigenous Australia is sufficiently committed to take it.

Conclusion

In this brief chapter, I have offered an outsider's reflections upon education in remote indigenous Australia. Like much that is written in this area, my reflections have focused more upon the challenges than successes. This is perhaps inevitable, but it is also unfortunate. One topic which Phillip Hughes has written about persuasively is the importance of inspiring individual student-teacher relationships to any successful education. I think it is important that all Australians remember this point when considering the gap in indigenous education – for it gives me a glimmer of optimism. Certainly, at a macro level, indigenous education in a post-colonial society presents policy issues of almost Byzantine complexity. However, my experience at the individual level suggests that it also presents many opportunities for ordinary indigenous and non-indigenous Australians to connect and help each other overcome these challenges. The inspiring friendships I have formed in Doomadgee are a rare privilege, and they remain an important part of my education as a young Australian.

Chapter 21
Two Sides of the Coin: Priorities for Good Schools

John Grant

We Know What We Do Not Know…

George Lee taught in schools in Aboriginal communities and on pastoral stations in the Northern Territory (NT) of Australia for much of his career. He is one of the unsung heroes of education in the NT. He preferred the smaller schools; though when I was appointed as a post-primary teacher to Maningrida, a remote indigenous community, in the 1960s, George was on the staff of this eight-teacher school, having been recently transferred from a pastoral station.

In welcoming me to the school, George invited me to visit his lower primary class. He was obviously loved by the children who responded well to his wry sense of humour mixed with a keen eye for discipline. Like all Northern Territory schools at the time, the curriculum and resources were largely sourced from those in use in South Australian schools. Hence, the standard set of primary school readers was the *Dick and Dora* series even though it was apparent to even the casual observer how foreign the stories and illustrations were when used in the context of a Northern Territory Aboriginal community. Elsewhere in the school, I saw posters depicting the lineage of the British Royal Family, and I heard a class chanting the names of Australian prime ministers.

George invited me to select a reader up to the grade 3 level, to open it up at random and to ask one of the children to read the story. This I did and the child responded with a word-perfect rendition. I was impressed. George then opened the book to another page, showed only the illustration to the child, and we again heard a word-perfect recitation. The children had heard so many teachers read the

J. Grant (✉)
Emeritus Faculty, Australian National University,
19 Loch Street, Yarralumla, ACT 2600, Australia
e-mail: j.grant@netspeed.com.au

P. Hughes (ed.), *Achieving Quality Education for All*, Education in the Asia-Pacific Region: Issues, Concerns and Prospects 20, DOI 10.1007/978-94-007-5294-8_21,
© Springer Science+Business Media Dordrecht 2013

stories on previous occasions that they knew the stories by heart (not that they could have identified with the double-decker buses and the gender-based family responsibilities of a 'typical' post-war South Australian family). As George said, 'Not all is as it seems'.

By way of introducing the children, George invited me to join in a conversation with him and the class. I learned that there were four main language groups represented in the class, that the level of English varied considerably but was nowhere near grade 3, that some children were hard of hearing and some had poor eyesight (in both cases George had them sitting at the front of the room), that school attendance was intermittent and that those who had been at the school for a few years had had more teachers than they could remember.

It was a valuable introduction to teaching in a remote Northern Territory school but more generally a reminder, to rework the words of Ausubel, that we must 'know the child and teach him/her accordingly'.

When I met my own class of 14-year-old boys (boys and girls were separated at the post-primary level), I was thus alert to the fact that if I were to be effective as a teacher, I would have to do my best to understand issues such as health, language, family and cultural responsibilities and previous school experience. Little was I to know at the time that with teenagers like David Gulpilil, the star of the film *Walkabout* and many later films, in my class there was a wealth of talent ready to be unleashed.

During the dry season, the water supply at Maningrida reduced to a trickle so the settlement superintendent asked the entire Aboriginal population to 'go bush'. This meant the closure of the school for several weeks, but with the permission of the school principal and of elders, I took my class on a week's bush camp where roles were reversed – I was the learner and they were the experts, particularly in living on bush tucker. It was then that I saw the boys in a new light, full of enthusiasm and engagement. In subsequent weeks, many of the boys were taken by their elders to a Kunapipi ceremony to which I was delighted to be invited. There I witnessed indigenous education at its most intense – meticulous preparations, all-night ceremonies, strict discipline and demanding expectations with no room for excuses.

I have often reflected on my teaching at Maningrida and wonder how well we know each student in our care, whether they live in a remote community or in an urban area. In subsequent years as a curriculum officer based in Darwin, first with the Aboriginal Education Branch of the Commonwealth Department of the Interior and then with the newly created Northern Territory Education Department, I met with staff of the Department of Health to explore ways of establishing lines of communication at the local level between health professionals and school teachers so that health issues affecting student learning could be better taken into account. I dreamt up a 'working title' for my concept: the IDEAL Testing Program (the interdisciplinary diagnosis of the early attributes of learners). Despite a sympathetic hearing for the health professionals, it was clearly going to be a long haul, and with a cyclone, staff turnover, ethical and legal considerations, etc., the dream was never realised.

Even today, in any school, there are students whose special needs (and talents) go unnoticed. They may be known to parents, to health professionals, to social workers or the like but they are not always known to the school. So if we are to take account of individual circumstances and needs, to capitalise on each individual's strengths and talents and to develop an enthusiasm for learning, we need to do more to 'know the child'.

Up the Creek

In Northern Territory schools, as elsewhere, absenteeism is a significant problem. Sometimes, the absence is for good reason – health issues, cultural demands, family travel, etc. But it could not be denied that lack of interest in classroom activities is a major factor. Hence, I was intrigued, as a Darwin resident commuting to work each day, to find that a group of some of the less-regular school attendees could be seen day after day at the same place near the bridge over Rapid Creek – playing with home-made boats, fishing, swimming, catching crabs, socialising and possibly engaging in some less-healthy activities as well. As one developing curricula for the new Northern Territory school system, I wondered why it was that the great variety of activities available at school was seen as less enticing than a daily get-together at a tidal creek. Was it necessary to rethink the curriculum so that at least for those turned off the typical school programme, there were activities which attracted them to attend?

And what about the undoubted merits of developing national curricula? How could curricula be devised which would be applicable in a place as diverse culturally, socially, geographically and economically as the Northern Territory let alone in places worlds away such as Australia's largest cities?

In attempting to come to grips with the undoubted need for some overall coherence in what teaching and learning takes place in Australian schools, I came to the conclusion that it is useful to differentiate between the 'curriculum domain' and the 'learning domain'. The first draws on the skills of a range of professionals including educators, subject matter specialists, psychologists, sociologists and practising classroom teachers. It produces curriculum documents and a wide range of supporting resources. It informs the training of teachers, the design of schools and the priorities for educational research. The second is the domain of the skilled teacher who must be given considerable flexibility and support in getting to know the students, devising activities that will interest them, assessing their progress and interacting with parents and the wider community. As most parents would probably agree, the most critical element in all of this is the quality of the teacher.

So the principal challenge is to attract outstanding and committed people into the teaching profession, to provide high-quality initial and ongoing professional development, to equip them with appropriate curricula and resources and to ensure that they have access to all relevant information about their students. Then teachers will be in the best position to stimulate and extend the particular students in their care.

Unfortunately some of the current national trends, particularly in educational assessment, but driven also by views about 'teacher-proof' curricula, seem more driven by the mantra of 'accountability' than by the need to put into the hands of teachers the tools to get to know their students better and to devise learning activities accordingly.

The Two Territories

The opportunity to test these thoughts came with my appointment in 1975 to Canberra as director (curriculum) to the second newly created Australian school system of the twentieth century, the Australian Capital Territory Schools Authority under its chair, Phillip Hughes, and its chief education officer, Hedley Beare.

It would be hard to find two places with such different educational challenges – the Northern Territory with its vast distances, harsh climate, remote communities, cultural diversity and highly mobile population and the Australian Capital Territory (ACT) with its highly educated and growing population, its high expectations, its compactness and its severance of the umbilical cord with New South Wales. There were perhaps only two common, though invaluable, features: first, the opportunity to break new ground, freed from some of the practices of the past which seemed less relevant to the needs of the late twentieth century and, second, the advent of the Commonwealth Teaching Service with its emphasis on teaching quality, peer review and teacher mobility. Consequently, in both territories, there was a sense of enthusiasm and even a pioneering spirit.

Not that the same educational solutions were appropriate in two such vastly different places. For the ACT, at least one distinguishing feature for which the Schools Authority will certainly be remembered is 'school-based curriculum development'. School boards with statutory powers were established with responsibility for determining curriculum policy. School by school, teachers found themselves as never before engaged in curriculum development.

Space here will not allow an analysis of the pros and cons, the lessons learnt and of subsequent developments, suffice to say that the advent of national curricula should be seen as a positive move, provided that they are devised so as to maximise the capacity of classroom teachers to apply their expertise. Equally, the current focus on student assessment should be welcomed, provided that it is recognised as both an inexact science and one which is at its most useful when it is applied as a diagnostic tool to assist the teacher in better understanding the needs and progress of individual students.

As different as these two Territories are, I conclude that there are at least two lessons which are as relevant for the future health of Australian schools as they were to the establishment of two new school systems. Put most simply, they are: know the child and develop and support teachers of the highest quality. These are the two sides of the educational coin.

Chapter 22
Getting Accountability Settings Right for Remote Indigenous Australians

Margaret Clark

With all the professional opposition to the ways in which the education transparency and accountability agenda has been prosecuted in Australia, one could be forgiven for thinking that the education profession is against accountability full stop. I believe that this is not the case and that there are things that we urgently need to do in Australia to improve educational accountability if we are to use it to drive good equity-focused policy, research and practice.

In this chapter, I focus on schooling in Northern Territory (NT) remote indigenous communities because this is where Australia's most desperately disadvantaged citizens live in hugely disproportionate numbers. I argue that in the NT, there are no votes in addressing indigenous disadvantage. This means there is an urgent need to develop strategies to make transparent what is happening for indigenous citizens who live in remote NT – strategies that will hold the Territory accountable.

I am not the only observer of NT government's performance to conclude this. Marcia Langton,[1] an indigenous woman who holds the Foundation Chair of Australian Indigenous Studies at the University of Melbourne and lived in the Northern Territory for many years, regards the NT Emergency Response (NTER) as necessary because of the failure of NT governments for a quarter of a century to adequately invest the funds they received to eliminate the disadvantages of their citizens in education, health and basic services.

In a recent article in *The Australian*,[2] Nicolas Rothwell, a journalist who has won awards for his coverage of indigenous issues, states that the NT's 33-year-long

---

[1] Jovan Maud, Marcia Langton on the NT Intervention, Word Press, 30 November 2007. http://culturematters.wordpress.com/2007/11/30/marcia-langton-on-the-nt-intervention/

[2] Nicolas Rothwell, The case against State 7, The Australian 16 April 2011.

M. Clark (✉)
Former CEO, Australian College of Educators, 1/268 Dryandra St, Lyneham,
ACT 2602, Australia
e-mail: megamd@tpg.com.au

P. Hughes (ed.), *Achieving Quality Education for All*, Education in the Asia-Pacific
Region: Issues, Concerns and Prospects 20, DOI 10.1007/978-94-007-5294-8_22,
© Springer Science+Business Media Dordrecht 2013

phase of self-government should be brought to a rapid close because of state failure across the board. He also makes it clear that this has nothing to do with which party is in power – the problems are structural and enduring.

He references Rolf Gerritson's new book (*North Australian Political Economy*) that details how the NT government diverts funds allocated by the Commonwealth Grants Commission for the purpose of addressing priority areas of disadvantage to other more politically useful domains.

He also notes the detailed work by Barry Hansen, treasurer, NT Council of Social Services (NTCOSS). His findings are described as *'beyond belief and yet … incontrovertible. Canberra provides more than 80 per cent of the NT's annual budget of almost $5 billion and much of this inflow is specific remote area remediation money, intended to help disadvantaged communities. Since 2001 the NT has channeled about $2bn from Aboriginal area spending. In the latest year alone, the shortfall in welfare spending was $200 m'.*

Nobody who has spent any time in NT government will be surprised by this. The mantra that there are no votes in indigenous issues is an oft-repeated phrase among government workers.

When in Darwin, I witnessed high levels of investment in a world-class conference centre and precinct with a wave pool, the building of state-of-the-art senior colleges and middle schools. I noted the extremely elaborate Parliament House and precinct – all for less than 230,000 people.

I also witnessed the appalling state of indigenous communities – where the average number of people to a room is over 3, children swim in open drains and there is no parity of amenity whatsoever. For example, in 2007 I observed the opening of a new school building in a remote community that was sub-standard from the outset – it would never have been built in Darwin. It was built on the only school oval. The school had no footpaths, no covered ways, no drinking faucets, huge mud puddles en route between classrooms, broken playground equipment, a very poor library with no librarian, no career advisors, no grassy play area and a staff room built for half the staff numbers. But at least it could (with this building) finally provide access to secondary schooling for the community of well over 2000 for the first time (this was in 2007). It is not at all surprising that in community consultations, a consistent refrain is 'we want a real school'.

Rothwell asks 'why this appalling state of affairs?' He answers by explaining the unique political setup and the demographic characteristics of the NT. These combine to render remote communities voiceless and powerless (not to mention sealed off and invisible) and also to pork barrelling of the worst kind.

He also makes the point that the NT Public Service is poorly managed across the board. Some of the failures have made national headlines. The most notable include:

• The $672 m *Strategic Indigenous Housing and Infrastructure Program (SIHIP)*
• The failures of child protection

- The lack of response to flamboyant evidence of corruption and fraud in many remote communities (as documented in one community in great detail by Russell Skelton)[3]
- A Commonwealth of Australian Governments (COAG) funded trial of joined-up government intensive service delivery in one of the largest remote communities – that failed to deliver on all counts because (as the evaluation concluded) of the intractability of government departments (both state and federal governments) that focused on their own turf, funding streams and outcomes[4]
- The Montara oil spill off the NT coast.

Education governance is no exception. During my time in the NT, I observed at close quarters many examples of programme failure, some of which can be attributed to incompetence, but most are more about politics than competence.

I observed:

- A string of ambitious indigenous education 'close the gap' strategies launched, with zero funds attached – the latest being the education component of the Territory Growth Towns strategy (called Working Future[5]) – also with no NT identified funds
- The development of Remote Learning Partnership Agreements (Commonwealth funded) with a number of remote communities and their schools but with no funds to implement any of the agreed initiatives until the Commonwealth Smarter Schools National Partnership funds came along
- A teacher forced to live in the staffroom of a very remote school for well over 6 months because housing (the responsibility of another department) was not available
- A literacy policy announced and published to the website only to disappear without explanation just weeks later
- The release of an NT-wide Accountability and School Improvement Framework – where 3 years after its launch almost no remote school has a strategic improvement plan in place
- The failure of the department to put in place any strategy to support students in remote communities to develop English language competency, when the bilingual policy was abolished – the controversial 4 h a day English language policy does not meet this challenge
- A decision to reclassify an East Arnhem outstation sub school as a proper school but no action taken to implement this for over 12 months (it may still be an outstation sub school to this day)
  - This means no teacher on site and reliance on an indigenous education worker with a visiting teacher 3 days a fortnight. There are remote schools with lower (non-indigenous) student numbers.

---

[3] Russell Skelton, *King Brown Country: The Betrayal of Papunya,* Allen and Unwin 2010.
[4] The evaluation noted that at the start of the trial there was an average of 17 people per (3 bedroom) house and that over the 3 years of the trial, a total of 4 new houses were built, 15 houses became uninhabitable and 200 babies were born.
[5] See http://www.workingfuture.nt.gov.au/Overview/overview.html

- The continuance of the policy of staffing schools on 'enrolment modified by attendance' in spite of agreeing with the Commonwealth to move to staffing by agreed student numbers (in exchange for funding for 200 additional teachers and a number of additional classrooms)
  - This has significant consequences. If a school has 315 enrolled students and a 60% attendance rate, it is funded for 220 students (at 70% of enrolment) – a shortfall of over 4.5 teachers (at primary level – more for older students). Yet, the number of students assigned to teachers and classes is 315 not 220 – they just attend irregularly. So the 10 teachers have over 31 students not 22 – attending in a highly irregular pattern.

While a small number of the above examples – both in education and beyond – can be put down to poor governance and lack of competence, there is a strong political element to almost all these failures. And it should be said that some of the problems implicate the Commonwealth Government just as much as the NT Government. Having worked with both levels of government in the NT, I would have to admit that there were inspiring talented individuals in both sectors and poor structures that allowed for myopic silos and empire building in both sectors.

When I joined NT Department of Education and Training in June 2008, the department was in the final phase of developing a revised 'needs-based' staffing formula for NT schools. It went to the executive for discussion in 2008 (this was when I first heard it said that 'of course it will never happen – it would mean taking huge numbers of staff out of Darwin schools').

In mid 2009, in response to a survey on funding for schools in 16 remote communities, the department reported that it was in the final phase of bedding down a new needs-based school staffing formula (the very same one) – but gave no details as to the current approach.

Then in 2011, in response to queries from *Education Review* journalists and myself about the staffing formula (among other things), the department again replied that it is in the process of finalising a revised needs-based staffing formula (again the very same one).

This is about politics not incompetence. For a long time, I puzzled over why the department put resources into something that will never be implemented, but it is an excellent deflector – worth the toll it places on staff who know their work is pointless. No one in the system is under any illusion about what is going on here.[6]

---

[6] While these observations about NT government are quite damming, it is important to put it in context. NT could also argue quite correctly that the way in which Commonwealth/State negotiations and decisions are conducted never takes into account their highly unique context. There have been strong cases put to the effect that the disadvantage loading provided by the Productivity Commission is in urgent need of review – because it has never taken into account the complexity of additional costs associated with remoteness, historical disadvantage and current disadvantage. Similarly when new programmes are rolled out, such as the Smarter Schools National Partnerships, they are based on the assumption that to place a teacher in a school only requires the costs of deploying that teacher. To place one additional teacher in a remote community requires that a whole house is built – these programmes only cover operational costs.

Rothwell's solution is to close down the NT Government experiment and have the Commonwealth take over. Having worked in the NT with both governments, I don't share his confidence in a Commonwealth takeover. However, I do believe that the Commonwealth can and should take strong action.

When I was involved in the COAG working group where the National Education Agreement and the National Partnership Programs were negotiated, the negotiation meetings were chaired by Julia Gillard herself (then Minister for Education and now Australia's Prime Minister), and she stressed that transparency, accountability and reporting would be key planks of the COAG approach. I had an expectation that the much-vaunted transparency and accountability process would lead to the extraction of data and reports that would bring this neglect to light. I was wrong.

So my question is, why do we have an educational accountability and reporting framework that utterly fails to do the one thing an accountability system ought to do? That is, to make governments accountable to the community for the money spent and the quality and effectiveness of services provided.

There are two parallel national schooling accountability systems in Australia – both products of the COAG school reforms of 2008. One is the high-profile school-level accountability system supported by the MySchool 2.0 tool (http://www.myschool.edu.au), and the other the poorly understood and known annual reporting against National Education Agreement measures and targets under the COAG Intergovernmental Agreement (IGA).

This is the government-to-government accountability strategy directed to 'improved accountability of governments to the community for the delivery of services, the quality and efficiency of these services and the achievement of outcomes'.[7]

The COAG Reform Council (CRC) is the body with responsibility to 'assess whether pre-determined milestones and performance benchmarks have been achieved and advise on the adequacy of the performance reporting framework to assist improved public accountability, and simple, standardised and transparent reporting'.

The CRC has argued that there are important data deficiencies (e.g. SES data and remote specific data) and that some targets are problematic or not fit for purpose (e.g. year 12 retention). These concerns and many others are valid and urgently require a critical review.

However, their critique does not get to the most important issues because they do not question the key assumptions upon which this accountability architecture is built. This is that accountability measures and targets should be small in number, simple to administer, standardised across the board and focus on outcomes to the neglect of outputs and inputs.

The challenge of closing the gap in indigenous education in remote Australia is a huge undertaking. The NT Government cannot guarantee a particular outcome over a few short years, but it can and should be held accountable for its spending of disadvantage-derived funds on addressing disadvantage, for ceasing the indirect

---

[7] COAG Reform Council, National Partnership Agreement on Literacy and Numeracy: Performance report for 2010, Report to the Council of Australian Governments, 25 March 2011, p. 5. http://www.coagreformcouncil.gov.au/reports/docs/npln_final_report_25_march.pdf

discriminatory practice of funding by enrolment modified by attendance (as agreed) and for implementing a transparent and comprehensive needs-based school funding regime. Indeed, until it is held accountable, with consequences for non-compliance, this change will never occur.

The measures selected by COAG for monitoring progress may well be a good fit for the bulk of school contexts, but there needs to be a recognition that for schools at the very bottom of the disadvantage end, their situation is not one of more disadvantages along the same dimensions – standard measures might be meaningless.

For example, Tom Calma[8] has noted that if all NT school-aged students were to attend school, the cost of building more classrooms and teacher housing alone would run to around \$375–\$400 million. How will measuring the year 10 to year 12 retention rate drive NT to focus on the non-enrolled or those that leave well before year 10? How will it help NT to focus on the year 12 completers who still can't read?

Tom Calma argues for a dedicated accountability framework, and this is in my view an urgent priority.

Some of the fitness for purpose measures could include:

- Input accountability – independently audited and covering issues outlined above.
    - The needs-based funding formula should include use of Australian Early Development Index, Index of Community Socio-Educational Advantage (ICSEA), remoteness, a new measure – English as a Second Language (ESL) stage of learning and school entry level assessments
- Extent of teacher cultural awareness and ESL training by geo-location
- Teacher experience and expertise in area of teaching by geo-location
- Teacher turnover and absenteeism by geo-location
- Experience of the school leadership by geo-location
- Development of a school capital works minimum standard for different school types and a regular audit of schools against this standard by geo-location
- Family literacy support programmes by geo-location
- Accountability for undertaking assessments of health issues relevant to student learning and disability needs
- Funded implementation of remote learning partnership agreements
- Professional development for teachers aligned with whole school improvement plans
- Holiday enrichment activities
- Local employment strategies aligned to education and training provision
- A funded comprehensive English language learning strategy
- Growth in the percentage of students attending more than 90% of the school year by geo-location (NT has commenced some of this work)

It is time intelligent, and appropriate accountability for remote indigenous education outcomes was given full consideration.

---

[8] Aboriginal and Torres Strait Islander Social Justice Commissioner, 2008 Social Justice Report, Australian Human Rights Commission Chapter 3, Remote Indigenous education.

Chapter 23
Quality and Equity in Education: A Perspective from Mexico

Sylvia Schmelkes

I write from the other side of the world, in both geographical and economic terms. Mine is a third-world country, Mexico. Over 50% of the population lives in poverty. Even though we are a member of the OECD, I do not really understand why we occupy the last places in the PISA exercises, together with many other poor countries. We are neighbors to the largest drug-consuming country in the world, the USA, and have lately become victims of drug-related violence. The country's average schooling is 8.4 years.

In spite of these differences with Phillip Hughes' country of origin and where his most important work has been carried out, Australia, I discover many similarities between his work and mine. We were awarded the Jan Comenius Medal in the same ceremony, celebrating inclusion in education, in Geneva, in 2008.

Phil and I both believe in education. Evidence has convinced us that education is the only legitimate avenue toward social mobility; that it is a powerful agent for values formation; that when it is quality education, it develops human beings that think, create, and serve their fellow humans; that it is the most important ingredient for building and strengthening social capital; that it has intergenerational effects; and that the children of educated parents will be themselves educated but also will more likely be healthy both physically and psychologically, open-minded and tolerant, and active and responsible citizens, and will have a better start in life.

S. Schmelkes (✉)
Institute for Research on the Development of Education,
Universidad Iberoamericana, Prol. Paseo de la Reforma 880,
Col. Lomas de Santa Fe, Del. Álvaro Obregón, México D.F. 01219, Mexico
e-mail: schmelkes@gmail.com

P. Hughes (ed.), *Achieving Quality Education for All*, Education in the Asia-Pacific
Region: Issues, Concerns and Prospects 20, DOI 10.1007/978-94-007-5294-8_23,
© Springer Science+Business Media Dordrecht 2013

Education has to meet certain requirements in order to develop its very powerful social potential. I will mention the two that I think are most important.

1. Quality Education

   Quality education emphasizes basic and higher-order skills, on the one hand, and values for living together on the other. Reading and comprehending, as well as communicating orally and in writing, are basic skills, but not because they are basic does it mean that their development is something that occurs only during the early years of schooling. They continue to be developed over the lifetime – I am still illiterate when it comes to understanding tax return forms, for example, and still doubt whether I really comprehend Ulysses by James Joyce; I would love to be able to write a very significant piece of literature and am sure that I can still learn if I try. Mathematizing the world and solving problems is another basic skill that is developed throughout the lifetime.

   Higher-order thinking skills begin to be developed from the very early years. They have to do with autonomous thinking, with argumentation, with analytical and synthesis skills, with discernment, with inductive and deductive reasoning, with hypothetical thinking, and with a logical and critical approach to the world.

   Higher-order thinking skills also refer to being able to take another's viewpoint and understand it and have to do with understanding and valuing cultural differences. Moral reasoning is at the heart of values formation and requires the development of higher-order thinking skills. But values formation also includes developing active citizenship and learning to participate creatively in democratic societies.

   Curriculum is important because it guides toward the attainment of educational results that are really important and because it should give teachers and schools the flexibility needed to make learning meaningful to children in different contexts and from different cultures as well as to children with special education needs.

   Quality education manipulates knowledge in order to develop these skills and values, but understands that knowledge is vast and changing, and that the most important higher-order skill to develop is the ability to learn throughout the lifespan, which includes the development of the ability to access and discriminate information and to gain knowledge.

   Quality education needs adequate and supportive educational policy, but in the end, it depends on the teacher. *Teachers Make a Difference* is one of Phillip's papers, written in 2000. The teacher has to be well trained in both the subject matter and how to teach it. General pedagogical knowledge is also a must. Teacher training is a continuous process that should respond to problems faced in the classroom and inform them. The state should help teachers train continuously to improve their educational results. There is also a crucial role of educational authorities in making teaching improvement possible.

   Quality education occurs in the school. Quality of school leadership, teamwork, school-wide planning and evaluation, and community and parent participation in schools are known factors central to educational quality.

What children learn in school is what educational quality is about. That what they learn is relevant to their needs and aspirations, both in the present and in the future, and will be useful for society at large, is the purpose of education, and should be carried out with ever-increasing quality. Lifelong educators, such as Phillip Hughes, are convinced that this is so and have dedicated much of their professional life to making it possible.

2. Equity in Education

   Quality education which is only for some and not for all cannot be considered quality education. Education is the only legitimate avenue for social mobility. Education is what gives societies the permeability that makes them governable. Equality in education supposes that all students are equal and thus is preoccupied with ensuring that all students receive the same amount and quality of resources. However, all societies are unequal; every context is different. Each school is unique because it faces sets of educational challenges and demands that derive from these very different contexts. Students also differ in their socioeconomic and cultural backgrounds, their talents and interests, and their ways of learning. In the face of this complexity and heterogeneity, equality alone cannot ensure that education can become an avenue for social mobility. Equity is necessary: Equity goes beyond equality, assuming that different people need different resources and types of support in order to reach educational objectives that are similar and also educational purposes that are different. The poorer the socioeconomic background of students, the more resources and support are needed to ensure their educational development. The larger the cultural distance between the home and the school, the greater the pedagogical support needed for students of different cultures to learn about their own culture but also to be able to perform adequately in mainstream society. The more diverse the students in a school, the greater the training and the teamwork required of the teachers for them to be able to teach inclusively and to achieve learning outcomes with all of their students.

   Equity and quality are related. Equity in education is a condition for quality education. In fact, once access to schooling for everyone is ensured, equity signifies the adequate distribution of quality education. Equity recognizes diversity and complexity as a pedagogical advantage and makes use of this possibility of learning from the different others. Equity supposes an inclusive approach to education, which among other things means that education develops each person's potential. Equity assumes complexity and discards uniformity in contents and methodologies because this represents a simple solution to a complex reality. Equity means giving more and better to those who need support the most, which is the only way of achieving similar education results and to be able to offer diverse avenues toward educational development.

   Phillip Hughes is preoccupied with equity in education. He has been worried, as I have, with opportunities for all students of accessing, learning, and finishing the different educational levels, from early childhood to higher education. He is convinced that equity in education contributes to equity in society at large.

Education is a basic human right. Though we know that there are no priorities among the different human rights, education is considered a key human right because, thanks to education, many other rights can be fully enjoyed. The concept of education as a right is important because the guarantor for this right is the state. Phillip has had very important roles in building capacity in state institutions for designing appropriate educational policies and for providing quality and equity in education and in his role as a consultant to many international organizations, notably to UNESCO, where this conception of education as a basic human right is key.

In Phil's lifetime work, educational research has played an important role. His research reflects the need for understanding the under-the-surface causes of educational problems, in order to have strong bases for reform proposals. Many of his articles deal with understanding and communicating educational innovations in different fields. Others are essays that pose questions relevant to research and practitioners. Educational research carried out by Phil is committed research, that is, research that contributes, directly or indirectly, to change and improvement in education. His contributions to education have been based on research findings but have also contributed to educational knowledge.

Persons that have a very rich professional life rarely carry it out without sharing their experience and knowledge. Phil has been a professor in many universities around the world. In so doing, he has been able to add to a long list of contributions to understanding and transforming education: that of forming others to carry out this work in different circumstances and latitudes. The opportunity of meeting strong, committed, capable, visionary personalities, and of having them as mentors and teachers, represents a landmark in the development of ethical and responsible professionals. I do not doubt this has been the case with Phil's students, and he can be certain that his preoccupation with quality education for all will be carried on by many.

Part IV
Prelude: Looking More Widely

Robert and Paris Strom from Arizona State University have developed a curriculum to help today's grandparents define their place in society. They consider them to be uncertain about their role in the family, and they are more likely to entertain their grandchildren than support the parents. They believe they assume too little responsibility and are not contributing as they could be. They suggest useful means for broadening contacts for learners especially for students for whom school is difficult. *'A more promising way of thinking about lifespan development is to encourage people from all ages to adjust to certain aspects of change together by learning from other generations. When reciprocal learning is recognized as essential, it is possible to facilitate harmony and ensure everyone stays in touch with the present and future of other cohorts'.*

The programme at Arizona State University introduced by Robert Strom has already proved to be a valuable source of help to many.

Paul Brock has been a wonderful example to Australians in his refusal to allow his almost total paralysis from motor neurone disease to contain his enthusiasm for life, his work output and his determination to continue his witness to the power of education. *'I saw on TV a distraught Sudanese mother holding her starving child who was asked by a reporter "what do you need most for your child?" "Food and education" was the desperate woman's immediate reply. Not only Australia, but our world needs the nurturing and irrigation of ideas, values, skills, knowledge, vision, hope, spirituality, and respect that education can bring to individuals, communities and societies'.*

Christine Deer, formerly Professor of Education at the University of Technology in Sydney, has first-hand experience with children who have more hurdles to jump than most to access appropriate education through her membership of the advisory board of the Salvation Army and also the board of the Royal Institute for Deaf and Blind Children. In her chapter, she focuses on four priorities:

1. *The centrality of the teacher*
2. *The importance of preschool education*

3. *The curriculum priorities*
4. *The need to establish an agreed and equitable system of financing education across all systems.*

Patrick Daunt, looking back after a distinguished career as teacher, school principal and a leading role for some years at the European Commission in Brussels where he headed the European action programme for disabled people, is very unhappy with the nature of the interaction between politics and education, seeing the political time span as being wildly out of kilter with the desirable pattern of change in schools. '*...education has become as hot as any political sector, a highly desirable staging post for young hopefuls, driven by the need to make their mark within two or three years by means of some loud but politically fragrant programme of parliamentary adventures*'.

Joanna Le Metais and Don Jordan in their Britain-Australia partnership start from the recognition of the depth of the problem.

On average across OECD countries, around one fifth of 15-year-olds did not attain proficiency Level 2 in three core areas of learning, namely reading (19%), mathematics (22%) and science (18%) and, consequently, lacked the essential skills needed to make sense of a complex world and to participate effectively and productively in society.

Joanna was the head of International Project Development at the National Foundation for Educational Research in England and Wales for many years and continues to work in the areas of curriculum review, reform and development through consultancies in many countries. Don is an experienced primary and secondary teacher whose recent consultancies are as varied as working with disaffected students in the United Kingdom and with Bachelor of Education students in the Gaza Strip. They are not content to end in gloom but map some realistic ways to move ahead.

Mal Lee focuses strongly on education's general failure to make more effective use of the modern technology which so many young people are so enthusiastically embracing. He feels that education in general has been reluctant to recognise a reality from which they might profit.

While individual schools are addressing these shortcomings there has not been from government a preparedness to take advantage of the shift to the digital and networked modes to ask how best their nation should school its young.

Don Aitkin is a widely experienced university administrator, most recently as vice chancellor of the University of Canberra. He also has a strong interest in the quality of school education and a deep concern for wasted potential. His concern goes deeper. '*More, it is doubtful that our community understands that while those first five years represent only a little more than five per cent of the future adult's life, they are very probably the most important five years of all*'.

Neil Dempster in his section takes up the same issue. He speaks from a broad background of higher education and also considerable experience in schools.

A great education starts with parents who know how dramatic their influence is on the architecture of the minds and bodies of their children. From birth, though Fiona Stanley, Australian of the Year in 2003, would say for at least two years before birth, children are mightily influenced by the behaviour, health and well being of their parents.

Chapter 24
Grandparents and Reciprocal Learning for Family Harmony

Robert Strom and Paris Strom

Records from archeology indicate that the average lifespan of ancient mankind was about 20 years, with few people surviving to age 50. In contrast, people in wealthy nations now can expect to live 85 years or perhaps even 100 if they were born since the year 2000 (Christensen, Doblhammer, Rau, & Vaupel, 2009). Expansion of the lifespan has introduced a new stage of development that is accompanied by unfamiliar challenges for policy makers, health care providers, employers, educators, religious institutions, and families. A common opportunity is that the longer the duration, the more individuals can anticipate being a grandparent. This additional time can allow them to provide continuity of affection, care, and guidance to grandchildren from infancy until early adulthood. More than 90% of retirees in the United States are grandparents; half of them will live to see their great grandchildren (Uhlenberg, 2009). This presentation explains how innovative education can equip grandparents to become a greater source of favorable influence in the family.

Learning throughout the lifespan is necessary so that, at every stage, people can adapt to change. However, obtaining widespread support to motivate growth in later life is difficult because educating older adults is unprecedented, and, in the past, they did not regard younger relatives as sources of learning. A related obstacle is the assumption that, because youth are the only subpopulation that has to attend school, they should bear the primary responsibility for reconciling society's goals of cultural preservation and cultural evolution. A more promising way of thinking about lifespan development is to encourage people from all ages to adjust to certain aspects

R. Strom (✉)
Professor of Educational Leadership and Innovation, Arizona State University,
6017 East Cambridge Avenue, Scottsdale, AZ, 85257, USA
e-mail: bob.strom@asu.edu

P. Strom (✉)
Associate Professor of Educational Foundations, Leadership and Technology,
Auburn University, 4036 Haley Center – Dept of E.F.L.T.,
Auburn University, Alabama, AL 36849, USA
e-mail: stromps@auburn.edu

P. Hughes (ed.), *Achieving Quality Education for All*, Education in the Asia-Pacific Region: Issues, Concerns and Prospects 20, DOI 10.1007/978-94-007-5294-8_24,
© Springer Science+Business Media Dordrecht 2013

of change together by learning from other generations. When reciprocal learning is recognized as essential, it is possible to facilitate harmony and ensure everyone stays in touch with the present and future of other cohorts (P. Strom & R. Strom, 2011a; R. Strom & P. Strom, 2011b; R. Strom & S. Strom, 1983).

The paradigm for education should be to expand beyond preparing people for work to include helping those no longer employed to continue learning over a lengthy retirement. This shift requires that grandparents become as critical of their development and maturity as they are about ensuring a quality education for grand-children. Grandparents may be unable to motivate one another to pursue the learn-ing they need. One reason is that many older adults define retirement as being the stage of life when they should be permitted to withdraw from responsibility and do whatever pleases them. Retirees commonly support the notion that they deserve a carefree lifestyle for having devoted many years to work. This aspiration overlooks the fact that people who choose to have no obligation cannot be defined as mature. A better outlook comes from recognizing that people stop work when they retire, but they should never stop learning and socially interacting.

Origins of Grandparent Curriculum

The concept of "productive aging" unites the efforts of professionals from many fields in recognizing that most older adults are physically as well as mentally capa-ble of contributing to society, the period between retirement and frailty is being extended, and elders want to remain active so life continues to have purpose, mean-ing, and satisfaction (Butler, 2008). In rapidly transforming societies, grandparents need education to acquaint them with the ideas, values, goals, and concerns of younger relatives and show how to apply modern methods of communication while building mutually beneficial relations (R. Strom & S. Strom, 1983).

A beginning step to establish relevant education for grandparents was curriculum development. Our efforts began a generation ago by offering a free class at senior centers, churches, and synagogues in Phoenix, Arizona. The 400 women and men, ages 50–80, who attended these weekly sessions were told that they would be helped to understand how the goals of parents change with the times, how growing up is changing, and how the resulting differences in lifestyle necessitate a corresponding shift in the grandparent role. In return, participants agreed to spend time during each session discussing questions about their aspirations, concerns, and satisfactions. Small groups of 4–6 participants also included a university gerontology student who acted as recorder. The topics identified were used to shape a tentative curriculum (R. Strom & S. Strom, 1990).

The next task was to determine whether the evolving curriculum was beneficial. A three-generational instrument was devised to assess the attainment of program goals. The Grandparent Strengths and Needs Inventory contains 60 Likert-type items, divided into six subscales, each focused on a separate component of grand-parent development (R. Strom & S. Strom, 1993). Respectively, the subscales portray grandparent satisfaction, success, teaching, difficulty, frustration, and information needs.

A curriculum field test was conducted during 1989–1990 with support from the Andrus Foundation, the research arm of the American Association of Retired Persons (R. Strom & S. Strom, 1990). The 400 grandparent subjects, from 50 to 80 years of age, were assigned to an experimental or control group. The experimental group, consisting of 200 members, attended a weekly session of 90 min for 12 weeks for the course, Becoming a Better Grandparent. Each experimental group member chose a school-age grandchild and one of that grandchild's parents to provide a confidential evaluation of grandparent attitudes and behaviors. Three generations were administered a separate version of the Grandparent Strengths and Needs Inventory before the classes began and when the instruction was completed. The control group of 200 grandparents did not attend classes but received an honorarium to complete the same assessments.

Grandparents attending the classes assigned themselves end-of-course scores that were significantly higher than before instruction began for the course. Specifically, they claimed improvements had been made in being able to define their role in the family, set goals for themselves in being more helpful, developing an optimistic outlook about family affairs, having a sense of purpose, feeling self-confident, gaining communication skills needed for intergenerational dialogue, and developing more satisfying relationships. Daughters, sons, and grandchildren corroborated these gains by assigning higher scores at the end of the course than at the outset. When the same instrument was administered a third time several months later, the gains that each generation had earlier identified were retained. In contrast, control group members made no progress from pre- to post-assessment. The conclusion was that grandparents could benefit from curriculum designed to improve their family influence (R. Strom & S. Strom, 1990; R. Strom, Collinsworth, Strom, & Young, 1991).

When participants were asked to suggest how the grandparent course could be improved, the most common recommendations were to add curriculum for supporting relationships with preschool- and college-age grandchildren. These suggestions were incorporated in two publications entitled *Becoming a Better Grandparent* (R. Strom & S. Strom 1991a) and *Achieving Grandparent Potential* (R. Strom & S. Strom, 1992). *Grandparent Education: A Guide for Leaders* was also published to design programs and support group facilitators (R. Strom & S. Strom, 1991b). Favorable reactions from grandparents and younger relatives were featured in national television interviews on *NBC Today, CBS This Morning, and ABC News* and print reports by *The New York Times, The Wall Street Journal, Newsweek,* and *USA Today.*

Grandparents in Other Societies

Modern nations are united by a belief that, in addition to health care and financial security, older adults need a sense of mission and to feel significant. Government can be expected to provide monetary support, but most elders have to rely on relatives to confirm their personal importance. Grandparents agree that their position in the family is eroding; they want a defined role instead of an ambiguous function and need education to guide their adjustment. They have gained wisdom from experience but should be encouraged to also acquire new knowledge that can preserve and enrich family relationships. Unless the education needs of grandparents are met, influence of elders is bound to diminish, they will experience more isolation, and young people will be denied observations of how to cope with change in later life. A more promising future is likely if nations decide to address common and unique learning needs of older adults. Toward this goal, we have collaborated with culturally diverse American groups and colleagues in Canada, China, England, Japan, Sweden, and Taiwan in exchanging views and carrying out large-scale studies to determine curriculum needs and providing facilitator training for educators, psychologists, and social workers. We are grateful to government agencies and private foundations that financially supported these initiatives (R. Strom, Buki, & Strom, 1997; P. Strom & R. Strom, 2011a; R. Strom & P. Strom, 2011b; R. Strom, P. Strom, Beckert, Lee, & Nakagawa, 2008; R. Strom, P. Strom, & Heeder, 2005; R. Strom et al., 1996; R. Strom et al., 1999).

Get to Know Grandchildren as Individuals

Classes for grandparents that help them explore the norms, values, goals, fears, and concerns of younger age groups should be widely available in longevity societies. Our work provides baseline assumptions about development in later life augmented by suitable goals for designing programs to meet the needs of grandparents (R. Strom & S. Strom, 1997). Understanding what to expect of grandchildren, at particular ages from preschool to adolescence, and young adults is examined in *Parenting Young Children: Exploring the Internet, Television, Play and Reading* (R. Strom & P. Strom, 2010), *Adolescents in the Internet Age* (P. Strom & R. Strom, 2009), and *Adult Learning and Relationships* (P. Strom & R. Strom, 2011a; R. Strom & P. Strom, 2011b).

The greatest learning need grandparents have is to get to know each grandchild as an individual. Lack of awareness can be costly because youth seek advice from people they believe understand their struggles, doubts, and concerns. There is not much benefit in identifying older relatives as being the most mature and then nullify their potential by refusing to keep them informed. In families where grandparents are seldom involved, grandchildren may assume that it is not important to share information with them. This conclusion reinforces ambiguity of the grandparent role and relegates their position to having honorific status without a purpose.

Mary describes a related obstacle many grandparents have to overcome: "I don't like it when my daughter and son in law report about my grandchildren. They tell all the good things that are happening, achievements at school, sports team victories, and other ways my grandchildren are doing well. Disappointing events or failures are not mentioned even though I feel certain my grandchildren have these experiences.

The difficult side of their lives is never told because it is supposed that I need to be proud of the family and not worry about anything. But, for me, it is important to be accurately informed. I want to provide encouragement when my grandchildren experience hard times; that is when I am needed most but cannot respond if told that everything is always fine. My grandchildren must wonder sometimes if I even care to console them."

Partial or biased reporting can prevent grandparents from knowing what is going on and deny them a chance to provide the emotional support children need for developing resilience. Parent reports that exclude difficulties of grandchildren mislead grandparents to suppose that growing up now is relatively easy and free of worries and concerns. This situation reveals how the grandparent function is defined in some families. Grandparents should question whether their family takes them into their confidence. Even friends share more with each other than just the good times. Grandparents can inform the whole family they want to hear directly from grandchildren and expect them to speak for themselves instead of parents assuming the role of intermediaries, family messengers, or interpreters.

Parents should let children know that grandparents want to be helpful but cannot offer worthwhile advice without enough information. Grandchildren who describe some of their experiences can acquaint older relatives with the complexities of growing up in the current environment and stimulate greater engagement of elders in family problem solving. Grandchildren will decide the extent to which they are willing to share feelings and information, but grandparents can increase child trust by understanding that people who ask for help are more likely to become a source of counseling. Asking grandchildren for advice is an uncommon sign of wisdom.

Adopt New Tools of Communication

Being a careful listener and sharing personal highs and lows demonstrate respect and the self-disclosure needed to get to know someone well. Grandparent influence also depends on a willingness to communicate using the tools of technology that are preferred by grandchildren, such as iChat, Skype, Facebook, texting, instant messaging, email, and cell phone. These tools make it easier to stay in touch and remain aware of grandchild views and feelings as a basis for being considered as an informed advisor. When we asked grandmothers from Taiwan whether they used technology tools in communicating with granddaughters, only 3% of them said they did (R. Strom et al., 2008).

Many young people suppose that peers of their same age are the only people who can understand them. Grandparents should challenge this false premise and attempt to convince grandchildren that, at every stage in life, it is a mistake to choose peers as the only audience to help process personal concerns simply because talking to them is easier. Adolescents who limit discussion of important issues to only their cohort friends forfeit the opportunity to gain broader perspective and communication skills that are needed to interact as team members with other generations at the workplace. The best support group is composed of loved ones who make themselves available to listen, try to understand feelings, provide comfort and emotional support, discuss options and possible consequences, recommend alternatives for reflection, and provide help during hard times. Relatives and friends who act in these ways are likely to be trusted advisors over time.

The Contribution of Time

In *The Fellowship of the Ring*, the wizard Gandalf declares that everyone must face the same daunting challenge in life. He observes, "All we have to decide is what to do with the time that is given us" (Tolkien, 2005, p. 50). The importance of time as an influence is portrayed by our studies of three generations of families involving thousands of subjects in many cultures. We consistently found that grandparents who spend the most time interacting and doing things with grandchildren are identified as the most successful in the estimate of grandchildren, parents, and grandparents. This means that the greater amount of time spent together matters more than has been recognized by researchers who focus on variables such as levels of education and income which are not malleable. Grandparents cannot alter their formal education or household income but can choose to benefit from the advantage that comes from spending more time with people they love.

Conclusion

A long-standing assumption is that the knowledge and skills needed to become successful can be acquired well in advance. Therefore, most nations try to arrange quality education for children, adolescents, and young adults. However, this plan is no longer sufficient since it fails to take into account the complex learning needs of technological societies that are characterized by an increasing life span. Harmony is more likely when successive generations express their expectations to relatives and respond to the needs of one another. Grandparents should be encouraged to establish new traditions that stimulate their adjustment to innovative ways of doing things while preserving valued customs. These traditions should affirm the mental capacity of older adults, identify societal expectations for their continued contribution to families, and facilitate reciprocal learning with younger relatives. Grandparent education can be a powerful way to support the achievement of these goals.

References

Butler, R. (2008). *The longevity revolution: The benefits and challenges of living a long life*. New York: PublicAffairs.
Christensen, K., Doblhammer, G., Rau, R., & Vaupel, J. (2009, October 3). Aging populations: The challenges ahead. *The Lancet, 374*(9696), 1196–1208.

Strom, P., & Strom, R. (2009). *Adolescents in the Internet Age*. Charlotte, NC: Information Age Publishing.

Strom, P., & Strom, R. (2011a). *Adult learning and relationships*. Charlotte, NC: Information Age Publishing.

Strom, R., Buki, L., & Strom, S. (1997). Strengths and education needs of Mexican-American grandparents. *Educational Gerontology, 23*(4), 359–376.

Strom, R., Collinsworth, P., Strom, S., & Young, D. (1991). Grandparent strengths and needs inventory. *Educational and Psychological Measurement, 51*(3), 785–792.

Strom, R., & Strom, P. (2010). *Parenting young children: Exploring the Internet, television, play and reading*. Charlotte, NC: Information Age Publishing.

Strom, R., & Strom, P. (2011b). A paradigm for intergenerational learning. In M. London (Ed.), *The Oxford handbook of lifelong learning* (pp. 133–146). New York: Oxford University Press.

Strom, R., Strom, P., Beckert, T., Lee, T., & Nakagawa, K. (2008). Strengths and learning needs of Taiwanese grandmothers, mothers and granddaughters. *Educational Gerontology, 34*(9), 812–830.

Strom, R., Strom, P., & Heeder, S. (2005). Performance of Black grandmothers: Perceptions of three generations of females. *Educational Gerontology, 31*(3), 187–205.

Strom, R., & Strom, S. (1983). Redefining the grandparent role. *Cambridge Journal of Education, 13*(1), 25–28.

Strom, R., & Strom, S. (1990). Raising expectations for grandparents: A three generation study. *International Journal of Aging and Human Development, 31*(3), 161–167.

Strom, R., & Strom, S. (1991a). *Becoming a better grandparent*. Thousand Oaks, CA: Sage Publications.

Strom, R., & Strom, S. (1991b). *Grandparent education: A guide for leaders*. Thousand Oaks, CA: Sage Publications.

Strom, R., & Strom, S. (1992). *Achieving grandparent potential*. Thousand Oaks, CA: Sage Publications.

Strom, R., & Strom, S. (1993). *Grandparent strengths and needs indicator*. Bensenville, IL: Scholastic Testing Service.

Strom, R., & Strom, S. (1997). Building a theory of grandparent development. *International Journal of Aging and Human Development, 45*(4), 255–285.

Strom, R., Strom, S., Collinsworth, P., Sato, S., Sasaki, Y., Sasaki, H., Makino, K., & Nishio, N. (1996). Developing curriculum for grandparents in Japan. *Educational Gerontology, 22*(8), 781–794.

Strom, R., Strom, S., Wang, C., Shen, Y., Griswold, D., Chan, H., & Yang, C. (1999). Grandparents in the United States and Republic of China: A comparison of generations and cultures. *International Journal of Aging and Human Development, 49*(4), 279–317.

Tolkien, J. R. (2005). *The fellowship of the ring* (p. 50). Boston: Houghton Mifflin.

Uhlenberg, P. (2009). *International handbook of population aging*. New York: Springer.

Chapter 25
Flying Upwards and Outwards

Paul Brock

What an honour it is to be invited by Professor Phillip Hughes to contribute to this book. Over the past decades as a distinguished member of what the Organisation for Economic Co-operation and Development (OECD) has described as the knowing and caring profession, Phil has made a stellar contribution to education within and across a broad and deep range of profoundly important Australian and, especially, international contexts.

At a personal level, through both his writing and his conference presentations, Phil has made a real impact on my own development as an educator. Furthermore, I was delighted to have been invited by him to be included in his *Opening Doors to the Future: Stories of Prominent Australians and the Influence of Their Teachers* (Hughes, 2007). In particular, I thoroughly enjoyed his thoroughness and insight when he interviewed me in order to tell my particular story.

In reflecting over my experience during my four decades in this profession, it strikes me that we educators seem to be too often finding ourselves in worlds of disconnect. For example, on the one hand, we are constantly reminded that an important focus of education in the twenty-first century has to be on innovation, creativity, stretching the imagination, problem-solving, cultivating and valuing effective personal and interpersonal relationships, and communication – flying ever upwards and outwards on the wings of sweeping advances in information and communications technology – while, at the same time, enhancing students' knowledge, understanding, skills, ethical values, discernment, critique and so on. Continuously teachers are quite rightly urged set the highest expectations both for themselves and for their students.

Many distinguished writers and thinkers have articulated what they believe should constitute the fundamental characteristics of twenty-first-century schooling.

P. Brock (✉)
NSW Department of Education and Communities, The University of Sydney,
Level 1, 35 Bridge Street, Sydney, NSW 2000, Australia
e-mail: paul.brock@det.nsw.edu.au

P. Hughes (ed.), *Achieving Quality Education for All*, Education in the Asia-Pacific Region: Issues, Concerns and Prospects 20, DOI 10.1007/978-94-007-5294-8_25,
© Springer Science+Business Media Dordrecht 2013

For example, in his *A Whole New Mind: Why Right-Brainers Will Rule the Future,* Daniel H. Pink asserts, among other things, that

The last few decades have belonged to a certain kind of person with a certain kind of mind – computer programmers who could crank code, lawyers who could craft contracts, MBAs who could crunch numbers. But the keys to the kingdom are changing hands. The future belongs to a very different kind of person with a very different kind of mind – creators and empathizers, pattern recognizers, and meaning makers. These people – artists, inventors, designers, storytellers, caregivers, consolers, big picture thinkers – will now reap society's richest rewards and share its greatest joys. Pink, 2006, cited at http://www.gurteen.com/ gurteen/gurteen.nsf/id/L002726/

Yet, when launching the draft Australian Curriculum for schools in the twenty-first century in March 2010, former Prime Minister Mr Kevin Rudd revelled in characterising it as merely a 'back-to-basics' prescription: the present prime minister, then education minister, strongly supported this view. Despite Australia's consistently very high ranking in international testing instruments, such as Programme for Individual Student Assessment (PISA) and Trends in International Mathematics and Science Study (TIMSS), the apparently assumed agenda then seems to have been that, for quite some time, Australian schooling had been moving away from the 'basics' and was in something approaching a precarious state brought about by some kind of rigour-less indulgence in educational mush. No evidence was produced to support any such inference. Furthermore, important educational concepts and values – such as those I referred to above – did not feature in supplementary federal government publicity concerning the launch of the draft Australian Curriculum that I (at least) read, listened to or viewed.

Too often, it has seemed to me that when framing educational policy, some ministers of education and some governments – from both sides of the political divide in Australia – have paid insufficient regard for the research, the scholarship and the wisdom of respected educators.

I have always tried to take a balanced view on educational matters. It is so easy for some people to be seduced by the black or white extremism resulting from what the Danish philosopher Soren Kierkegaard called 'the either/or fallacy' (in his *Either/Or,* published in 1843). For example, I fear that the pendulum hanging between those two interdependent and necessary components of schooling – learning and teaching on the one hand, and assessment and testing on the other – has sometimes swung too much away from learning and teaching.

The point about the potential tension between learning/teaching and assessment/ testing is nicely made in a poem which was given to me nearly 26 years ago by one of my closest friends, the late Mike Hayhoe, a colleague of mine when I was the visiting fellow at the University of East Anglia, UK. Mike was given this poem by an elderly teacher in Halifax, Nova Scotia. It is called 'The Lesson', based on the famous "beatitudes" speech in the gospels:

Then Jesus took his disciples up the mountain and gathering
    them around him he taught them saying

    blessed are the poor in spirit for theirs is the kingdom of heaven
    blessed are the meek
    blessed are they that mourn
    blessed are the merciful
    blessed are they who thirst for justice

blessed are all the concerned
blessed are you when persecuted
blessed are you when you suffer
be glad and rejoice for your reward is great in heaven
try to remember what I'm telling you

Then Simon Peter said - Will this count?
And Andrew said - Will we have a test on it?
And James said - When do we have to know it for?
And Phillip said - How many words?
And Bartholomew said - Will I have to stand up in front of the others?
And John said - The other disciples didn't have to learn this
And Matthew said - How many marks do we get for it?
And Judas said - What is it worth?
And the other disciples likewise.

Then one of the Pharisees who was present asked
to see Jesus' lesson plan and inquired of Jesus
his terminal objectives in the cognitive domain

And Jesus wept.

Most of my energies as an educator have been devoted to the field of English in education. English provides a good example of what is *necessary* is not always *sufficient*. The subject English as a whole has been at considerable risk of being diluted by the necessary, but not sufficient, focus on basic literacy skills. English incorporates reading, writing, speaking, listening and viewing within and across classical, popular and other forms of literature including poetry, fiction, non-fiction, the prose of persuasion, the imaginative writing and forms of textual creation by students themselves, participation in drama, making and critiquing films and so on.

Therefore, the rich tapestry of English is far broader, richer and deeper than that defined by the skills of basic literacy. Just as the school subject mathematics – incorporating arithmetic, algebra, trigonometry, quadratic equations, calculus, statistics, three-dimensional geometry and so on – is far broader, richer and deeper than the area defined by basic numeracy skills.

The importance of the leadership exercised by the school Principal, and her or his being supported by the appropriate personnel and *materiel* resources, is a most crucial influence on the quality of her or his school. Educational research has proved beyond any doubt, however, that the most critical school input into quality learning for students is the quality of their teachers. This is made even more apparent by research that indicates that the differences in the quality of learning and teaching *between* schools of relative similarity can be less than the differences *within* each of those schools. To put it rather simply, it can be said to come down to a matter of who is teaching whom – what, how, when and where.

What then might be the characteristic features of quality teaching? Of course, whole books have been written on this. If I were challenged to sum up an answer in just one paragraph, it would be along the following lines.

Accomplished teachers have the appropriate intellectual command of the curriculum areas within or across which they teach – but they are also skilled in connecting and 'engaging' with their students in the processes of learning. They like working with students and treating them with respect while, at the same time, attempting to ensure that their students also treat them with respect. Accomplished teachers have a sense of humour. They ensure that the prescribed curriculum is taught in its rigour and richness, and exercise whatever flexibility is possible in adapting that curriculum to take account of their specific learning and teaching contexts. They operate on the principle that learning is an active process. They encourage their students to exercise their imagination and creativity – and to 'do' and to generate, and not merely to soak up and to react. Accomplished teachers assess student learning fairly, accurately and in a consistent manner – and what they learn about their students from this assessment process richly informs their subsequent teaching. They accept professional responsibility for the welcoming, induction and ongoing mentoring of beginning teachers into the profession. They are committed to abiding by the highest ethical standards of the education profession.

I now want to broaden the focus. I look upon the *Melbourne Declaration* (http://www.curriculum.edu.au/verve/_resources/National_Declaration_on_the_Educational_Goals_for_Young_Australians.pdf) as the 'Magna Carta' to guide the direction of the education of young Australians – at least until 2018, when this document will be due for review. There is insufficient space in an article of this length to address the *Melbourne Declaration* in detail. It suffices to ask how often do we see all of the rich and challenging dimensions articulated in the *Melbourne Declaration* being acknowledged, celebrated, disseminated and demonstrated in our public, political and media discourses about the goals of Australian schooling? Not often enough, I believe.

Consistent with this broader focus, school education can, indeed must, play a most important role in confronting issues of national and global significance in the twenty-first century – many of which issues are hangovers from the twentieth and earlier centuries. For example, education on a global scale should expose and educate the citizens of the world about the global obscenity revealed by the United Nations that in 2005 (for example) almost six million children were sold into slavery: the vast majority of these poor children being sold into sexual slavery.

People in many parts of the world yearn for both material and, in the broadest sense of the word, spiritual replenishment. Merely a few seconds exposure to a powerful visual image can leave an indelible impression about these matters on the mind and heart. For example, a couple of years ago I saw on TV a distraught Sudanese mother holding her starving child who was asked by a reporter 'what do you need most for your child?' 'Food and education' was the desperate woman's immediate reply.

Not only Australia, but our world needs the nurturing and irrigation of ideas, values, skills, knowledge, vision, hope, spirituality and respect that education can bring to individuals, communities and societies. Through education – in the fullest sense of the word – the foundations of wisdom should be acquired and developed in ways that should enable the inhabitants of our world to identify and expose contemporary intellectual, religious or spiritual ignorance: wherever manifestations of such ignorance flourish.

We need to celebrate a quality of education which, among other things, is committed to helping students satisfy the universal human search for truth and meaning, in particular a quality of education that is informed, honest, critiqued and properly resourced; that is both properly idealistic and properly sceptical; that celebrates the virtues of compassion, justice and human rights; and which repudiates tyranny, ignorance, fundamentalism of all kinds and terrorism – whatever and wherever be its sources around the globe. And this quality of education can and should be found in all schools – whether public, faith-based or any other category.

By way of prefacing my final remarks, I need to point out that I am afflicted with motor neurone disease, a still incurable and an inevitably terminal disease. Given by a neurologist, the prognosis of having at worst 3 years and at best 5 years to live when diagnosed in 1996 when all that was apparently 'wrong' with me was a weak right forearm, I am still 'hanging in' there.

Eight years ago at the end of Chap. 10 of my autobiography *A Passion for Life* (Brock, 2004), I attempted to sum up my ideals, hopes and aspirations as an educator by putting these within the personal context of my two young daughters – Amelia (Millie), who was then 9 and in year 4, and Sophia (Sophie) who was then 13 and in year 8. Amelia is now 17 and is in year 12 at Cherrybrook Technology High School; Sophia will turn 21 later this year and is in her honours (fourth) of study in the Faculty of Arts at The University of Sydney.

This is the challenge I set in 2004 for their future public school teachers:

> Therefore, not just as a professional educator, but as a Dad, I want all future teachers of my Sophie and Millie to abide by three fundamental principles that I believe should underpin teaching and learning in every public school.
>
> First, to nurture and challenge my daughters' intellectual and imaginative capacities way out to horizons unsullied by self-fulfillingly minimalist expectations. Don't patronise them with lowest-common-denominator blancmange masquerading as knowledge and learning; nor crush their love for learning through boring pedagogy.
>
> Don't bludgeon them with mindless 'busy work' and limit the exploration of the world of evolving knowledge merely to the tyranny of repetitively churned-out recycled worksheets. Ensure that there is legitimate progression of learning from one day, week, month, term and year to the next.
>
> Second, to care for Sophie and Millie with humanity and sensitivity, as developing human beings worthy of being taught with genuine respect, enlightened discipline and imaginative flair.
>
> And third, please strive to maximise their potential for later schooling, post-school education, training and employment, and for the quality of life itself so that they can contribute to and enjoy the fruits of living within an Australian society that is fair, just, tolerant, honourable, knowledgeable, prosperous and happy.
>
> When all is said and done, surely this is what every parent and every student should be able to expect of school education: not only as delivered within every public school in New South Wales, but within every school not only in Australia but throughout the entire world.

References

Brock, P. (2004). *A passion for life* (pp. 250–251). Sydney, Australia: ABC Books.
Hughes, P. (2007). *Opening doors to the future*. Melbourne. Australia, ACER Press.
Pink, D.H. (2006). *The whole new mind: Why right brainers will rule the future*. New York, USA: Riverhead Books.

Chapter 26
Four Priorities for Australian Education

Christine Deer

H. G. Wells wrote more than 90 years ago in 1919:

'Human history becomes more and more a race between education and catastrophe'. It seems to me in 2011 these words are very true. As a result, I have four priorities for education in Australia today. They are:

1. The centrality of the teacher
2. The importance of preschool education
3. The curriculum priorities
4. The need to establish an agreed and equitable system of financing education across all systems

I shall now address each of these priorities in turn.

I believe the teacher is central to school education. The quality of the teacher determines life in classrooms and the learning that occurs outside these classrooms under the guidance of teachers. So many people, in later years, long after schooling is finished, pay tribute to teachers who sparked their interest in a school subject that became a career or a lifelong passion or, who by their teaching, gave lessons that have never been forgotten. I remember our brilliant biology teacher, Mrs. Joan Webb, who in fourth year at Hornsby Girls' High School in 1953, brought in a horse's lungs and pumped them up so we could see how much they expanded when filled with air. It was quite astounding to see the size they became. It is a lesson I have never forgotten. The respiratory cycle became real in a very vivid way. In the same way, we all sat enthralled as she explained how eggs divided and the Canadian Dionne quintuplets developed.

C. Deer (✉)
Former Head of Teacher Education, University of Technology,
Sydney and Macquarie University, 4 Thompson St, Drummoyne,
NSW 2047, Australia
e-mail: christine.e.deer@gmail.com

P. Hughes (ed.), *Achieving Quality Education for All*, Education in the Asia-Pacific Region: Issues, Concerns and Prospects 20, DOI 10.1007/978-94-007-5294-8_26,
© Springer Science+Business Media Dordrecht 2013

Given the importance of teachers in our education systems, it is vital that they receive high-quality pre-service teacher education that combines theory and practice. To achieve a combination of theory and practice requires a partnership with skilled practising teachers who believe in working with beginning teachers to enrich the profession as a whole. Skilled teachers with their principals need to see initial teacher education as important and to firmly believe they have an integral part to play as a result of their own teaching experience.

However, such teacher education is just that pre-service education in whichever university it is undertaken. Ongoing, high-quality professional development must be a requirement of continued employment as a teacher. All systems employing teachers must devote funds to allowing this process to be ongoing, partly funded by the teachers themselves but also by the systems that employ them. The recent institution of national standards for teacher education is an important part of this process.

Second, I believe access to high-quality early childhood education should be the birthright of every child in Australia. The early years lay the foundation for so much that is to follow. Love of learning, the foundations of literacy and numeracy and the wonder of the world about them can flourish in these early years or these years can leave children with disillusionment about their capabilities. High-quality early childhood education also gives teachers the chance to work with parents, many of whom are first-time parents.

There are significant advantages for all concerned, where early childhood education is located adjacent to baby health clinics and to primary schools. Such locations enable a seamless transition between important nodes in our communities. They can be places for parent education courses at significant stages of their children's development as well as making it simpler for families to provide for their children and for their own work environments.

Early childhood education is *not* babysitting. It is introducing young children to the joys that come from education. It therefore demands high-quality teachers who are well educated and who, like those teachers in primary and secondary schools, are required to upgrade their qualifications at regular intervals.

Third, what should go into the curriculum for the years of schooling say from 5 years to at least 15 or 16 years of age? I believe there should be breadth and opportunities for depth where appropriate.

Even though I completed geography I, II and III at the University of Sydney for my Bachelor of Arts degree and became a geography teacher, later in 1969 I went on to Macquarie University to help begin their teacher education program, teaching students to become high school geography teachers, but I did not place much emphasis on planet earth in the curriculum during all those years. There was even then at Macquarie University a First Year School of Earth Sciences subject called *Planet Earth*. Now, as rainforests disappear in equatorial regions and climate change is a reality, I believe that planet earth deserves much more emphasis in the curriculum. In my first year of teaching in 1959, there were large areas of rainforest in the Congo Basin, in the Amazon Basin and across South East Asia. These areas are now much diminished. There is an obvious focus in geography and history lessons in schools but also in studies in the local area, in the sciences and in the arts and in literature.

There is no reason age and development appropriate sessions cannot be introduced from the beginning of schooling in preschool education. The generations who are entering school in the next decades deserve to know all we can teach about planet earth and its fragility. There is only one planet earth with all its beauty and its terror. H. G. Wells' words seem to be more than ever true (Wells, 1951).

Everyone deserves to know about the human body: How it operates and what is inside and how it can be maintained in good working order? What are the various systems such as the circulatory, respiratory, excretory, digestive and reproductive and how do they work? The developing obesity epidemic is becoming a worldwide phenomenon in many parts of the Western world. Learning about our insides can be fun and a way to learn how to keep the systems in good working order. I remember a student at Macquarie University in the first year of his Teacher Education Program who, in working out a way to motivate students, donned a white T-shirt that was emblazoned in black with an outline of the digestive system. He then proceeded to talk about each of the elements in his diagram. His fellow students were 'hooked' and clearly motivated.

Developments in technology make our world interconnected and offer the possibilities for students in our schools to be connected with schools in areas remote from where they live. A great living example is Teleschool operating at the Royal Institute for Deaf and Blind Children (RIDBC) at North Rocks in northwest Sydney. Deaf and blind children and their parents in remote areas of Australia can now be connected in their own homes via their own TV sets with skilled staff at North Rocks. In this way, RIDBC staff teach both parents and children so that the children start to develop language using what is available in the home and sets of toys provided by RIDBC. Developments in technology are removing what Geoffrey Blainey called 'the tyranny of distance'. Schools today regularly link their students with those in schools far removed from them. Cross-cultural communication can be a daily reality not only within the school but far beyond it.

The arts and particularly music deserve a place in every early childhood and primary school education. Music has the potential to develop the skills of listening. It gives the opportunity for creativity as children can imagine what the music is saying and act out in movement to the tune of whatever music is played. They can start to play an instrument, in however elementary a way, and in effect learn another language.

Of course literacy and numeracy are essential elements of the curriculum for as long as it takes children to grasp the essentials. The good teacher in the early years is able to match the method of teaching to the needs of the child. I remember well Miss Celia Styles who was infants mistress at East Lindfield Public School in Sydney in the 1970s. She was called in as a last resort as a young boy in her infants department could not read, and his teacher and parents were becoming increasingly anxious. She went through in her mind her repertoire of ways of teaching reading and after trying various methods such as '*whole word*' and '*look and say*' it was the one she personally least favoured that suited this boy. It was a '*stimulus response*' method. The symbols on the page began to make sense to the youngster. He began to read! At night, he did not want to stop reading, and his parents were elated. This skilled teacher knew how to individualise instruction to the great benefit of all, not least the young boy. However, in doing so, she had on display her skills as a wonderful teacher who knew many ways to teach reading and was able to choose a method that suited her pupil, thus individualising instruction.

Scientific literacy is vital. Many early childhood teachers and primary school teachers do not feel comfortable teaching science, and so particular efforts are necessary to equip them for this task. Initial teacher education and ongoing professional development is essential owing to changes as a result of scientific research. The human genome project was unknown when I was a schoolgirl, unlocking the genetic code was but a dream. Now it has been revealed there are all sorts of issues for discussion as well as the basic explanation of what it is. Ethical issues such as stem cell research provide the subject matter for enthralling discussions such as those I had in high school about the Dionne quintuplets.

More and more the benefits of knowing and speaking a language, other than that of the family home, are becoming clear. 'Walking in another's shoes' is much easier when the nuances and idioms of another language are part and parcel of daily life. I am more and more convinced that learning a language other than English is vital in education. There is always the question of which language. It used to be that to go to the University of Sydney you had to have a language other than English. For my Leaving Certificate in 1954, I studied French and German. After university, I began studying Bahasa Indonesia as Indonesian students came to study in the School of Education at Macquarie University and later Italian, which continues today. Study of a language other than our own native tongue gives insight to other ways of thinking. It accentuates the need for listening skills and provides insights to our multicultural world.

Finally, in Australia today, school finance is a vexed issue. Under the Australian Constitution, education is a state responsibility, but in the 1960s, the federal government first intervened to provide funds for improving science laboratories. This need arose partly as a result of the 1957 Sputnik launched by the Russians much to the consternation of the United States. Later, the move came from the federal Menzies government for funds for the hardware of language laboratories but not, unfortunately, their maintenance. Funds were then provided for non-government schools, and in New South Wales the group called *Defence* of *Government Schools* or *DOGS* became a major pressure group. For more than 50 years, school funding has been a vexatious issue. I believe the time is ripe now to resolve how funding should be managed between the taxing authority, federal government and the states and territories. The federal government initiated review, chaired by David Gonski to report later in 2011, has a great opportunity to set new ways of proceeding that are equitable and that will fund government schools appropriately. School funding should not remain the political football it has become. All schools deserve some government funding, but the government schools must be revitalised so that they do not become the poor relations.

In conclusion, each generation will work out how to organise schooling. There is no one way. However, standards of excellence are vital in all aspects. The environment or culture in our education centres should be such as to inspire everyone in them to achieve his or her personal best. Teaching is a great profession, and I am extremely fortunate to have had the opportunities it has provided me.

Reference

Wells, H. G. (1951). Chapter 40. In *The outline of history*. (Rev. ed.). London: Cassell & Company. First published by George Newnes in 1919.

Chapter 27
Rotten at the Core: Paideia Politicised

Patrick Daunt

It is a classical, though strangely unrecognised, tactic of polemics to divert attention from one's own most critical defect by flatly attributing it to the opposition. So, it was common practice to accuse those promoting British comprehensive schools of social engineering, as if God or nature or some other transcendent force had decreed that there should be two sorts of child, the academic and the other sort, so that dismantling the structure that assumed this dispensation was a gratuitous infringement of unwritten law. Yet, human dynamics are not constrained by logic, least of all when the status quo is assailed by innovators in a hurry. Non-rationally but acutely, once its implications began to be understood, the comprehensive movement was felt to be ideological, and so in that subjective sense it effectively was.

An unintended effect of this, especially in England, was the increasing politicisation of the forms and objectives of secondary schooling. And an implication of that has been the dramatic change in the political status of the Secretary of State for Education. Traditionally, to be Minister for Education was its own reward, the career apex of a relatively enlightened and no more than modestly ambitious statesman or stateswoman. More recently and quite quickly, education has become as hot as any political sector, a highly desirable staging post for young hopefuls, driven by the need to make their mark within 2 or 3 years by means of some loud but politically fragrant programme of parliamentary adventures.

It might have been supposed that the dramatic change of government as a result of the Labour landslide of 1997 would mean a grand change too, not certainly in the political status of educational policy, but in its direction. To expect that however was to fail to reckon with Blair's New Labour, proclaimed as the end of ideology but reinforcing the ideology already in use. In education, this was immediately made clear by the retention of League Tables and of Chris Woodhead as chief inspector.

P. Daunt (✉)
Education Consultant, 4 Bourn Bridge Road, Little Abington,
Cambridge, CB21 6BJ, UK
e-mail: patrick.daunt@talktalk.net

P. Hughes (ed.), *Achieving Quality Education for All*, Education in the Asia-Pacific
Region: Issues, Concerns and Prospects 20, DOI 10.1007/978-94-007-5294-8_27,
© Springer Science+Business Media Dordrecht 2013

The Establishment Polarised

A consequence has been the continuing tendency for the concerns of educational theorists and politicians to polarise. Comprehensive reorganisation in Britain, like democratic psychiatry in Italy, was professionally driven, devised by powerful and proactive administrators, taken on by academics, inspectors (both national and local) and teachers, then adopted by Old Labour parliamentarians; the role of university institutes of education in promoting and enabling the abolition of selection at '11 plus' was prominent and effective. Since then, the relative 'deprofessionalisation' of teachers has been part of the new orthodoxy which has seen a general replacement of professional by commercial ethos; skill, not vision, is what makes the good teacher; in training, the theory, history and sociology of education are to be decried and diminished; schools are run by management teams, where there is no collegium. Business rules.

Little wonder if there is in the academy a certain squeamishness in face of political realities. I suspect that any theoretically expert reader of what I have so far written may already be scorning my whole approach, seeing me as politically obsessed and biased. I deny the former, but confess to the latter; like M. Swann, I have reached the age when I need to take sides. But I would defend my stress here on the political dimension without reserve or apology. To ignore it is to end up kicking field goals by moonlight – that is surely obvious, but the problem is much worse than that. That there are no principles worth the name in British politics now is as much an intellectual failure as a moral one; unless what in other countries it is permitted to call 'intellectuals' dig deep and produce some ideas that deserve to be taken seriously, there is no hope in that department.

The Pathology of 'Reform'

And so, since the rules of spin mean that all changes are reforms, to be in perpetual (albeit factitious) need of reform has been the fate of the whole secondary system in England, regardless of its high achievement since the 1960s in vastly enhancing the personal expectations of the majority of the nation's children and their families. A number of features common to both political colours have characterised this process.

At the bipartisan heart of policy has been the pretence that severe educational problems, affecting only those areas where authentic reform is actually needed, can be solved by educational measures alone. This is a notion so stupid that no one, even in our times, really believes it; but the alternative, as Chesterton said of the Christian ideal, 'has been found difficult and left untried'. These areas of real need are, of course, those of urban blight. The idea that secondary education throughout (for example) East Anglia is in need of 'reform' is an insult to the whole 'educational community' of the region – children, families, teachers, administrators and local politicians; yet, there are a few schools in the city of Norwich which are barely sustainable. As in the successful new towns, holistic programmes of redevelopment comprising employment, schooling, social and health services, public amenities and (perhaps the most crucial of all) housing are – it surely should not need to be said – the only way forward. The challenge is daunting, certainly; but for years both the experience and the financial and other resources have been there, and the failure to address it has been abject. New Labour did not hesitate to make clear its intention to make a virtue of that failure, by announcing that 'poverty is no excuse for educational failure'. But if, whether excuse or not, it is a reason which would not go away, what then?

The bleak result of this is that the schools have had to bear the blame for the whole mess, in defiance of the fact that what some spad called with deadly malice 'bog standard comprehensives' have no option but to draw most of their children from bog standard housing estates inhabited by folk operating at a bog standard in all aspects of family life. These truths about some urban situations must never be openly displayed in their entirety; no minister can risk his/her reputation for this, both because solutions are unknown and because the reality is so awful that anyone would be reviled for drawing attention to it. Blackguarding schools on the other hand is always a safe procedure in England (not so in Scotland), for a number of reasons deeply set in the tribal culture, among them the perceived academic excellence and undoubted cultural superiority of the major independent (so-called public) schools and the uncertain rank of state school teachers in the English class system. At the same time, schools are such easy prey, always stuck where they are, at the mercy for any minister to slander, manipulate and bully.

Linked to this, and conveniently supportive of it, has been a process remarkable for its continuity in the political life of England over the last three decades, the determination of Whitehall to demolish piecemeal the power of local government. That it was in the interest of the Thatcher regime to break up the London County Council and the more recently created huge metropolitan boroughs was obvious enough; the chances of ever achieving let alone retaining Conservative majorities there were evidently poor; so, if you could not win them, then it was expedient to go for the second best, to fragment and debilitate them. But there was also another motive at work, more primitive than that factional one. When New Labour, having as expected and hoped, announced its intention to restore the influence of local authorities, surprisingly set about doing the opposite, it became clear that central government, regardless of party, was set on plundering local powers merely in order to have them for itself. Inevitably this was going to affect above all education, the jewel in the local crown. Thatcher's offer of money to secondary schools if they agreed to 'opt out of local authority control' was a mere political bribe, without a hint of any actual educational advantage involved for anyone, man, woman or child, other than the money itself, a striking example of invasion by commercial ethics of a realm which had until then operated on different moral principles. When in the 1990s I resigned as governor of an excellent 11–16 school because the chairman and local authority representative had persuaded the governing body, some with difficulty, to accept the bribe, the fact that the authority was Cambridgeshire and the school one of the famous village colleges founded on collective principles by the chief education officer Henry Morris in the 1930s is what journalists would call 'ironic', though 'shameless' would be a better word.

Commercialisation of the whole primary and secondary educational process has been the most prominent operational characteristic favoured by both parties since the 1980s. Since schooling is both compulsory and free, schools are as a fact not providers of a product in a market, but for several reasons it is thought to be essential to treat them as if they were. For one thing, dogma demands the belief that without competition there can only be inefficiency. So, what a professor in the London Institute of Education has called the 'inveterate mendacity of the market' has taken charge; in spite of occasional ministerial protestations which deplore a narrow emphasis on test results, children are formally tested almost every year of their secondary careers, and their schools are judged only by what can be expressed in figures. 'Failing' schools are first 'named and shamed', as witches or whores once were, then treated exactly like businesses, either merged (taken over) or closed down (bankrupted). *Of all this, a critical instrument are the League Tables which, as well as publicly humiliating those schools and those teachers battling with the most difficult tasks, violate the humanity of all the children, by reducing their learning to the figures of a market report for the benefit of the commercial management and of those consumers worth targeting.* While at university level education has become a mere commodity, in schools the commodity is the children themselves, the raw material put through an industrial process aimed to fit them for the open market of real life which lies ahead. And in all this, the parents are deceived, unaware that they are condoning a reversal of roles, government not serving the schools but the schools serving the government and the ambitions of its ministers.

With this commercial transformation of schools into factories goes the diversification of their type, a means for enabling another essential of policy, parental choice – though to what extent choosing the school transmutes into the favoured school choosing the child is already an interesting question. It is both a strength and a weakness of comprehensive schools that they can only work well if they are virtually universal; once too the belief that 'comprehensive' can mean 'common' is current, then to the ambitious middle-class parent, any school that one has not chosen in preference to another cannot be good enough. The promotion of choice from a personal recourse to a national policy has been driven by the predicament of more or less lefty politicians and journalists, living in fashionable but relatively affordable and socially heterogeneous parts of London, whose children were approaching secondary school age. In the words of Peter Mitchell, a former chief education officer, 'If a good local comprehensive school were located on Horse Guards Parade, then Blair's policy would be a good local school for everybody'. So, like the development of adult education and the integration of children with disabilities into the mainstream, the community school movement, once so full of promise, has been marginalised when not brought to a halt. There was a certain inevitability that the programme which Mitchell, then head of Quintin Kynaston School, created in the 1970s and 1980s to break down the barriers between the education of school children and adults should be closed down as soon as the Inner London Education Authority was abolished.

The Follies of Government

However disagreeable, this account would be incomplete without mentioning that the intransigence of successive governments has been matched by their bungling. There has not once in the last 60 years been any clear declaration of the respective roles of central and local authorities. Selection at 11 years for grammar or secondary modern schools still goes on throughout the county of Kent. The free-for-all allowed to local councils in response to the 1967 Plowden Report on primary schools meant that children under the various schemes were being moved from one level of secondary school to another at every age other than 14. Just as how schools should be inspected, so too how school leavers should be examined are questions repeatedly but fruitlessly debated; the Tomlinson Report commissioned to devise a single diploma did exactly that, only to be binned because of an approaching election. The recent pace of bright ideas, apparently picked up at random, some discarded as quickly as they were taken up, has become manic. The programme of secondary 'academies' devised by one government for struggling schools is taken on by the next for 'outstanding ones'; when this is called 'freeing schools from local government control', the public and the media are so spin-drunk they cannot see that the words 'freeing' and 'control' are propaganda. Grants to support music and sport in schools are abolished only to be partly restored; hundreds of school building programmes are cancelled at one sweep; a programme of free schools, paid for by tax payers but publicly unaccountable, is launched after the example of the not particularly successful Swedish model (Alas! 'Where are the snows of yesteryear?'). Now that it has been discovered that it is Finland where things actually work, one wonders which particular feature we should adopt first, the abolition of League Tables or uniforms, the delay of formal education until 7 years, the weak private sector or the actual commitment to fully comprehensive schools. Meanwhile, the chief inspector explains to us that, whenever schools are assessed, 'satisfactory' means 'unsatisfactory'; whether 'not satisfactory' means 'not unsatisfactory' she does not say.

Equal Value or Nothing

I am aware that all I have said is open to one or the other of two charges, that it is hysterical, the merely irritating exaggerations of a maverick, or that there is no point in saying it since it is all been said before and everyone knows about it. My response to the first of these is that it is simply false. There is no exaggeration, the reality is as bad as I have painted it, and I know of no evidence of tendencies which might prevent it getting worse. There are new enlightened ideas of course, for example, the work of Michael Fielding in the London Institute on 'schools within schools' and pupil democracy, but what is lacking is the least sign that these are themes our political masters have a taste for. As for the second, what matters is not how often the truth has been told but who was listening, while it is no use knowing it if it is not admitted, proclaimed and then dealt with. As things are, does it not come to this that the educationists have given up on it and have no hope of doing more than tinkering with technical details? If that is so, then while government is Pozzo, blind and virtually insane, the academy is lucky, dragged round on a string, all those impressive bibliographies recording no more than 'the labours unfinished of Testew and Cunard'.

This old man's Jeremiad has not been an attractive read, though not at heart as ideological as it may seem. It is true that without an ideological shift, revolution rather, the sad farce of schools harassed into attempting an impossible task and castigated for failing to perform it will simply go on and on. *Anthropos politikon zôon,* man is a social animal. You can throw money at individual families for as long as you like, and at the end of it, your urban blight problems will merely have gone on getting worse, cultural and moral poverty untouched. So, for educational 'failure' in England, it is a choice between a communitarian solution and no solution, not a conclusion with one drop of hope in it.

Yet, what matters most is at an even deeper level than that. Compulsory education is an essentially collective idea; in itself it is incompatible with the individualism which dominates and looks likely to go on doing so for the foreseeable future, but it is a fact. That we make all children come to school whether they or their parents like it or not establishes an obligation from which there is no escape: As I tried to show in *Comprehensive Values* nearly 40 years ago, it follows that we are bound both to value the education of all children equally and to value all schoolchildren themselves equally. This is not quixotic, still less utopian, but a question of deontology, defining the categorical scholastic imperative. Recognition of this and its implications is the rock, the only rock, on which a structure of authentic educational principles can be refounded. Till that day, if it ever comes, school policy will continue to be built on sand.

Chapter 28
Let Us Turn Around and Face the Future

Joanna Le Métais and Don W. Jordan

In her 2002 study, *Does Education Matter? Myths About Education and Economic Growth,* Alison Wolf concludes that

> The lesson of the last century must be that, for individuals, [education] matters more than ever before in history. And not just any education: having the right qualifications, in the right subjects, from the right institutions, is of ever growing importance. Fewer and fewer jobs and opportunities are open to those who are denied, or reject, formal education; and, for the young, long periods in school and university increasingly appear not as an option, but as pretty much a necessity. (Wolf, 2002, p. 244)

Most developed countries now require young people to pursue a full-time education for about 10 years, with an encouragement or expectation that they continue, at least on a part-time basis, until the age of 18.

Full-time education might be described as a process during which young people prepare for a harvest, which, it is implicitly assumed, will form the basis of their nourishment throughout life. Those whose harvest is rich are valued and enjoy the greatest advantages in life.

Many people enjoy their education and reap lifelong benefits. However, despite considerable investment of finance, human resources and time, education systems are not achieving their goals for a significant minority of their students. In 2009, the OECD's Programme for International Student Assessment (PISA) found that, on average across OECD countries, around one-fifth of 15-year-olds did not attain proficiency level 2 in three core areas of learning, namely, reading (19%), mathematics (22%) and science (18%), and, consequently, lacked the essential skills

J. Le Métais (✉)
Le Metais Consulting, 19 Geffers Ride, Ascot, SL5 7JY, England, UK
e-mail: jlemetais@gmail.com

D.W. Jordan
Education Consultant, 19 Lynden Road, Bonnet Hill, Taroona, TAS 7053, Australia
e-mail: donjordan1@bigpond.com

P. Hughes (ed.), *Achieving Quality Education for All*, Education in the Asia-Pacific
Region: Issues, Concerns and Prospects 20, DOI 10.1007/978-94-007-5294-8_28,
© Springer Science+Business Media Dordrecht 2013

needed to make sense of a complex world and to participate effectively and productively in a society where science and technology play a large role in daily life (OECD, 2010).[1] This is endorsed by employers, who often complain that young people are inadequately prepared for working life.

How Has This Situation Come About?

Is It Because the Aims of Education Are Unclear or Volatile?

The aims of education in most developed countries are expressed in terms of the development of individuals, their integration into society and their preparation for active participation in the economic life of the society and the wider world. New formulations of curricula use these personal, social and economic strands as a starting point to identify values (e.g. equity, integrity, diversity and excellence), dispositions (e.g. perseverance, resilience, connectedness) and competences (literacy, numeracy, creative and critical thinking, leadership and team work).

However, although 'lip-service may still be paid to learning for personal enrichment and development, … in politicians' speeches the emphasis is unremittingly on what education can do for the economy' (Wolf, 2002, p. 13). Perceived economic benefits determine the activities for which resources are provided (in terms of trained staff and facilities) and, especially in countries with centralised curricula, the objectives and content of those curricula.

Individuals live within communities that have predominant racial, cultural, social, religious and political landscapes that may reflect, or differ from, those of the country as a whole. Where these are shared and homogenous, the implementation of values into aims and educational activities is relatively straightforward. However, change and mobility – whether voluntary or forced, such as in the case of refugees – are fixtures in our lives.

It no longer is possible to consider our lives in isolation from other countries. The global economy, mobility and electronic communications open our eyes to other possibilities and raise our expectations. They equally require us to take into consideration the political, social, economic and environmental impact that our day-to-day activities have on others around the globe.

These two factors mean that we constantly need to review our beliefs and values to ensure that all citizens are treated fairly and given the chance to develop to their full potential.

---

[1] PISA evaluates the quality, equity and efficiency of school systems in some 70 countries that, together, make up nine-tenths of the world economy. PISA considers students' knowledge in these areas not in isolation, but in relation to their ability to reflect on their knowledge and experience and apply them to real-world issues. The emphasis is on mastering processes, understanding concepts and functioning in various contexts within each assessment area.

Is It Because the Locus of Control Has Moved?

Given the claim on public funds and the personal (and increasingly financial) investment required of students, it is not surprising that education is asked to meet the dual criteria of 'quality' and 'value for money'. This concern becomes particularly prominent at times of economic recession, and practices of education 'have tended to become overly rationalistic, scientistic (*sic*), corporatist, managerial, and narrowly results based' (Van Manen, 2000, p. 1).

In the last quarter of the twentieth century, two strategies were adopted to raise the quality of education in many developed countries. Central or regional governments increasingly devolved authority for governance and financial decision-making to schools. School boards, representing the school and its wider community, were held accountable for efficiently 'delivering' prescribed standards of student achievement and behaviour, commonly measured in terms of examination results and attendance, respectively. Second, an assumption that competition would 'drive up' standards led to the introduction of a market model, whereby parents' choices would channel resources to schools. The best would thrive and grow whilst the unsatisfactory would perish (Le Métais, 1992, pp. 29–33).

As the provision of education changes from a national (or provincial/state) service to local 'offerings', analogous to a franchise business, virtuous and vicious circles emerge. Schools in socio-economically advantaged areas have a ready supply of individuals with the expertise necessary to manage an 'educational business' and willing to commit their time and energy to serve on their child's school board. These schools have the pick of the best teachers, and their students tend to come from homes where education is valued and which have a rich cultural capital (Bourdieu & Passeron, 1973). In contrast, schools in deprived areas not only attract disadvantaged students, but they often lack the support of parents and generally find it hard to attract members to their governing board and to recruit good teachers. Without external moderation, the quality of education available to young people depends largely on where they live, leading to what is sometimes described as a 'postcode lottery'.

Is It Because the Organisation of Education Constantly Looks Backwards?

A brief glance at formal education shows that it lacks flexibility, focusing on cohorts rather than on individuals. The evolution of this system is well illustrated by William Spady's (1997) metaphor of an educational iceberg 'drifting in a sea of the ingrained habits, past practices and institutional inertia'.

At the bottom of the iceberg, the Feudal Age constitutes an agenda 'of sorting and selecting the most able and deserving students so that high educational opportunities are not wasted on others' (Spady, 1997, p. 9). This focus on the élite has largely determined the content of the curriculum. Even now, irrespective of individual aspirations or abilities on the one hand, or the needs of society on the other, many curricula still primarily serve those students aiming for an academic, university education.

Next from the bottom is the Agrarian Age calendar, which 'limits teaching and learning around the traditional holidays to harvest crops' (Spady, 1997, p. 9). Long summer holidays allow students to forget much of what they have learned. In Christian countries, the alignment of other holidays with Christmas and Easter leads to a further imbalance in the duration of school terms.

Next up is the Industrial Age, representing a 'delivery system' that organises student placement, curriculum, teaching and assessment around the 'major features of the factory assembly line, with everyone doing pre-assigned work at a pre-scheduled work station for the proper amount of time' (Spady, 1997, p. 9). In most countries, pupils are organised in groups according to age and progress to a new grade each learning year. This lockstep progression means that fast learners come up against a bottleneck and slow learners fall progressively further and further behind. Both groups risk becoming disaffected. Moreover, as 'repeating a grade' is rejected for its demotivating effect on students, it is often only at the end of ten or more years of education that students are declared 'a failure'. Many students turn away from learning and, in some cases, disengage from society itself.

Just below the surface of the water, Spady places the Bureaucratic Age, whose culture 'defines and operates everything in the system on the basis of time spent, resources, programs, means, procedures and roles rather than on outcomes, results, standards, achievements, ends and goals accomplished' (Spady, 1997, pp. 9–10).

Blowing across the tip of the iceberg are the challenging 'winds of change' of the New Information Age. Above the water, suggests Spady, 'educators attempt to respond to the constantly evolving and increasing challenges of today's information age, blinkered to the rest of the iceberg [which] remains sheltered from and largely uninfluenced by … future conditions and realities' (Spady, 1997, p. 9) because each stage has been added without consideration of the way in which previous models could – or should – be rejected or adapted in the light of new developments.

If computers allow for tailored learning programmes and individual progression, asks Spady, why are students still arranged in age-based classes? Is it because schools are accountable, not to their students, but to parents and political authorities who are reluctant to abandon the models of their own education?

Is It Because We Mainly Teach What Is Measurable?

It is common for governments to focus on quantitative targets that allow them to monitor progress and pronounce success in terms of what can be counted and measured. The most extreme manifestation of this trend is outcome-related funding. Whilst centralised, target-driven controls with financial pressures are inherent in any large-scale expansion of state-funded compulsory education, they undermine quality and invite abuse.

This may occur, for example, by a narrowing of the learning experience and, in some cases, by manipulating assessments to secure the desired outcomes.

Schools are motivated to teach what is measured rather than what is valued. Attitudes and dispositions such as self-esteem, self-management, commitment, perseverance, resilience, confidence, creativity, entrepreneurialism, independent thinking and interpersonal relationships are difficult to measure, not included in examinations and therefore less often taught. We want self-reliance, but teach conformity; we want creativity, but constrain learning to timed lessons; we want critical and creative problem-solving, but teach that there is one right answer. Managing uncertainty and taking risks, so important for learning, are discouraged.

Is It Because Teaching and Learning Are Becoming 'Technopolised'?

The nature of learning is changing significantly, as more and more technologies are assimilated into our lives. *How* learning happens: for example, taking part in a discussion with people from all over the world. *When* it happens: for example, listening to a podcast whenever it is convenient for us to do so. There are more opportunities to access, create and instantly share content with others. The nature of teaching and the measurement of learning have also changed. We have created a diverse range of technologies for educational purposes, from multimedia learning to mobile measuring and sensing equipment. Interactive whiteboards and Wi-Fi are also more commonplace in schools. The way teachers engage with their students, using computers or online assessment to provide feedback and reports, is very different from the 'chalk and talk' model of the past. What will learning be like in 2020? Will the exercise books and report cards of today even be recognised? Will these technologies ultimately replace even teachers?

Spady suggested that computers in schools could be the 'winds of change' of the new information age, and new technologies have been seized upon as *the* solution to the perceived inadequacies of education (Cuban, 2001, p. 195) and of teachers. However, many writers have argued that technologies are not neutral.[2]

Neil Postman (1993) highlights the dangers of uncritical dependence on technologies by tracing their effect on humanity over time. He identifies three stages. In *theocracies,* or tool using cultures, tools are subordinate to and integrated in ways that do not challenge a society's belief system or ideology. In *technocracies,* social and symbolic worlds become increasingly subject to the requirements of technologies. In *technopolies*, where the primary goal of human labour and thought is efficiency and technical calculation is deemed superior to human

---

[2] See, for example, Weizenbaum (1976), Street (1984), Winner (1986), Perelman (1992), Idhe (1993), Pursell (1994), Armstrong and Casement (2000), Bowers (2000).

judgement in all respects, subjectivity 'is an obstacle to clear thinking; … what cannot be measured either does not exist or is of no value; and … the affairs of citizens are best guided and conducted by experts' (Postman, p. 87). *Technopoly* involves the 'submission of all forms of cultural life to the sovereignty of technique and technology' (Postman, p. 52). Both a state of mind and a state of culture, *technopoly* is an 'affliction of individuals and societies in which technology becomes the chief source of authority, definer of life-goals and provider of satisfaction'. *Technocracy* becomes *technopoly*, says Postman, 'when tools win the battle for dominance and become the sole determiners of a culture's purpose and meaning and in fact of its very way of knowing and thinking or of not thinking' (Postman, p. 55). Where does this leave human relationships and the emotional connector in learning?

In Fig. 28.1, Jordan builds on Spady's metaphor to introduce his notion of 'cusp', a signal to break away from the past and face the future (Jordan, 2009, pp. 54–55). The 'Journeyman' passes through the foothills of *theocracy*. He then climbs the slopes of *technocracy*, where the adoption of technology helps mankind achieve more, faster but requires individual and community adaptations which break up communities and impair the quality of life. Like the Journeyman, educators are encumbered by their past and walk backwards into the future, facing towards where they have been (Jordan, p. 53). When they reach the top of the hill, will they make a 180-degree turn towards the brave new world of Spady's information technology, be caught by the winds of change and be blown into an exciting high-tech world?

Over time and through personal knowledge, experience and understandings as a classroom teacher, Jordan has found that the computer has not (yet) brought about the cusp, the 'facing forwards' for which many had hoped. Rather, there is a danger that, instead of enjoying the freedoms offered by technology, teachers and students will find themselves in the realms of *technopoly,* where tools define what and who humans are and where there is no 'transcendent sense of purpose or meaning, and no cultural coherence' (Postman, 1993, p. 63).

So What Now?

> To teach is to create possibilities for the construction and production of knowledge rather than to be engaged simply in a game of transferring knowledge [and that] when I enter a classroom I should be someone who is open to new ideas, open to questions, and open to the curiosities of the students as well as their inhibitions. (Freire, 2001)

As has been indicated already, the majority of schools and teachers do not espouse this approach. In our view, those of us committed to high-quality education need to face forwards and embrace the unknown with courage, responsibility, flexibility and trust.

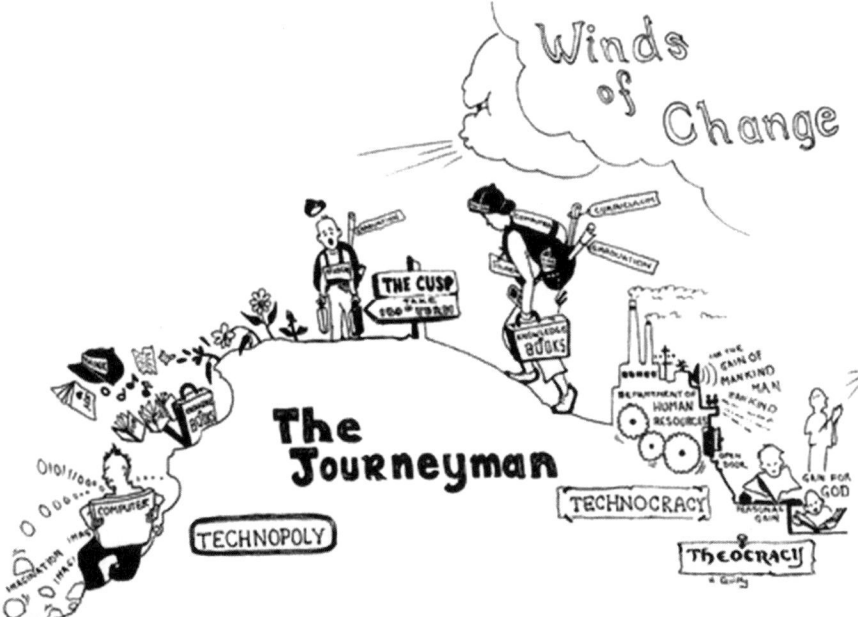

Fig. 28.1 The Journeyman (Jordan, 2009; Illus. Helen Quilty)

Embrace the Unknown with Courage

The future is unknown. The pace and scale of change will continue to increase. Whilst it is important for students to learn the specific principles and methods of the different disciplines, 'real life' requires them to understand, integrate and apply knowledge and skills from a range of disciplines to address problems effectively and creatively. An integrated, 'competence-based' approach offers students a more holistic and coherent way of learning and making connections between different subject areas.

Continuing the analogy of the 'harvest' with which we started this chapter, individuals need to produce harvests throughout their lives, in unpredictable conditions. A successful harvest depends upon the quality of the soil and the skill with which the gardener uses the land and other resources to meet 'climate change'. In our metaphor, the 'soil' represents the dispositions of the gardener. Under this heading, we would include resilience, persistence and an ability to reflect on and learn the lessons of experience. The gardener needs to know which plants grow best in his local conditions and climate. He needs to use tools and other resources competently and flexibly to compensate for deficiencies in the soil, adverse weather and so forth. He needs to reflect on and evaluate what worked and what he needs to change to achieve a better crop. The ability to cooperate with others will enable the gardener to share advice, support and seeds, increasing her and her fellow gardeners' yield in a mutually beneficial way.

Two examples of this dispositions and competences approach which have been implemented in a substantial way are the Tasmanian *Essential Learnings* curriculum and the Royal Society for the encouragement of Arts, Manufactures and Commerce (RSA) *Opening Minds* project.

The Tasmanian *Essential Learnings* curriculum[3] was 'organised around five "essentials" – *Thinking, Communicating, Personal futures, Social responsibility* and *World futures* – which young people need to succeed in the 21st century'. Examples of the 18 underpinning elements include being ethical, maintaining well-being, building and maintaining identity and relationships, being literate, being numerate and inquiry (Tasmania. Department of Education, 2005).

The RSA *Opening Minds* project (now being used in over 200 schools in England) promotes innovative and integrated ways of thinking about education and the curriculum, whereby school leaders, teachers, students and the wider community design their own curriculum based round the development of five key competences: citizenship, learning, managing information, relating to people and managing situations. Broad areas of capability are developed through a mixture of instruction and practical experience: students plan their work, organise their own time and explore their own ways of learning (RSA (Royal Society for the encouragement of Arts, Manufactures and Commerce), n.d. (a)).

Take Joint Responsibility

Successful education requires the cooperation of teachers, parents and students and the support of communities, governments and other agencies. We need to replace the current emphasis on rights and blame with a willingness to accept individual and collective responsibility for the upbringing of our young people. We therefore need to communicate with one another and explore how each of us can best contribute to the achievement of common goals.

Rather than relying on external examinations that measure only a narrow range of knowledge and skills, we need to develop the individual student's capacity to evaluate, and give feedback on, their own and others' behaviour and outcomes, in accordance with relevant criteria. This skill will not only enable students constantly to improve their own performance, but it will prepare them for leadership in later life. The ability to give relevant, specific feedback on performance, rather than criticising the individual, undermines many a manager's effectiveness.

---

[3] Implemented state-wide until 2006, when it was revised as part of curriculum reform, but now largely superseded by the Australian Curriculum.

Be Flexible

We need to acknowledge explicitly that each young person is an individual and that one curriculum size, even when modified, does not fit all. Shedding the shackles of the iceberg and reconsidering the what? who? where? when? and how? of schooling may better take account of the lived worlds and identities of young people and maximise engagement and achievement.

What can students learn from the local community? How do local history and environments add to students' understanding of knowledge and concepts? How can theories be applied in concrete situations?

Who can be involved with education, and in what ways can we engage a wider community in curriculum development?

Where does learning happen? By involving a wider community, can we move education beyond the classroom walls and enrich the experience and the perceived relevance for students? To what extent would such an approach contribute to greater cost effectiveness, giving students access to 'real-life' expertise and equipment?

When does learning happen? Could a more flexible model give (working) parents more time with their children?

How can we best create circumstances in which students can develop and practise attitudes and dispositions, and apply knowledge and skills in different practical contexts, working with people of different ages and backgrounds, reflecting the 'real world'?

The RSA's *Area Based Curriculum* project offers one model for co-creating a curriculum. The aim is to engage a wide range of people and organisations, in particular students, in the development of a curriculum that is meaningful and challenging; that recognises and values their neighbourhoods, communities, families, cultures and wider locality; and that equips students to shape their own futures and that of their local area for the better. The curriculum builds on local characteristics and resources, whilst encouraging students to consider critically the relationships between local, national and global dimensions of learning (RSA (Royal Society for the encouragement of Arts, Manufactures and Commerce), n.d. (b)).

Trust

National and regional authorities have established criteria for and expend considerable sums on the training and employment of teachers and school leaders, and yet they tend to micromanage the work of these professionals. This suggests not so much a lack of trust in the professionals as a lack of trust in their own judgement and systems. Micromanagement may reduce, but cannot totally prevent, failure (see the PISA results). On the downside, it undermines the potentially favourable outcomes of individualised and innovative teaching practices.

Education – and especially educational change – is a long-term process. Unfortunately, the evidence suggests that politicians (constrained by the short period between elections) tend to respond to criticisms with a succession of quick-fix solutions. As a result, few initiatives are meaningfully implemented. Educators become increasingly demoralised by the ongoing (overt and implied) criticism, and expectations to achieve ever-higher standards that may not be reasonable and for which the support and resources are generally inadequate. This is similar to constantly uprooting and replanting vegetables during the growing process: uprooted carrots do not improve in yield. If educational aims were to be agreed between political parties, there would be less need to introduce change as a proxy for 'improvement'.

Conclusion

Courage, responsibility, flexibility and trust: yes, it *is* a challenge, but no greater than dealing with the consequences of failing some 20% of our young people.

References

Armstrong, A., & Casement, C. (2000). *The child and the machine: How computers put our children's education at risk*. Beltsville, MD: Robins Lane Press.

Bourdieu, P., & Passeron, J.-C. (1973). *Reproduction in education, society and culture*. London: Sage.

Bowers, C. (2000). *Let them eat data: How computers affect education, cultural diversity and the prospects of ecological sustainability*. Athens, GA: The University of Georgia Press.

Cuban, L. (2001). *Oversold and underused: Computers in the classroom*. Cambridge, MA: Harvard University Press.

Freire, P. (2001). *Pedagogy of freedom: Ethics, democracy and civic courage*. Lanham, MD: Rowman & Littlefield Publishers.

Idhe, D. (1993). *Philosophy of technology: An introduction*. New York: Paragon House Publishers.

Jordan, D. W. (2009). *Invisible cusps and unintended outcomes: A response to two influential documents as heralds of computers in Tasmanian government schools*. Doctoral thesis, Curtin University of Technology, Perth, Western Australia, Australia.

Le Métais, J. (1992). *Conservative values and education policy 1979–1990*. Doctoral thesis, Brunel University, Department of Government, Uxbridge, UK.

OECD. (2010). *PISA 2009 At a Glance*. Paris, France: OECD Publishing. Retrieved April 20, 2011, from http://dx.doi.org/10.1787/9789264095298-en

Perelman, L. (1992). *School's out: Hyperlearning, the new technology and the end of education*. New York: William Morrow.

Postman, N. (1993). *Technopoly. The surrender of culture to technology*. New York: Vintage Books.

Pursell, C. (1994). *White heat*. London: British Broadcasting Corporation.

RSA (Royal Society for the encouragement of Arts, Manufactures and Commerce). (n.d. a). *Area based curriculum: Engaging the local*. Retrieved April 20, 2011, from http://www.thersa.org/projects/education/area-based-curriculum#concept

RSA (Royal Society for the encouragement of Arts, Manufactures and Commerce). (n.d. b). *Opening minds curriculum*. Retrieved April 20, 2011, from http://www.rsaopeningminds.org.uk/about-rsa-openingminds/

Spady, W. (1997). *Paradigm lost: Reclaiming America's educational future*. Alexandria, VA: American Association of School Administrators.

Street, B. (1984). *Literacy in theory and practice*. Cambridge, UK: Cambridge University Press.

Tasmania. Department of Education. (2005). *Essential Learnings – A curriculum for the 21st century.* Hobart: Retrieved April 20, 2011, from http://www.education.tas.gov.au/annualreport/04-05/pre-compulsory/essentiallearnings

Van Manen, M. (2000). Moral language and pedagogical experience. *Journal of Curriculum Studies, 32*(2), 315–327.

Weizenbaum, J. (1976). *Computer power and human reason: From judgement to calculation*. Harmondsworth, MX: Pelican Books.

Winner, L. (1986). *The whale and the reactor: A search for limits in an age of high technology*. Chicago: The University of Chicago Press.

Wolf, A. (2002). *Does education matter? Myths about education and economic growth*. London: Penguin.

Chapter 29
Providing a Balanced Schooling in a Networked World

Mal Lee

Introduction

As the place called school finally begins to go digital and to experience the same irrevocable transformation that all other organizations that have gone digital have undergone, it is opportune for governments to look from high at the appropriateness and effectiveness of the schooling provided by the nation to its young in an increasingly networked world.

The nature of schooling has remained basically unchanged for centuries, and the perception has naturally grown that its form is somehow immutable.

It most assuredly is not, and in the last decade, early adopter schools across the developed world have moved schooling from the traditional paper-based operational mode to one that is digital, and in some instances networked.

Schooling is evolving at pace, with virtually all schools in the developed world moving to the digital stage and as such from an era of constancy and continuity to one of ongoing, often rapid and uncertain change and evolution, where more than ever the desired future needs to be proactively shaped.

It is timely to reflect on the current concept and nature of schooling, its appropriateness for a networked society, to identify its shortcomings, to envision its desired form and to begin shaping the schooling for a networked world.

In examining the evolution of schooling over the decade, and the profound impact the technology has had upon the learning of the young, there are major shortcomings to do with the disinclination to revisit the reasons nations have schools, to ask what schooling should entail and to critique the established ways and as a consequence continue to perpetuate the lack of balance in the educative process. Added to this is

M. Lee (✉)
Education Consultant, 2 Martin Place, Broulee, NSW 2537, Australia
e-mail: mallee@mac.com

P. Hughes (ed.), *Achieving Quality Education for All*, Education in the Asia-Pacific Region: Issues, Concerns and Prospects 20, DOI 10.1007/978-94-007-5294-8_29, © Springer Science+Business Media Dordrecht 2013

the seeming inability or unwillingness of the vested interests to redress those imbalances and use very considerable untapped community resources.

While individual schools are addressing these shortcomings, there has not been from the government a preparedness to take advantage of the shift to the digital and networked modes to ask how best their nation should school its young in a world where learning occurs continuously.

Nor does it appear to have been prepared to ask the most basic of questions; what constitutes a school in a networked world where students no longer have physically to attend to be taught and to learn? As Lipnack and Stamps noted in 1994 in a networked world, the requirement to physically attend is no longer apposite; yet today, the place called school is still defined by its physical location and form (Collins, 2007).

There is much to be said for defining schooling in the networked world by its function and purpose to enable schools not only to teach students but also to use their educational expertise to wider advantage such as preparing others like parents, grandparents, community elders, coaches and older students to assist in the holistic 'teaching' of the young from birth to graduation.

At this point in history, one sees across the developed world two distinct, unlinked educational 'streams': the formal, run by the education professionals within schools that focus on an academic education, and the informal, provided everywhere but the classroom 24/7/365 by the parents and the young that address all other learning.

Little the wonder, the literature speaks of the escalating home-school divide and the growing irrelevance of formal schooling:

> Kids lead high-tech lives outside school and decidedly low-tech lives inside school. This new 'digital divide' is making the activities inside school appear to have less real-world relevance to kids. A blend of intellectual discipline with real-world context can make learning more relevant, and online technology can bridge the gap between the two. (Illinois Institute of Design, 2007, p. 24)

Nearly a century ago (1916), John Dewey advised curriculum designers to secure due balance between the informal and formal, presciently noting

> there is the standing danger that the material of formal instruction will be merely the subject matter of schools, isolated from the subject matter of life experience. Dewey (1916, p. 10)
>   This danger is never greater than at the present time, on account of the rapid growth in the last few centuries of knowledge and the technical mode of skills. (p. 11)

No nation wanting to provide all its young a quality, balanced education that will enable them to thrive within and contribute productively to an information society can afford this current divide and imbalance to continue.

Restoring Balance

The lack of balance is to be found in the schools, the bureaucratic control of schooling and the homes, although not surprisingly that imbalance stems from the lack of professional advice.

While the schools have for centuries had an academic focus, in the last couple of decades that imbalance has become ever more pronounced and skewed with the more holistic education of the young being neglected in favour of an emphasis on what are termed the basics. Increasingly, the educational professionals and bureaucrats decide what is appropriate for their clients, with the students and parents not only having no real voice but are given no recognition or support for the vital role they play in their children's holistic education.

While leading educational thinkers of the likes of Arnold, Dewey, Montessori, Whitehead, Hilda Taba and Goodlad have rightly identified the importance of providing a balanced total education of the young and while for decades schools sought to provide that kind of education, of recent years governments have chosen to forego to equate a quality education with success in literacy and numeracy.

Ironically this is happening at a stage in history when the digital and networking technology has fundamentally changed the nature of work and life and placed ever greater importance in having a balanced holistic education that will enable the young to thrive in an increasingly networked and collaborative world and has opened the way for the students' homes to play an ever greater role – intentionally or not – in the education of the children.

While most nations seeking to provide a quality holistic education for every one of its young people apposite to the C21 know learning occurs in some form from birth onwards, that students don't physically have to be in a school to learn, the schools under their control continue to be skewed towards a subset of the academic, aided by basic skills tests and simplistic national and international 'school performance' tables that further accentuate the imbalance.

The current perception of 'schooling' is limited to the approximately 200 days of the year, 6 h a day, the 5–18 group and, physically a place called school. Learning in the other 80 plus per cent of the young's time awake is neither recognized nor supported by the school.

The organization of the school, particularly in the secondary years, is strongly hierarchical, with those atop the apex the only ones with a macro view of the total workings of the school and the vast majority of the staff having only a limited micro perspective that markedly disempowers them professionally (Lee & Finger, 2010b). In brief although supposedly nurturing collaborative teaching and learning, schools as organizations, particularly in the secondary years, are inordinately skewed in favour of decision making by a few.

Needless to say, the parents, grandparents, students and the wider school community have little more than a symbolic role in those schools where the governance and ultimate control is vested in government bureaucrats and not a legally constituted board or council.

The strongly hierarchical organizational structure invariably continues through into the bureaucracy and the ultimate control of the schools. Control is usually with an elected official, such as a minister of education. Operationally, that official rarely has any direct dealings with a school community and is strongly influenced by his/her bureaucrats who have as their prime purpose supporting that elected official and not the children for whom the schools are supposedly provided.

Perhaps the greatest imbalance and shortcoming is to be found in the fact that in virtually all developed nations the vital 0–5 years of education are still not viewed as part of the nation's schooling nor are they the responsibility of the schools. Few today would question the fundamental educational importance of this phase of a person's development and that if the key educational building blocks are not sufficiently developed before the children enrol at school, and in some instances like vocabulary and self-control by age 3 (Hart & Risely, 2002), the child has scant chance of success at school. Their fate is largely decided before they enter school, destined to years in remediation.

Yet despite this awareness, 0–5 'teaching' has invariably been left to a hodge-podge of agencies, church and charitable groups – excluding the schools – to work with the parents.

One can understand why this occurred. The young developmentally were not ready to attend a place called school.

The 'missing' 0–5 'teaching' has to be viewed as part, a vital part of the nation's 'schooling' and incorporated astutely as part of a fundamentally reconceived model of primary 'schooling'.

While not for a moment suggesting the 0–5 physically attend the place called school or in any way diminish the vital primary 'teaching' role of the parents, with a little imagination, an astute redeployment of existing early childhood educators and the use of networked primary school communities nations ought to be able to develop a birth to graduation model of 'schooling' that incorporates the age group.

Sadly, national governments, possibly unwittingly, perpetuate the myth, usually at or around the time of an election that there is a simple, magic panacea that will solve the nation's problems with its schools and the education of its young.

It is just that, a myth. Schooling and the appropriate education of the young is a highly complex process, which if anything is growing more complex by the day. A young person's success at school and in life depends on a multitude of interrelated developmental, social, academic, pedagogical, emotional and attitudinal factors. Diverse variables like the home learning culture, the mother's level of education, parents' conversations with the young, the child's degree of self-control and home Internet access all have their impact on ultimate educational attainment.

The Untapped Resources

In *Developing a Networked School Community* (2010), Lee and Finger examined the immense, underdeveloped community resources outside the classroom that were impacting on the learning of the young, which with greater acumen being shown by educators could markedly enhance the quality, balance and appropriateness of the young's schooling.

A simple glance at those potential resources will reveal how they could be used to help redress the current imbalance.

- Developed nations have in their parents historically the most educated cohort ever, with most not only motivated but educationally ready to collaborate in the 'teaching' of their young and in particular the teaching of the educational building blocks. The expertise remains underused and undeveloped.

- The same nations have in their grandparents a similar highly educated, underdeveloped resource that is rapidly growing in size with the influx to their ranks of the 'baby boomers'. In many situations with both parents working or the single parent working, the grandparents provide the after-school 'teaching'. However, once again, not only are the grandparents' current efforts not recognized or supported, the potential contribution has not been considered.
- The 'Net Generation' have long since normalized the everyday use of the digital and are using it to shape their lives and learning, but despite their acknowledged interest and competence in the technology, they are rarely listened to or drawn upon by their teachers.
- The burgeoning digital capacity of the student's homes has far surpassed that of the classroom. A study by Lee and Ryall (2010) compared the digital technology in the homes of six 30-year-old students with that in their classroom in 2009 and found that in the home was conservatively a factor of 15 greater than in the classroom. That home-school digital technology disparity is growing daily with the surge in young people's acquisition of a range of handheld mobile computing.
- However, once again this immense potential resource remains untapped, banned from use in most classrooms as too do most of the resources of the school's community and its social networks. While education authorities continue to block the networked world and the young's mobile computing from school operations, the imbalance will remain.

That vast and probably growing difference between the kind of education provided in the home and the school is not as some would contend a digital divide but rather a difference of circumstances that if approached positively can be soon turned into a far more collaborative, networked and indeed balanced mode of schooling.

Collaboration

The synergies possible by pooling the very considerable resources and efforts of the home, the young, the school and the school's community are immense, far exceeding the current imbalanced efforts of the schools acting alone. So too are the potential educational, social, economic, organizational and political dividends.

Facilitation

What is already apparent is that pathfinding schools of their volition are moving swiftly to achieve that collaboration and can readily do so if they have the desire, the leadership and readiness to move.

However, before they can make the shift to the networked mode and embrace a collaborative approach, all the teachers in the school need to have normalized the use of the digital in their everyday teaching – the school has to have moved to the digital operational stage.

The schools can make the move even within a tightly controlled bureaucratic and hierarchical structure, but ultimately to take maximum advantage of the opportunities opened, they will require facilitating organizational structures, a significant degree of school autonomy and leadership and teachers attuned to the ways of the networked world.

Conclusion

Schooling historically is at a watershed moment. Judging from their track record, most educational authorities and school leaders will be loath to cross that watershed and will strive futilely to retain the ways of the paper-based school.

The national government needs to seize the moment, support the pathfinders and develop a balanced model of schooling 0–18 appropriate for a networked world.

References

Collins. (2007). *Australian dictionary*. Glasgow, UK: HarperCollins.
Dewey, J. (1916). *Democracy and education*. New York: Macmillan.
Hart, B., & Risely, T. (2002). *The social world of children learning to talk*. Baltimore, MD: Paul Brooks.
Illinois Institute of Design (ID). (2007). *Schools in the digital age*. Illinois Institute of Technology. http://www.id.iit.edu/635/documents/MacArthurFinalReport1.pdf
Lee, M., & Ryall, B. (2010). Financing the networked school community: Building upon the home investment. In M. Lee & G. Finger (Eds.), *Developing a networked, school community: a guide to realising the vision* (pp. 109–24). ACER Press: Melbourne.
Lee, M., & Finger, G. (2010). *Developing a networked school community: Guide to realizing the vision*. Melbourne, Australia: ACER Press.
Lee, M., & Finger, G. (2010b). The impact of school organisational structure on teacher agency and educational contribution. Australian College of Educators Notepad, no 9.

Chapter 30
Educating Everybody: Properly!

Don Aitkin

It seems that I have been involved in education all my life. I started in first class at Ainslie Infants School in 1943, listened to my parents, both teachers, talking about the New Education Fellowship after the war, wanted to be a primary school teacher, then wanted to be a high school teacher, then wanted to be a university teacher—and became one for a time. I have talked to almost every kind of class, from kindergarten to postdoctoral to University of the Third Age (U3A), in Australia and overseas, been a school Parents and Citizens' Association (P&C) member and continue to be a 'grand friend'. I have helped to review a lot of Commonwealth principles and practices in education and chaired a review of school legislation in the ACT. And the longer I live, the more important I think education to be for any society.

Although I no longer have grand remedies to propose, it is always possible to suggest incremental improvements to this or that aspect of any educational system. Nevertheless, I do not think that 'fixing' education will fix all society's problems. It is true that almost every human baby comes into life with immense potential, but not necessarily with potential for good. The baby's parents themselves; the odd genetic quirk; the nature and extent of the child's parenting, sibling order, gender; the circumstances of the time, the availability of extended family; and the quality of schooling—all these factors will be important in the development of the human adult. Education cannot do everything and should not be asked to. Indeed, schools are in danger of serving in part as therapy centres for children who are already strongly and wrongly shaped when they reach school at age 5.

Of course, I agree that every child should have 'effective, relevant, high-quality education'. How could one argue the reverse? But that goal comes with two major problems. The first is establishing, for a particular child, what kind of education will be relevant, effective and of high quality. The second is making it available, for that

D. Aitkin (✉)
Former Vice Chancellor, University of Canberra,
80 Banks St, Yarralumla, ACT 2600, Australia
e-mail: donaitkin@grapevine.com.au

P. Hughes (ed.), *Achieving Quality Education for All*, Education in the Asia-Pacific Region: Issues, Concerns and Prospects 20, DOI 10.1007/978-94-007-5294-8_30,
© Springer Science+Business Media Dordrecht 2013

child. For the moment we look at a particular child, rather than at children, we move into a new world of educational provision. Our current schools, at every level, and our tertiary institutes, no matter how ingenious their provision of alternatives, are based on the 'one size fits all' principle. And it is plain to me, especially after 12 years in a university that prided itself on its capacity to give young people a second chance, that our educational institutions are not especially effective in what they do. There are just too many failures, too many uninterested kids, too little real learning. And that is not in any way to disparage teachers and their often more-than-wholehearted efforts.

If we were to take seriously the notion that every child needs to be well educated, then we would organise education rather differently. Howard Gardner, the Harvard scholar whose work has greatly affected my own thinking in this area, has said that the major advance in school education in the last 1,000 years has been in bringing children in out of the rain. Ideally, we would have much more knowledge than we now do about each child's portfolio of skills and interest, and we would design a programme for that child so that his/her development proceeded steadily. We would try to balance that development, so that we did not in the end produce lopsided adults who were extraordinarily proficient in one field but quite undeveloped in others. Since we would not know what occupation that child would have, we would do our best to prepare him or her for a variety of possible areas of life and work, recognising that by late adolescence the future career path or paths might be quite plain.

The child would still be in a school, but the school would have quite a lot more staff, both teachers and support people. It would be organised differently too. High schools might start after lunch, in recognition of the different circadian rhythms that come in adolescence. Some might be co-educational in part, but mostly single sex in specific areas, recognising that puberty can interfere with good learning. The desired outcome would be the development of skilled, self-confident, productive, altruistic adults who would in time become the parents of children whose development they supervised with encouraging, disinterested love.

It is not that today's parents and our educational institutions do a bad job in this domain. In my judgement, and comparing now with the 1940s and 1950s, when I was in school, things are a lot better than they were. Every time I visit a school or a university, I am encouraged by what I see. The problem is a little like that in road safety. In that domain, there have been dramatic improvements in mortality and morbidity in the last 40 years. But the improvements have 'flatlined'. If we are to achieve even lower death and injury statistics, we will have to tackle road safety in a new way—by involving all drivers in what amounts to an ethical examination of our attitudes when we drive, our attitudes to other drivers, our vehicles, other drivers, our time and so on. This is part of the 'Vision Zero' goal that is being adopted slowly by each jurisdiction in Australia.

To do that in education, we will have to go past thinking of improvements to our schools, our teachers and the timetable, important though they are. We will need to start with the decision to make a new baby, the circumstances in which that baby will emerge into the world and its likely course over its first 5 years. At once we face a major hurdle, because making a baby is regarded as an absolutely private matter, one in which the state ought to have no interest. And that is paradoxical, because the moment the baby is born the state moves to take notice of it. Why not start earlier? The Howard Government set up an initiative in parenting, and today there are most useful websites that are there to help new parents, if they know about them and are able to take advantage of their assistance.

But I think we are long way from a community understanding that every baby is a future adult, and that babies are not possessions, or someone to love who loves us, or achievements to justify our own lives, or warriors sent out into the world to achieve what we have so far been unable to achieve. More, it is doubtful that our community understands that while those first 5 years represent only a little more than 5% of the future adult's life, they are very probably the most important 5 years of all. In fact, during our own lives, we will encounter our children mostly as fellow adults, not as small people dependent on us for almost everything. From this perspective, or so it seems to me, we should be striving to ensure that our adult children are equipped to cope with life in a resilient, confident and helpful way and likely to see us as special friends, rather than as 'parents'.

This is a hard ask, but it seems the obvious next stage. Is it worth it? I think so. Australia's prisons are vastly oversupplied with young men for whom the education system was not helpful and, in so many cases, for whom parenting was not very helpful either. The school cannot replace good parenting and, to repeat, it should not be asked to do so. Our social welfare system consumes billions of dollars each year patching up problems whose genesis, in so many cases, can be traced to inadequate or indifferent parenting, or to the making of a baby at a most injudicious time, given the real needs of the growing infant. In my opinion, the making of a baby is arguably the most important decision we will ever make, and the consequences of that decision should be beneficial to the community in which we live.

I would go further. Each of us has creative potential that is, in most cases, only poorly developed. It is true that human life is finite, and that even in a long life, we will never be able to do all the things we would like to do or have the capacity to do. And to do anything well requires time and energy which will therefore not be available to undertake some other creative activity. Having said that, it seems to me that by concentrating on ensuring that high school graduates are ready for jobs, important though that is, we neglect the development of that part of us that leads to our having joy in creation, in having an art form that we can turn to when work is over, in having creative skills that lead us to others and in possessing the right sort of self-esteem in our ability to do something creative quite well. To use the prison example again, the great majority of the young men in prison do not possess any creative skills at all and have never been encouraged to develop them.

The success of 'el sistema' in Venezuela ought to be an example for us, the much wealthier Australians. 'The system' in question is the national network of youth and children's orchestras of Venezuela, which has been operating now for more than 30 years. A publicly funded state foundation watches over 125 youth orchestras and the instrumental training programmes that make them possible and draw the 250,000 children who attend its music schools around the country, nearly all of them from poor socio-economic backgrounds. There are several studies which link participation in the programme by the two million children who have been in it to improvements in school attendance and declines in juvenile delinquency. 'El sistema' is moving into Venezuela's jails, with the same overarching goals. Other countries have seen the Venezuelan experience as something they could emulate. It is time that we did.

I focused on music because it is my own creative partner. But, in principle, the same system could be applied in painting, in sculpture, in dance, in writing—in any and all creative pursuits. To be good at something creative seems to be a life enhancer, and the faster we acquire those skills and interests, the better. I could add 'sport', with two provisos: first, that the sporting pursuits not focus too heavily on team sports, which cannot easily be continued through life, and, second, that built into sport is the recognition that there is a role later in life for sports people to act as coaches, administrators and mentors.

In sum, if we are to greatly improve the life chances of our children, in the next 50 years, we must address the need for would-be parents to be prepared and ready to nurture the babies they create so that their child's experience of the educational system will be productive and enjoyable. That is a huge ethical challenge, and we have hardly begun to debate it. Then, we will need to recognise that the creative side of our potential is as important as the money-earning side, and that we need to develop mechanisms in our society that make it easy for children to acquire appropriate creative skills and develop them through adolescence. This too is hardly recognised at the moment.

There is, then, a long way to go. But I am not disheartened. When I left high school in 1953, only 2% of my age group went on to any form of further education. Today the proportion is some 60%. In the 1940s and early 1950s, most girls were not educated past age 15, on the grounds that they would only marry and have babies and that the money and energy should be devoted to boys. That is no longer the case, and the country is vastly better for it. I remain of the view that we can build a better society along the lines I have suggested, and this little essay is a contribution to that goal.

Chapter 31
Three Priorities for a Great Education

Neil Dempster

Introduction

What makes for a great education for children and young people in Australia? Phil
Hughes, a man whose career has been dedicated to seeking answers to this question
has asked it again at a point in his life when retrospection dominates most people's
thoughts. Not so with Phil. It is a testament to his lifelong commitment to education
that he has continued to search for better futures for Australia's young and is doing
so through this his last book.

When Phil asked for my views on the question that drives him, I wondered where
I would start; such is the complexity of educational provision in the modern era. It did
not take me long, however, to decide to write a purely personal response. In doing so,
I step aside from my training as an academic to write from the heart, so to speak, about
what I think is essential for a great education for the young. I have three unshakeable
priorities, great parents, great teachers and great leaders.

Great Parents

A great education starts with parents who know how dramatic their influence is on
the architecture of the minds and bodies of their children. From birth, though Fiona
Stanley, Australian of the Year in 2003, would say for at least 2 years before birth,
children are mightily influenced by the behaviour, health and well-being of their
parents. Great parents understand how important their own health and well-being
are to the health and well-being of their children. They know that they are the

N. Dempster (✉)
Professor Educational Leadership, Griffith University,
76 Felstead Street, Everton Park, Brisbane, QLD 4053, Australia
e-mail: N.Dempster@griffith.edu.au

P. Hughes (ed.), *Achieving Quality Education for All*, Education in the Asia-Pacific
Region: Issues, Concerns and Prospects 20, DOI 10.1007/978-94-007-5294-8_31,
© Springer Science+Business Media Dordrecht 2013

primary educators of the young, and they dedicate the time needed to carry out this responsibility. They also know how critical their role is in their children's acquisition of language. Rich oral language experience is the foundation for learning to read, and children cannot have enough of it.

Recently, I passed through a small rural Australian town with some colleagues on our way to a seminar on leadership for literacy learning no less. We stopped at the local pub for a quick cup of coffee as we had been driving for about 2 h, and we were looking for a break. In the little bistro adjacent to the public bar was a family of four, mum, dad and their two kids, a boy and a girl. We were the only other customers present. We ordered our coffee which took a little time to arrive, so our break lasted for about 30 min all up. During that time, the waiter brought the family its order which they commenced to eat in silence. While we were in the bistro, not a word was spoken by the four. As we returned to the car to continue our journey, my colleagues and I could not help but make reference to what we had seen. How could a mother and father sit with their two children for half an hour and say nothing? Of course, this snapshot of family life may have been quite out of character. They may have been talkative most of the time. But we as educators were disappointed by the fact that silence seemed to prevail at a time when the voices of both parents and children should have been intermingled. Both language and social learning occur on occasions like this in informal ways provided that the adults know and understand that opportunities like this are critical to the creation of the rich language environment so important in children's learning.

A great education starts with parents who automatically understand that whatever they do with their children in the formative years of their lives sets up the springboard from which youngsters dive deeply into the 'waters' of life. It happens with everything they do. Parents influence children's attitudes to people, to animals, spiders and fish, to giving, to taking, to music, to stories, to race and religion, to politics and parties, to science and the environment, to technology and social networking, to music and the arts, to marriage, to loving, to old age and to taxes and death. There is nothing about the formation of children's lives in which parents are not implicated.

The upshot of this fact carries very important messages for those responsible for the policies and practices of education systems – policies which recognise parents as the primary educators of their children, which create opportunities for the inclusion of parents as key contributors to children's learning at home and at school, and practices which are built on positive views of parents rather than the deficit theorising that has dominated much of the profession's outreach to parents and families since formal schooling began. The old adage 'teacher knows best' should be seen for what it is – a relic of the past. In the future, a great education will have faith in parents and their aspirations, it will respect their backgrounds, and it will automatically involve them as leaders of their children's learning with inclusive strategies developed through authentic partnerships between home and school.

Great Teachers

The second of my priorities for a great education for young Australians concerns the quality of their teachers. First and foremost, teachers need to have an allegiance to the pedagogical equivalent of the medical profession's Hippocratic Oath. By this, I mean that they should be committed to improving the lives of their students through learning, no matter the circumstances. To be so committed, they need to have a love of young people. Teaching is no profession for the ephebiphobic. In other words, those with antipathy towards the young should not apply. Those who do need a deep knowledge of human growth and development, an equally deep knowledge of learning, a love of their subject and qualifications to teach it, and they should have the command of a wide range of effective teaching and learning strategies to engage the young, no matter the field of learning. Above all though, they need dedication to their role as professional educators. Such teachers understand learners, their cultural and linguistic backgrounds, their needs, interests and abilities and their motivations and aspirations. And they use this understanding to assist their charges achieve to the best of their abilities. A great education rests on teachers who don't give up on students, even the most difficult ones.

All that said, outstanding teaching is informed by robust research. Teachers are no different from members of other professions in that their practice should be based on the weight of convincing research findings about *what works and why*. Evidence-informed practice is intrinsic to the work of medical specialists and it should be no different in the work of teachers. I illustrate this claim with another personal anecdote. I recently watched two cardiologists at work. They were discussing my *atrial fibrillation*, a condition where the electrical impulses governing the heartbeat in the upper, or atrial chambers in the heart, are quite irregular. The older cardiologist was briefing his younger colleague because I was being transferred as a patient to the latter on the imminent retirement of the former. With me present, they discussed the accumulated record of evidence in my case – the onset of the fibrillation, frequency of the changes in rhythm, data from 24-h heart monitoring, stress tests, echocardiographs, blood pressure checks, a score of graphic heart rate printouts, my body mass index over time and my personal accounts of how I had managed the condition for many years. They noted that there had been no change in the evidence for several years nor a change in the medication prescribed. They mined the data together in discussion about what my records were telling them, occasionally referring to me and how I felt. Once the younger doctor had exhausted his questions about the evidence, they discussed the treatment options available, including the medication I had been taking for some 7 years. They moved then to lay out the pros and cons of each optional treatment, citing research evidence on the effects of each option. At the end of this interchange, they recommended that my best course of action was to continue with the same treatment until the research evidence on one of the options, a procedure to adjust the heart's electrical currents, was producing much more reliable results than was the case at present. The other option, a pacemaker, though the research evidence was positive, was not judged to be necessary at my age and stage.

As I watched these two professionals at work, I was thinking that for a teacher, making decisions about what to do when a child is struggling to learn should always be based on evidence. Analysis of records about the child's learning and achievement is essential to understand what has been happening and why. Both are precursors to making judgements about what it would be best to do. In my view, there is no difference in the general process employed whether the professional is a cardiologist or a teacher. Both base their view of the patient or child on evidence, both seek explanations of why particular symptoms or behaviours are occurring and both use their professional knowledge to make judgements about strategies for maintenance or improvement.

The major message I want to convey on this, my second priority, is that quality teachers are fundamental to a great education. They should be vocationally committed; research-minded; they should use a wide range of evidence to better understand their students; they should exercise their professional judgement in the pursuit of improvements in teaching and learning; and ultimately, they should gain job satisfaction through the personal achievements of each and every learner.

Great Leaders

My third priority for a great education is quality school leaders. In saying this, I am not referring only to principals, although I see them as critical leaders of learning. Principals are the ones who are able to see what is occurring across the school because they have a different vantage point from that of their teachers. Great principals know how to connect what they do with the learning and achievement of their students. They do so by holding firmly to high expectations and the moral purpose of all educators, improving the lives of students through learning. They lead actively in coordinating the school's curriculum and in monitoring teaching, learning and student achievement. They encourage, facilitate and engage in the kinds of professional conversations that are focused on improvements in teaching and learning. They enable their teachers to gather and examine helpful evidence about their students so that diagnosis of problems on the basis of that evidence precedes improvement action. Principals also participate with their teachers as co-learners in the professional development activities so necessary to ensure that teaching is research informed. Notwithstanding these kinds of leadership actions by principals, it is essential that they recognise leadership in others. I believe that accepting responsibility and being accountable for what occurs in schools require a commitment to shared leadership. Principals should be the champions of this, making sure that they and their teachers share agreement on the school's vision and values, structures and strategies. When this occurs, leadership is distributed broadly and deeply in a school.

What I take from this priority is the fact that great leaders make great schools but only when they and their teachers pursue agreed goals in consistent ways with all accepting and taking leadership roles as the circumstances demand. Consonant with my first priority, leadership in the future should be extended as a matter of course, beyond the school into families and the wider community. When this point has been reached, a truly great educational environment will have been achieved.

Conclusion

You will notice in my set of three priorities that I have not mentioned the content or subject matter of a great education. This is not to say that the 'what' is not important but rather to emphasise that it is through knowledgeable, skilled and dedicated people and processes that a great education is possible. With great parents, great teachers and great leaders, the education of Australia's young will be in good hands.

Part V
Prelude: Concluding Comments

Alexandra Draxler writes from the perspective of her many years in the education section of UNESCO in Paris. Her emphasis here is on the wider purposes of education and the danger of seeing it too narrowly. '*It is not wrong either to attempt to track the effectiveness and the cost-effectiveness of educational efforts. However, the time-frames of education are long: their effects, good and bad, last a lifetime. The aims we have for education have to be just as expansive. Measuring immediate and short-term effects of schooling will give us only part of the picture.*

The rest of the picture is how education contributes to individuals' abilities to act purposefully and positively, to create, and interact within successive social entities and broader society'.

John Fien is passionate about sustainability and the social change processes that will be required for advancing sustainable development. His paper also appeals for a wider emphasis. '*Developing a vision of, and a commitment to, a vibrant civil society is core to education in a democracy, and this means helping students to develop criteria for determining what is best to conserve*'.

Edna Tait has had wide experience of education not only in New Zealand but also in the Pacific countries where she has played a major role. She notes the need for traditional skills but points out broader aspects. '*It now seems we need more than reading and writing. Sputnik 1 brought not only a concern for numeracy and science but also an expansion of literacy imperatives. We stopped being identified as packaged economic work units (farmer, bushman, wife, machinist, lawyer, nurse) and became individuals with new needs*'.

Raj Bhowon's search to help his country of Mauritius has taken him to many countries and broadened his outlook as he looked and sought ways to lift his country and its citizens out of poverty. '*Transformation will succeed only if we align the five organizational elements namely, capacity, stakeholders, culture, structure and systems. Information and Communication Technologies (ICT) have changed the learning environment*'. He sees the need for change but also the need to make plain why and where change needs to occur.

Philip Hallinger and Allan Walker – these two educators bring together unrivalled experience of a variety of settings from Australia and the USA to Thailand,

Hong Kong and China. Their emphasis here is strongly on the values we bring to our task but also our consistency in applying them. '*Explicit leadership actions can involve taking a stand on a program that the school will or will not adopt, or on what is defined as acceptable behavior of a student or teacher, or how instructional time will or will not be used*'.

Rupert Maclean has been one of the major forces behind this book, bringing his unrivalled international experience to the task. He has had a lifelong interest in addressing disadvantage in education, particularly in South East Asia. '*The enormous disparities between rich and poor are brought home graphically if one considers that it is estimated that 60 per cent of those living in the region* (Asia Pacific) *have never used a telephone, while at the same time millions of others can afford access to the latest computers and communications technologies in their own homes*'.

Rupert's career is based on his genuine concern to work effectively in this situation.

Chapter 32
A Humanistic Education

Alexandra Draxler

Why Do We Need a More Humanistic Education? And What Do Teachers Have to Do with It?

This chapter is a plea for doing the obvious: considering people as the most important ingredient of the quality of education.

Contemporary anxiety about quality of education seems to focus principally on its practical societal functions: preparing people to participate in the economy and educating people against dangers and behaviours that have negative societal consequences (violence, war, gender inequality, substance abuse and so on). Powerful sources of finance, whether they be international institutions, bilateral donors or national parliaments, scrutinize education policies for evidence that they contribute to economic growth. Many reforms address institutional structures and mechanisms, management rather than philosophy and material changes rather than people. Debates rage about financing, school choice, increased competition, standardized measurement, management information and techniques and especially about methods of organizing education that can be teacher-proof, notably through the use of technologies.

It is certainly not wrong to try to ensure that formal education provides practical skills for work and for citizenship. Although economic growth does not by itself lead to more inclusive societies, it has become a generally used, although contested, measure of human progress. Nevertheless, directly aiming to provide 'just-in-time' skills for the job market through the school system has not been demonstrated to be the most effective way overall, either to long-term economic growth or to more inclusive societies. Trust and cohesion are inversely related to inequality; schooling and education are major tools for tackling inequality (McPike, 2003).

A. Draxler (✉)
Independent Consultant, 12, rue Notre-Dame des, Champs, Paris 75006, France
e-mail: a.draxler@gmail.com

P. Hughes (ed.), *Achieving Quality Education for All*, Education in the Asia-Pacific Region: Issues, Concerns and Prospects 20, DOI 10.1007/978-94-007-5294-8_32, © Springer Science+Business Media Dordrecht 2013

It is not wrong either to attempt to track the effectiveness and the cost-effectiveness of educational efforts. However, the time frames of education are long: their effects, good and bad, last a lifetime. The aims we have for education have to be just as expansive. Measuring immediate and short-term effects of schooling will give us only part of the picture.

The rest of the picture is how education contributes to individuals' abilities to purposefully and positively act, create and interact within successive social entities and broader society. For that, I think it is essential to defend a humanistic vision of education that has as principles the discovery and development of individual competencies. Learning specific skills should accompany the acquisition of competencies for life that are based on understanding where we come from and what potentials we want to enhance. This type of education is firmly human centred and involves quality human interaction between teachers and learners.

How to define a humanistic education? It is inclusive, it is of quality, it is adaptable, it is people-centred and it promotes both individual excellence and social responsibility. How can one develop, system-wide, a humanistic education? I believe this can be done only by focusing on people. Can there be, as we are trying to discover through these chapters, an education system that works equally well for all citizens and that has guaranteed results? While that has to be the aim, all human endeavours and interactions include risk, and that there will be failures, both of the system and of individuals within the system. Education institutions need to be conceived and managed with the aim of reducing this risk for both individuals and groups and providing additional opportunities at each stage of the educational experience of learners.

However, '…schools do not exist in a vacuum. They cannot succeed in their civic mission without a supportive culture. The prevailing ideas of that larger culture, for better or for worse, seep through the bricks and mortar of their walls' (Schleicher, 2011).

Visions of education are rooted in philosophy and history much more than in science. The practice of teaching is based as much on each individual's lived experience as on learned techniques. While no education system, or even perhaps education institution, can fully fulfil the aims it sets for itself, it is fundamental principles that should govern and adjust educational experience. Observation and evidence can provide strong features for setting and correcting the course, but in the end most of successful education is based on human interaction. The fundamental and noble aim is to make this interaction as successful as it can be in each case.

Inclusive Education

Inclusiveness is the best antidote to prejudice, clannishness and intolerance. It is best caught, not taught, and demonstrated by practice at every level. Inclusive education is one that offers and guarantees for all access, second chance and response to special needs. Inclusive education is humanistic because it recognizes individual differences; it recognizes that not everyone brings the same tools and abilities to the learning experience. It recognizes the responsibility of quality education to recognize, analyse and take account of these differences. Above that it ensures an opportunity for each learner as well as recognizing that not all learners begin with the same tools and capacities. Inclusive education means of course availing all learners the opportunity to benefit from the public education on offer for the privileged. In most cases this will mean including children with special needs in 'mainstream' classrooms; in some special cases, it means making provision for extra learning opportunities with the help of trained specialists in addition to or partly separate from the mainstream. But inclusive education is more than that: it means an understanding on the part of education decision-makers of the tremendous value for all those involved in education, learners and children alike, of diversity. Inclusiveness promotes democratic values, trust, mutual understanding and empathy. It must permeate the legal system, the management techniques and processes, teacher training, school mapping, linguistic policy in multilingual environments, physical infrastructure, pedagogy and out-of-school activities.

The foundations of inclusiveness are rigour and history. Differences cannot be an excuse for abandoning demanding education. Making education demanding requires leadership, the ability to distinguish individual differences and persistence. Each learner has to be encouraged to make an effort according to her or his capacities, not being judged according to a uniform standard. This requires, again, patient and dedicated human interaction, with teachers who are committed and respected.

Nor can differences be accepted and understood properly if a strong grounding in history is not part of education. Embracing the richness of cultural, ethnic, religious and individual differences can happen only if we have some idea both of our differences and what unites us. It is in this sense also that education must be inclusive: inclusive of people and also inclusive of what has shaped humanity and our particular place in it.

However, inclusiveness is based not only in pedagogy and in approaches to individuals. Social inclusiveness means ensuring equality of opportunity to all, throughout institutions and throughout life. Inequality can be firmly laid at the door of schools' characteristics and the role and status of teachers,[1] and reducing inequality means focusing on people-centred solutions.

Adaptable Education

All good education is founded on the principle that one must use and understand the past in order to prepare for the future. However, this task was simpler in societies that were relatively homogeneous, with a more or less agreed historical narrative and a common national identity. Contemporary societies and nations are much more

---

[1] Even the impeccably credentialed right-wing thinkers, Gary Becker and Richard Posner observed recently on their blog that 'analysis of the PISA [Programme for International Student Assessment], results has revealed … that higher teacher salaries dominate small class size as a factor in high PISA scores. Another finding … is that private schools on average do not outperform public schools after adjusting for the quality of students upon entrance and that competition for students does not seem to improve average performance either' (February 2011).

heterogeneous ethnically and culturally. Education, therefore, has to be adaptable and contextualized. This means taking into account differences of identity and of learning styles and needs, providing for linguistic and ethnic minorities. It means ensuring real equality of opportunity. Finally, it means that schooling and learning have to incorporate diverse, sometimes conflicting, narratives about the past.

Education for Purpose, Responsibility and Community

Humanistic education focuses both on the individual and on the individual's roles and responsibilities in larger groups: family, community and society. It must negotiate and equilibrate tensions between continuity and change and between individual rights and individual responsibilities. While the development of a strong sense of identity is important, it is equally important to understand that each of us has multiple identities and that many of these overlap and unite us to others. Skilful classroom pedagogy should help children understand how identities evolve over time and how democratic processes favour recognition of needs emerging from these identities.

People-Centred Education

Education is principally based on human interaction. Even the most sophisticated distance education offerings and technology-based learning experiences use—and require—human interaction to be successful. Individual learning, successful as it can be, thrives best when human communication enriches, challenges, reinforces, validates and encourages what individuals do. In spite of many efforts over the years to bypass teachers in improving education, the intractable fact is that schools are only as good as their principals and teachers. In trying to reduce the element of human error, through rigid lesson plans, detailed instructions of what is expected, perversely, this results in teachers that become disempowered and less effective. The most important lesson from the OECD-led PISA experience and the resulting national scores is the benefit of 'investing in the preparation and development of high-quality teachers, while at the same time taking steps to elevate the status of the entire profession to a higher level of respect and regard'.[2] This is more important than class size, than infrastructure, than most management issues. Two other factors that strongly impact learning are also people-based: time of presence in the classroom (and therefore with teachers) and the quality and role of school principals. Moreover, a focus on learners shows that spending more per pupil on children (and adults) with greatest needs (due to poverty, special learning needs due to disabilities, contextual issues related to conflict, displacement and so on) is productive. Since research has amply shown that what children bring to school is as important in learning achievement as what they acquire there, acknowledging the centrality of parents' engagement in schooling is crucial.

Pitfalls and Practicalities

Naturally, a philosophy of education can only do so much to help solve the intractable problems, many of them unrelated to educational institutions, of reaching and including marginalized groups or individuals with particular needs who are not well served by typical educational institutions and offers. Education does not take place in a vacuum: poverty, geography, societal conflicts and many other external features impact the potential of individuals and groups to fully profit from mass education. Our contemporary world is marked by large population migrations. These are not the first in modern history, but they do pose unique linguistic, cultural and logistical problems for the organization of education. Models based on teaching to groups that are largely homogeneous ethnically or through rapid assimilation are no longer adapted to a contemporary world where strong identities are affirmed and held close.

My proposal is again a people-centred one: accept and strengthen public participation in decisions about education reform. Embrace and foster strong teachers' and community organizations. Allow for diversity, messy as that can be. Governments must ensure basic rights and allow for diverse paths to achieve them.

Conclusions

Experience and research have demonstrated the powerful, indispensable role of teachers and of school leadership in quality education. Material inputs are certainly essential: appropriate infrastructure, materials, community and government support and regulation. Equality of opportunity includes equality of access to resources and special measures for those with special needs. But none of these can guarantee a quality education if the teachers do not have motivation, training and respect.

The elephant in the room of these observations is of course financing. The major expenditure of formal education is on teachers. Education budgets all over the world are under threat, as financial crises make them easy targets, and ideology about choice and limiting government action get more and more traction. Building on examples of poor teaching and uncooperative teachers' organizations, the case is made that saving money on teachers' salaries and working conditions won't change much. And yet the opposite is true. The foundation of good learning is good teaching, and good teaching comes from teachers who are competent, motivated and recognized.

Where the state retreats in the name of choice and freedom, it is those with less information and fewer resources who end up with less of both choice and freedom. In turn, this contributes to societies that are less cohesive, more confrontational, more violent and ultimately also less creative both economically and scientifically.

It is alarming when in country after country voters democratically decide to slash budgets for teacher education and teachers' salaries in order to reduce or avoid raising taxes. The antidote is to mobilize energetic and widespread public discussion about and defence of quality education for all, supported and regulated by governments. Defence of humanistic, people-centred education has to come from collective and individual effort. This initiative by Phillip Hughes, who has dedicated his life to building and preserving quality, inclusive education, is an admirable contribution to such a defence.

References

McPike, E. (2003). *Education for democracy*. Washington, DC: Albert Shanker Institute.

Schleicher, A. (2011). "How the U.S. educational system looks to a leading expert abroad" by Justin Snider in the Hechinger Report, May 10.

Paine, S. L. & Schleicher, A. (2001). What the U.S. can learn from the world's most successful education reform efforts. Policy Paper: Lessons from PISS, McGraw-Hill research foundation. New York, USA

Chapter 33
Democracy and Pedagogy Count

John Fien

The famous law professor Lloyd L. Weinreb once reflected on his career teaching criminal law by analysing how he began his teaching at Harvard in 1965. He recalls that his first choice was to select the textbook for his course, and that he found it in 'a very fat book of more than 1400 pages' published in 1940 and still in its first edition. He justified his choice by noting that the book not only contained all the representative legislation but also 'an abundance of additional material: reports, essays, questions, problems, [etc.]' (Weinreg, 2009, p. 279).

He recalled that he still admires the book as 'the most intelligent, thorough, and interesting approach to the subject that was available' (p. 280), but, more than 40 years later, he was unsettled about the impacts of his use of the textbook on his students. There were two reasons for this. First, the textbook he chose represented the case method of teaching, which he described as good for learning 'what the law is' (i.e. precedents) but not for active enquiring into the normative issues around 'what the law ought to be' (p. 282). Second, and as a result, the textbook failed to address the interdisciplinary social, economic, political and cultural foundations of law and, hence, subliminally promoted a view of the law as a 'hermetically sealed' body of knowledge to be learnt rather than as a dynamic reflection of sources of power in society to be analysed and critiqued.

In these reflections, Weinreb was showing us the entwined *dualism* (not mutually exclusive *duality*) of education and democracy – and the consequent politicisation of the curriculum that flows from the choices of pedagogy, textbooks and assessment methods, etc., that we make. He noted, of course, that he did not fully perceive the political agenda of his choice of textbook at the time. Indeed, he argued that 'It never occurred to teachers at that time ... to explain the intellectual premises of their

J. Fien (✉)
Professor of Sustainability, Innovation and Leadership Program,
RMIT University, GPO Box 2476, Swanston Street,
Melbourne 3001, Australia
e-mail: john.fien@rmit.edu.au

P. Hughes (ed.), *Achieving Quality Education for All*, Education in the Asia-Pacific
Region: Issues, Concerns and Prospects 20, DOI 10.1007/978-94-007-5294-8_33,
© Springer Science+Business Media Dordrecht 2013

pedagogy', and that teachers 'would mostly have disclaimed' any overt or even hidden political or social agenda in their work.

Professors and teachers do not have the luxury of such naivety today. We are very aware of the impacts of globalisation and its ideological 'sister', neoliberalism, and their impacts on increasing global and national inequalities. And, as teachers, we live daily with the economic steerage of education and the resulting narrowing of the curriculum through inappropriate emphases on 'the basics', standards and national testing. We have no excuse for not knowing that education is political.[1] As Shaull (1970, p. 15) argued in his *Foreword* to Frieire's *The Pedagogy of the Oppressed*:

> There is no such thing as a neutral educational process. Education either functions as an instrument which is used to facilitate the integration of the younger generation into the logic and practice of the present system and being about conformity to it, or it becomes the 'practice of freedom', the means by which men and women deal critically and creatively with reality and discover how to participate in the transformation of their world. The development of an educational methodology that facilitates this process will inevitably lead to tension and conflict within our society. But it could also contribute to the formation of the new person and mark the beginning of a new era in Western history.

Or as Tyler asked in his *Basic Principles of Curriculum and Instruction* in 1949:

> Should the schools develop young people to fit into present society as it is, or does the school have a revolutionary mission to develop young people who will seek to improve society? (p. 35)

The answer to this question is, of course, 'both'. Developing a vision of, and a commitment to, a vibrant civil society is core to education in a democracy, and this means helping students to develop criteria for determining what is best to conserve in their cultural, economic and natural heritage, as well as to discern values and strategies for addressing national and global concerns. Recognising this democratic basis of education is not indoctrination. Nor does it involve encouraging students to adopt only one view of what society could be like or undermine their capacities for independent, critical thinking. Rather, emphasising democracy in education encourages teachers and students to engage in a 'shared speculation' about possible and alternative futures and 'reflectively construct and reconstruct' their visions of the future (Huckle, 1991, p. 61).

This is where pedagogy and democracy come together. Pedagogy involves more than the traditional concept of teaching and learning strategies; pedagogy includes the teacher's visions of what education is for and how society might be. Whatever curriculum themes and topics are adopted, or whatever curriculum structures are established, the teacher's beliefs and attitudes, together with the teaching strategies chosen, significantly affect the nature of students' learning experiences and the objectives achieved. Such choices and attitudes determine whether or not education reproduces the existing social and cultural mores or contribute to empowering students for participation in civil society.

---

[1] See the timeline flow chart of the development of this way of thinking about education at URL: http://www.21stCenturySchools.com/Philosophical_Foundations_Flow_Chart.htm

This Deweyian or reconstructionist tradition in education provides for learning experiences in which students analyse alternative positions on important social, economic and environmental issues. However, contrary to the seemingly fair-minded approach which would tend to treat all positions equally, irrespective of issues of power and influence, teachers seeking to enact a democratic pedagogy would be mindful that balanced *teaching* might not necessarily result in balanced *learning* if certain positions are more privileged than others in public discourse. Thus, a democratic education requires teachers to invite students to analyse alternative positions on these issues within a set of fundamental questions about power and social reproduction in both public policy and personal decision-making. Thus, it would replace values relativity with invitations and guidance for students to:

- Identify and challenge the assumptions in all positions on sustainable development
- Imagine, explore and critique alternatives of their own
- Question the influence of context and the social interests served by all positions
- Use the values of ecological sustainability, social justice and democracy as criteria in the evaluation of all positions
- Adopt a reflective scepticism to their own and other people's ideas and actions

Such a democratic framework for pedagogy can help educate for a body politic comprised of 'people able to act to maintain the best of what we have, to challenge the unsustainable, and to build the desirable' (Hoepper, 1993, p. 36). Continuing the sustainability example, Huckle (1991) describes a democratic approach to education, which displays a commitment both to democratic values and to professionally ethical ways of dealing with facts and issues. He describes this approach to education as:

> ... a shared speculation with pupils on those forms of technology and social organization which can enable people to live in harmony with one another and with the natural world. It should be a form of social education cast in ... the liberatory mould. This seeks to empower pupils so that they can democratically transform society. It does this by encouraging them to reflect on their experience in the light of critical theory and to act on the insights gained. It is a form of praxis ... which by allowing pupils and teachers to reflectively construct and reconstruct their social world, develops the critical and active citizens who are capable of bringing about the transition to sustainable development. (p. 61)

A simple but very effective model of democratic pedagogy has been developed by Jensen and others from working in classrooms in Denmark (as well as in the Czech Republic, Portugal and Australia) to develop a flexible approach to empowering students through social analysis and community action. The approach is called 'IVAC' which is an acronym for the four interchangeable and cyclic steps of '*I*nvestigation, *V*ision, *A*ction and (evaluate for) *C*hange'. The series of guiding questions which has been developed with the teachers – and from their practice – to guide an IVAC enquiry is illustrated in Fig. 33.1.

It should be noted, however, that the steps in Fig. 33.1 are not seen as either comprehensive or fixed, but rather as open to change (as represented by the blank spaces next to some dot points). Similarly, the model does not represent a linear

1. **Investigation** of a Question, Issue or Problem
   - What is the question, issue or problem?
   - What is its significance to us both now and in the future?
   - Who is being advantaged and who disadvantaged?
   - What were things like before, and how/why have they changed?
   - What do we see as the root causes of the question, issue or problem?
   - What influences do personal life styles and living conditions play in these root causes?
   - How do other people interpret the causes and effects?
   - How open to change and alternatives are we/others?

2. Development of **Visions**
   - What alternatives are imaginable?
   - How have people in other times, places and cultures thought about this question, issue or problem?
   - What alternatives do we prefer and why?
   - What critiria can be used to evaluate alternative visions?
   - Who would gain and who would lose if different alternatives were implemented?
   - What is our preferred vision?

3. Planning and Taking **Action**
   - What sort of changes will bring us closer to our visions, especially our preferred vision - changes within ourselves, in the classroom, and in society?
   - What action possibilities exist for realising these changes?
   - What barriers might prevent carrying out these actions?
   - What barriers might prevent actions from resulting in the desired changes?
   - What actions will we initiate?
   - How will we do them?
   - What skills do we have that will assist us in these actions?
   - What other skills might we need? Where can we learn them?
   - What other persons and groups could help us with our actions? How could we enlist their support and encourage coalitions of mutual benefit?
   - How can we best deal with possible conflict and help neutralise opposition?

4. **Evaluate** for Change
   - What sort of changes will we look for when evaluating changes within ourselves, in the classroom, and in society?
   - How can our actions and these changes be monitored?
   - What criteria could be used to evaluate our actions and these changes?
   - What should we do as a result of the evaluation?

Fig. 33.1 IVAC-based enquiry (After Jensen, 1995)

process but one in which some steps may be returned to during the learning experience. Thus, Jensen states that 'instead of looking at the boxes and the questions as goals to be worked on in a set order, the process can be described as a circle, or spiral perhaps, where one keeps going back to points several times in order to further elaborate on them' (Jensen, 1995, p.168).

Especially significant in democratic pedagogy is the potential to help students acquire and value the skills to be fully active in society. As Starr (1991) notes such an approach to teaching would mean:

> ... a lot of heavy traffic between schools and their communities. It means participatory decision making. It means getting involved with learning projects that can have political and tangible outcomes. It means learning critical powers of analysis, of working collectively, of critical reflection, 'problem-posing' and of having power in the learning situation. (p. 23)

And, surely, isn't this what education should be all about?

Extending the sense of community from the local to the global is an important dimension of democratic education. This may involve understanding manifestations of globalisation in the local community (through what Ira Shor (1980) calls 'extraordinarily re-experiencing the ordinary') and critically analysing the consequences of personal choices and local community practices in global patterns of social and ecological sustainability (or the lack thereof). This could involve the investigation of the reasons, dimensions, directions and impacts of flows of goods and services and the development of small-scale alternatives and locally relevant alternatives to them.

In such a democratic approach to education, we may be able to stand with those whom Orr (1992) has described as having refused to 'stand aloof from the decisions about how and whether life will be lived in the twenty-first century' (p. 145) and say with Kirk (1977) that our work has contributed to the task of education as:

> ... the catalyst that not only saves the human race from extinction, but (which) also ... serves to unite all the people of the world in a common effort to find solutions to the perplexing and difficult problems that threaten life on the planet. (p. 350)

References

Hoepper, B. (1993). Seeking global citizens in the history classroom. In D. Dufty & H. Dufty (Eds.), *We sing of a world reshaped: Readings and reflections on global citizenship* (pp. 35–37). Brisbane, Australia: Social Education Association of Australia.

Huckle, J. (1991). Education for sustainability: Assessing pathways to the future. *Australian Journal of Environmental Education, 7*, 49–69.

Jensen, B. B. (1995). Concepts and models in a democratic health education. In B. B. Jensen (Ed.), *Research in environmental and health education* (pp. 151–169). Copenhagen, Denmark: Research Centre for Environmental and Health Education, Royal Danish School of Educational Studies.

Kirk, J. J. (1977). The quantum theory of EE. In *Current issues in EE – III*. North American Association for Environmental Education, pp. 29–35. Washington: DC.

Orr, D. (1992). *Ecological literacy: Education and the transition to a postmodern world*. Albany, NY: State University of New York Press.

Shaull, R. A. (1970). Foreword. In P. Freire (Ed.), *The pedagogy of the oppressed*. New York: Seabury Press.

Shor, I. (1980). *Critical teaching and everyday life*. Boston: South End Press.
Starr, K. (1991). What is social justice? *Curriculum Perspectives-Newsletter Edition, 11*(3), 20–24.
Tyler, R. W. (1949). *Basic principles of curriculum and instruction*. Chicago: University of Chicago Press.
Weinreg, L. L. (2009). Teaching criminal law. *Ohio State Journal of Criminal Law, 7,* 279–291.

Chapter 34
Literacy Ain't Everything

Edna Tait

> *Cogito, ergo sum: literacy is not enough for high quality,*
> *relevant and effective education for the future*

Over the centuries, many aspects of life have improved. With work, homes, health care, transport, communication, justice and political systems, people may now live safer and more interesting lives. Even recreation offers new possibilities. People who can throw, hit or catch a ball well, hold a tune or pretend in front of a camera are now able to earn more than their doctors, teachers or local police. The launch of Sputnik 1 in 1957 is a useful marker for many of the improvements. With the space age came concern for rights, including those of women, children, indigenous peoples and animals and, more recently, teachers and police on the streets. The space age saw organ transplants and better control of the spread of infectious diseases. The space age brought the microchip and a communication revolution. To live in the twenty-first century is to enjoy many possibilities for a good life. Schools may be praised for their contribution to some of these riches.

However, in this space age, all is not well. It is marked by increased military production and powers, depletion of natural resources, degradation of the environment, decreased opportunities for paid employment and a rise in terrorism. We have had 50 major violent conflicts and 5 recognised holocausts since 1945. The world still has people living with the same levels of illiteracy, poverty and pain as their ancestors did centuries ago. It is estimated that worldwide one in four adults cannot read or write while as many as 40% of developed nations' adults do not have the literacy skills needed to benefit from the opportunities of the space age. It is also estimated that worldwide, one in seven people is hungry. We have approximately one billion people starving, more than the total world population in 1800. In too

E. Tait (✉)
Education Advisor, New Zealand National Commission for UNESCO,
20 Wolfe Street, Regent, Whangarei 0112, New Zealand
e-mail: ednatait@xtra.co.nz

P. Hughes (ed.), *Achieving Quality Education for All*, Education in the Asia-Pacific
Region: Issues, Concerns and Prospects 20, DOI 10.1007/978-94-007-5294-8_34,
© Springer Science+Business Media Dordrecht 2013

many developing countries, people lack food, water and medicines. In the so-called developed world, those horrors are paralleled, in opposition, by obesity, alcoholism and drug addiction. It seems life may have improved for some, but it is still difficult for too many. Schools have been unable to help these people.

Who can guess what the world will be like in another 50 years? What will be the riches and inequities of 2061? How do schools prepare learners to live in, and contribute to, an unknowable future, as peaceful and productive citizens rather than as one of those who harm people and the planet? Answers might be found in different school organisation and teaching styles or increased family participation. Perhaps more emphasis on a love of learning or respect for others or caring for the environment would be useful?

For centuries, we thought we knew what to do. Until the nineteenth century, the world carried on with most people not schooled at all, and although life for most was hard and short, that was expected and accepted. Then along came the industrial revolution. The invention of factory and agricultural machines required literate workers not only for the new machinery but also, and especially, for the management of its products. So, many countries in the 1870s set up national systems of primary schooling and emphasised basic reading and writing for work. This certainty about literacy continued into the twentieth century. Even in the late 1950s, the school's message was still 'learn to read and get a good job'. Of course, then, jobs were available for all. By this time, many learners had access to secondary schools. Here they were streamed with literacy tests and then taught according to the school's perception of their ability and probable work as an adult. The drive for literacy improved many lives but for most, although it was a little longer than their ancestors, life was, and is, still hard.

It is important that schools continue to teach the skills of reading and writing. All people and all nations need literacy. It helps us to express feelings and intentions and enables us to create the magic of literature, explore the promises of the sciences and examine the challenges of philosophy. It helps us to look for better laws and medical care, improved food supplies, more secure buildings, safer transport and, possibly, how to use communication technology to find information or friends. Literacy provides and protects so much that is good in life. For many, literacy enables escape from the poverty of body, spirit and mind and, we are told, it brings peace and development to nations.

However, literacy has also brought us paparazzi, libel, internet scams, cell phone bullying and white-collar crime. Generally, no pun intended, it's literates who take us into wars. Here's the problem and it's a paradox: although many of those who commit crime have literacy problems, most illiterates do not become criminals. They live quiet, decent and sometimes difficult lives, and we hear nothing of them. Instead, most of the worst crimes against people have been, and are still being, committed by those who are literate. Literacy, therefore, ain't everything if we want relevant and effective schooling for a better future.

Further, it now seems we need more than reading and writing. Sputnik 1 brought not only a concern for numeracy and science but also an expansion of literacy imperatives. We stopped being identified as packaged economic work units (farmer, bushman, wife, machinist, lawyer, nurse) and became individuals with new needs. In the space age, it turned out that we needed not work literacy or basic literacy but *functional* literacy to read road maps, the instructions for completing forms and the directions on medicine bottles. The space age also brought the microchip and so we needed *technological* literacy. Then came concerns about dwindling oil resources and problems of waste management, and we needed *environmental* literacy. In troubled economic times, *financial* literacy is added to the list. The space age brought a meteoric burst of change to the concept of literacy, and today, it seems we need *multiple* literacies instead of just reading and writing for work.

Schools face another problem with literacy. It is being complicated by new communication methods. Cell phone texting, email brevities and television advertising are changing the symbols of literacy. We are witnessing the death of vowels, punctuation and grammar, and, consequently, we are losing not only best language use but also and ironically clarity of meaning, universal uniformity with the printed word and possibilities for schooling, the very things Gutenberg's printing press made possible. Somehow, the romance and single person intent of 'I love you also' seem to be lost in 'i luv u 2', but this may be the literacy of the future. Should, therefore, schools try to provide all of these literacies and literacy symbols for the adults of 2061? Will such skills be of any use in the future to maintain the best we have and decrease the problems we confront?

Schooling is often a scramble for all kinds of knowledge. This approach reflects the claim that we live in a knowledge society. We do not. We live in a world filled with information that communication technology brings into a rapidly increasing number of cities and homes. The world is e-mailed, Internetted, Facebooked, My Spaced, Twittered, YouTubed, Skyped and otherwise entangled with information networks. Only some of this information requires high levels of literacy. Only some of this information is reliable, safe or helpful. We need more than literacy to guide us through these webs of viscid so-called knowledge.

The way forward is to remember that literacy, of any kind, ain't everything. Literacy is only a tool. It contains no sense of what we ought or ought not to do, what we can or cannot do. The challenge for schools is not whether learners have this or that sort of literacy, or how well they read. It's what learners and adults do with their reading that matters. This is not about teaching law because, although important, laws are human constructions and change with the views of those in power. Nor is it about teaching logic. Logic is also important, but we can plan quite logically harmful actions. Further, this is not a proposal that schools teach more ethics. Although the poverty and violence in the world show that a sense of right and wrong will remain a need for all in the future, the cultural and religious complexities of morality are still beyond any universal application in schools.

Instead, the best thing schools can do is to teach learners what to do with the products of their literacy tool. We might call this a critical analysis of information or, more simply, better thinking. Schools have always taught thinking, but the new emphasis would be on deeper, broader, more vigorous thinking. This teaching can be justified easily with explanations of human dignity and civic utility, and quality schooling will recognise both as imperatives for citizens of the future. Of course, all people think but many are unaware that their information processing is inadequate. The result is that the limits of their thinking are the limits of their world. Cogito, ergo sum is actually: *as* I think *so* I am.

This call for increased thinking skills is not a call for great minds only. We must, of course, continue to produce people such as Archimedes, Aristotle, the Curies, Goethe, Beethoven, Florence Nightingale, Jenner, Bell, Shakespeare, Wright brothers … and more. We note, incidentally, that they gave so much to the world without technological, environmental or any of the new literacies of today, and this reminds us again that literacy ain't everything. The great minds of the past did more than just read. They 'read' the right or best thing to do and turned information into something useful or creative. The future will continue to need such people, but, to enjoy the gifts of great minds, the citizens of 2061 will need better thinking in their everyday lives.

Here a caveat must be noted. Thinking ain't everything either. We all know that the silence of good people supports the harm in the world. We generally believe that actions speak louder than words as did Eliza Doolittle who begged: 'Don't talk of love, show me!' As with literacy, it is what we do with our thinking that matters. Nonetheless, vigorous thinking is a necessary, if not sufficient, teaching goal for a better future.

Is it possible to teach vigorous thinking? Yes, it is and here's the irony: it has to begin with some basic literacy. Literacy may not be *everything,* but it is *something*. As most flowers depend on spring, so best thinking depends on literacy. All learners, regardless of their intellectual, physical and emotional abilities, need some literacy to develop thinking skills and even as they begin to gain literacy, they can learn to examine its products critically. They should, at least, learn to ask about the accuracy of information and the positive and negative, short- and long-term consequences of its use. Learners can be taught the skills of questioning, examining sources and looking for assumptions, contradictions, similarities, differences and possible unintended side effects. Learners can be taught to be comprehensive in their checking and information-inclusive in their processing. Learners can be taught to be deeper, broader and more vigorous thinkers.

So, literacy is something but it is not everything. If today's children are to live in 2061 with wellbeing and safety, the world must have more than literacy. High-quality, relevant and effective schooling for the future will develop as many literate *and* critical analysts of information as possible. Although the world's problems may not disappear even if most people are critical thinkers, those problems will not be resolved if thinking skills do not improve. People need to be able to think critically. All nations need critical thinkers. The vision is that one day, and without qualification, people may say 'Sum, ergo cogito'. I am, therefore, I think.

Chapter 35
A World-Class Education for Mauritius in the Twenty-First Century

Rajesh Bhowon

This article has been inspired by the statements made by Professor Phillip Hughes, Head of the Centre of Education at the University of Tasmania in a UNESCO Study entitled "Futures and Education" (1983). This document has been seminal as I used many ideas from it in my doctoral study under his supervision. This international study has been used extensively by me as Director of Education in Mauritius and as Education Specialist at the World Bank and the International Financial Corporation in Washington DC and as Parliamentarian in the National Assembly of Mauritius.

The inspiration emerges from the UNESCO Study "Education acts as the inheritor and communicator of what is valuable in our culture, largely in terms of the creation of the past… it is from the past that we can discern what is enduring about human values… even as we acknowledge the importance of the future … a recognition of the limits of the possibilities in the areas of human interest and a determination to utilize the possibilities for the enhancement for the value of life" (Hughes, 1983).

The Mauritian Minister of Education at the inauguration of Brian Caldwell's Workshop in Mauritius in 2007 on "Re-imagining School Leadership towards Quality Education for All in Mauritius" within the context of the International Networking on Educational Transformation (iNet) said that:

> We cannot reinvent the wheel, but we can certainly make it travel along well-surfaced and time-tested roads. Hence international good practices have informed a number of reform projects in Mauritius, albeit those practices have been suitably indigenised to suit the local context. In some cases, obviously, we have had to chart completely new grounds for the sake of offering learning opportunities to those who would otherwise have been irretrievably lost.

R. Bhowon (✉)
Member of Parliament in Mauritius, Equal Opportunities Commission,
Prime Minister's Office, Mauritius, 1st floor, Belmont House,
Intendance Street, Port Louis, Mauritius
e-mail: rbhowon@hotmail.com

P. Hughes (ed.), *Achieving Quality Education for All*, Education in the Asia-Pacific Region: Issues, Concerns and Prospects 20, DOI 10.1007/978-94-007-5294-8_35,
© Springer Science+Business Media Dordrecht 2013

Mauritius is a small island state struggling to reinvent itself. It has to make difficult choices for its survival in a variety of complex areas: technological development to create a world-class educational system and a knowledge hub, ecological conservation and resource depletion in the context of an additional one million overseas tourists arriving in Mauritius, food security, social justice and world peace. Continued improvement requires a relentless coherent strategic approach and a framework for sustained development. Standards, accountability, innovation and system-wide excellence in student learning should be attainable at reasonable cost using differing strategies including the virtual media to reach the maximum number of students. Education should also help to cultivate truthful citizens, with a strong emphasis on professionalism and teachers to be models of global citizens, while respecting the traditional teaching-learning, respecting past success and fostering sustainable development. Transformation will succeed only if we align the five organisational elements, namely, capacity, stakeholders, culture, structure and systems. Information and Communication Technologies (ICT) have changed the learning environment. There need to be ways of integrating the cultural dimension directed towards peace, social justice and creating sensitivity. It is the firm intention of government to go beyond access, equity, quality and relevance to a new educational architecture that would change the piecemeal approach to a broad-based, comprehensive, holistic and interdependent strategy to cut across all levels of education.

The educational system of Mauritius has strong two-century old roots in the British system. Through the passage of time, it has continued to depend on developments in Britain with inputs from United Nations agencies like UNESCO, UNICEF, United Nations Development Programme and with the rest of the world through multilateral and bilateral relations. Its relationships with the World Bank and the International Monetary Fund and the Francophonie are considered essential. Two major public examinations, Cambridge School Certificate and Cambridge Higher School Certificate have been conducted by the Cambridge University Syndicate for over a century. The nation at large has the firm conviction of the role played so far by the Cambridge University in creating a platform for social justice, fairness and excellence in education.

The Mauritian educational system is linked to the British system through history and geography. After independence in 1968, the Mauritius Constitution handed over to us from Britain provides us with the constitutional framework within which Mauritius, an independent sovereign state, has to operate. In fact, the Constitution requires that nobody is barred from access to school irrespective of the child's socio-economic background or denomination. The Education Act, designed by R. L. Butler, the then Minister of Education in England, was handed over to Mauritius. It was intended to provide an education "according to age, ability and aptitude of the child". The Act further stipulates that English is the official language of the country and that the English language will be further developed. It has been found useful to look at ways in which this nation has managed to maintain and nurture its welfare state that put its people first and that the future potential of the country requires the full potential of the youth and the investment in youth through access and opportunity to education. It is considered legitimate that all those who make the grade at secondary level have the right to proceed to tertiary education. The government has created the Tertiary Education Ministerial Portfolio to focus on the tertiary sector and the reorganisation of the two universities and the creation of two more universities with the framework of the creation of a knowledge hub to serve the Sub-Saharan region. All these developments require heavy investments despite the difficult national and international economic context.

In line with its welfare policies, government has earmarked its largest share in the budget devoted to education and health which are considered the pivot for all developments. The appropriate conditions are created to provide equitable learning opportunities to all so as to acquire the necessary skills, knowledge and capabilities of learners who will be able to cope with future challenges and initiate developmental changes that will lead to the retransformation of our multicultural society. Government has to reckon with the fact that most of the children at school will be working in many countries across the globe and that the education provided should be flexible and adaptable. In order to celebrate the Year of Technology in 2007, the Minister of Education proclaimed school transformation with the support of a wide range of ICTs to allow greater access to resources. These resources were intended to develop a global network of students whose voices would be heard and networking on programmes on school leadership, research networks, personalising learning for students, a range of online and real-world support for rapid dissemination of best practice and pushing the boundaries to develop new ways of transferring knowledge and experience for the benefit of all students. A significant achievement has been the creation of the digital library at the Head office which is in the process of being linked to schools. The implementation of the state-of-the-art network infrastructure is critical for organising and sustaining online conferences and dissemination good practice nationwide.

Brian Caldwell and "The New Enterprise Logic of Schools"

Experience around the world in nations where transformation has occurred suggests a "new enterprise logic" that is shaping the way a school is organised and operated. This concept was coined by Zuboff and Maxim (2004) and unfurled by them at the iNet Conference at Boston College in 2007 and by Brian Caldwell in Mauritius and around the world. This concept adapted to schools show six elements which are of relevance to Mauritius and their application is underway. These are (a) the student is the most important unit of the organisation, not the classroom, not the school, and not the school system; (b) schools cannot achieve expectations for transformation by acting alone or operating in a line of support from the centre of a schools system to the level of the school, classroom or student. The success of a school depends on its capacity to join networks to share knowledge, address problems and pool resources; (c) leadership is distributed across schools in networks as well as within schools, across programmes of learning and teaching and the support of teaching and learning. Synergies do not just happen of their own accord. Personnel and other resources are allocated to energise and sustain them; (d) networks involve a range of local, national and international institutions, public and private sectors in educational and noneducational settings; (e) new approaches to resource allocation are required to take account of developments in the personalising of learning and the networking of expertise and support and (f) significant, systematic and sustained change that secures high levels of success for all students in all settings require coherence among the strategies at school and the alignment of various forms of capital, namely, intellectual, social, financial, spiritual, ecological within a framework of good governance (Caldwell, 2007).

In the final analysis, the success of any educational enterprise, including coping with the future, depends on the response at the school level. What happens with and for students is the final reality rather than decisions made at other levels. If education is to prepare young people adequately for the future, the genuine participation of the educational community of each school is a necessary condition. In Mauritius, it is mandatory that every school should have a Parents' Teachers Association (PTA).

SSAT and iNet

At the inauguration of the setting up of iNet, an arm of the SSAT, in July 2006, the Prime Minister of Mauritius said that "We are a centre of excellence where we strive for perfection with a pure heart and beauty of action with the determination to serve the country and pave the way for it to shine at the international platform". On the eve of this inauguration, Elizabeth Reid, the Chief Executive of the SSAT signed a Memorandum of Understanding with the Minister of Education of Mauritius for the block affiliation of all schools and tertiary institutions in Mauritius, Rodrigues and the Agalega Islands to the iNet an arm of the SSAT based in London. This is a unique event in education for out of the 30 countries and 400 schools in England affiliated to SSAT, Mauritius is the only one where all educational institutions are affiliated to the iNet. This was necessary to internationalise our educational system and to position ourselves on the global launch pad to make a global citizen out of every Mauritian child. Since this vision has been translated into activities where the students share and participate in community activities together with the PTA as responsible citizens by opening the doors of their school to the world and to learn to live as one people and as one nation in peace, justice and liberty. In 2007, the visit of ten distinguished heads of schools from England under the iNet programme visited the schools in Mauritius and found out that schools were excellent and that with iNet their doors will be opened to the rest of the world. Professor Brian Caldwell and Associate Director of the SSAT/iNet conducted six workshops for all heads of schools of primary and secondary schools on the theme "Re-imagining school leadership".

iNet is a fantastic gift to children around the world. It is an initiative for schools by schools by a London-based Specialist Schools and Academies Trust (SSAT) that provides an opportunity achieving systematic change in all settings. It is a global web-enabling playing field with ICT linking the Mauritius Cyber-Island sharing same ideas without regard to geography, distance or language. It is aligning the best practices. Some 4,000 schools in England alone and some 30 countries are a part of the SSAT/iNet. This institution set up by Prime Minister Tony Blair is being extended worldwide and represented an extraordinary platform for tapping an expertise in managing schools especially in the domain of leadership and the sharing of knowledge about a world-class education in a changing society. This institution has already demonstrated excellence in achievements in all settings. It is the largest network of schools. It is building up powerful, innovative and sustainable networks of schools underpinned by new technologies introduced in all schools in Mauritius. It has also provided an opportunity to review the curriculum to ensure the relevance of subjects taught in the light of changes occurring across the globe. It has also taken into consideration the functionality of the domains of human development by taking into consideration the multicultural aspect of the society and the ways of integrating culture with the teaching-learning transaction.

References

Caldwell, B. (2007). Foreword: Jousting for the new generation. In *Jousting for the new generation: Challenges to contemporary schooling*. Melbourne, Australia: ACER (Australian Council for Educational Research Press).
Hughes, P. (1983). *Futures and education – UNESCO study*. Hobart, Australia: University of Tasmania, Centre for Education.

Chapter 36
Values: The Core of Successful School Leadership

Philip Hallinger and Allan Walker

> *I am firm in my belief that a teacher lives on and on through his students. I will live on if my teaching is inspirational, good, and stands firm for good values. Good teaching is forever and the teacher is immortal. (Stuart, 1949)*

Jesse Stuart was a teacher and international educator whose career spanned, defined, and reflects the American twentieth century education experience. Jesse Stuart's career as an educator began as a 16-year-old teacher in a one-room school house in the mountains of Eastern Kentucky in the 1930s. He went on to become a school principal and superintendent as well as an important writer. We wish to suggest that Phil Hughes' remarkably broad experience as an educator helped to define the experience and evolution of education in Australia in many of the same ways as Jesse Stuart's did for the USA (Beare, 2007). Phil Hughes taught leaders, mentored leaders, and was a leader in every sense of the word.

Working to change the lives of their students under the most difficult conditions, Hughes and Stuart believed that values were at the core of good teaching and successful leadership. As Fien (2007) wrote of Hughes, "The importance of values in educating for a better, fairer, and less troubled world is central to the work of Hughes" (p. 197). Both shared the values of hard work, caring, self-discipline, trust,

---

Portions of this chapter appeared in Hallinger, P. (2011). Leadership for learning: Lessons from 40 years of empirical research. *Journal of Educational Administration, 49*(2), 125–142.

P. Hallinger (✉)
The Joseph Lau Luen Hung Charitable Trust Asia Pacific Centre
for Leadership and Change, The Hong Kong Institute of Education,
10 Lo Ping Road, Tai Po, New Territories, Hong Kong, China
e-mail: hallinger@gmail.com

A. Walker
Department of Education Policy and Leadership, The Hong Kong Institute
of Education (HKIEd), 10 Lo Ping Road, Tai Po, New Territories,
Hong Kong, China
e-mail: adwalker@ied.edu.hk

P. Hughes (ed.), *Achieving Quality Education for All*, Education in the Asia-Pacific
Region: Issues, Concerns and Prospects 20, DOI 10.1007/978-94-007-5294-8_36,
© Springer Science+Business Media Dordrecht 2013

results, sacrifice, and mutual respect. Likewise, they both articulated and modeled their values through the lives they lived as education leaders in their respective societies. Hughes (2004) asserted that, "The study of teaching, like teaching itself, should include humanity and warmth" (p. 6). Sharing a similar perspective, Stuart entitled one of his later books on education, *To Teach, To Love* (Stuart, 1987).

We take both Phil Hughes and Jesse Stuart as inspiration for this chapter which reflects on the role of values in successful school leadership. The chapter begins with a brief presentation of a values-based conceptual model that has guided our own work over the past several decades. Then we elaborate on how values underlie successful school leadership.

Values Leadership

The leadership model portrayed in Fig. 36.1 is a values-based leadership framework. In the words of McCrimmon (2004, p. 1):

> I refer to Kouzes and Posner's theory as values leadership, because asking people to undertake a risky journey with you depends on your credibility, as they rightly argue, which in turn depends on what you stand for as a person – your values. Moreover, the changes advocated by such leaders generally entail a shift in cultural or personal values (Kouzes and Posner's, 2007).

The model of school leadership shown in Fig. 36.1 shares a similar normative assumption. It conceptualizes leadership as explicitly aimed at the improvement of student learning (i.e., the model presumes a focus on improvement in learning *should* be the aim or goal). A decade ago, Ronald Wolk (2000, no page), the founder of *Education Week,* stated, "What we need more than anything else today are principals who are asking hard questions about what it is we want from our schools,

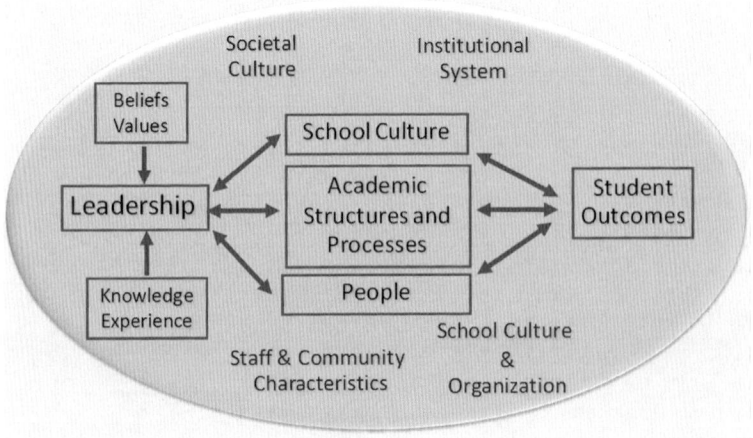

Fig. 36.1 A model of leadership for learning

what it is we want from our students and how we get it." When he said, "what we want from our schools and students," Wolk was referring to the principal's role in defining and prioritizing the school's "terminal values" (e.g., learning growth, academic achievement, social development, virtue, community service, equity in learning). "How we get it" refers to the "instrumental values" that leaders manifest and nurture to achieve shared goals (e.g., self-discipline, integrity, fairness, caring, mutual respect, risk taking, interdependence). Every school has a mix of values that shape the day-to-day behavior of principals, teachers, and students regardless of whether leaders are aware of or seek to impact them (Barth, 1990; Deal & Peterson, 1999; Saphier & King, 1985).

Indeed, this perspective is not meant to suggest that principals "dictate" the values that guide the school. New principals entering a school must begin by taking the time to understand values that already predominate in the corporate culture and the extent to which they are creating a healthy productive learning culture (Deal & Peterson, 1999; Saphier & King, 1985). Principals may choose to subtly or, at their own risk, dramatically introduce changes into the value mix of the schools. Dramatic changes in core values are, however, generally reserved for crisis or turnaround situations, and even then school cultures demonstrate a surprising ability to return to the "norm" after overt pressure is removed (Deal & Peterson).

Principals also act as "gatekeepers" monitoring and managing the introduction of new values as they are introduced into the school (Hall & Hord, 2002). Saphier and King (1985) highlighted this role of the principal as values leader, stating that principals are responsible for "protecting what's important." Implicitly, "what's important" refers to the school's values. The principal acts in this role more explicitly through decisions made on a day-to-day basis concerning, for example, resource allocation, staffing, problem finding, and problem resolution (Dwyer, 1985). Explicit leadership actions can involve taking a stand on a program that the school will or will not adopt, or on what is defined as acceptable behavior of a student or teacher, or how instructional time will or will not be used.

Values play an instrumental role in the principal's decision making in another way. Research conducted by Leithwood and colleagues (e.g., Leithwood & Stager, 1989) found that expert principals tend to have a high degree of clarity about their own personal values. They use their values as a "substitute for information" when solving problems in ambiguous and information poor situations. In sum, values both shape the thinking and actions of leaders and represent a potentially useful tool for working with and strengthening the school's learning culture.

Vision and Goals

A prominent synthesis of the school leadership effects research identified vision and goals as the most significant avenues through which school leaders impact learning (Hallinger & Heck, 1996). More recently, in a meta-analysis of the school leadership effects literature, Robinson, Lloyd, and Rowe (2008) reaffirmed this conclusion.

Indeed, they placed vision and goals as the second most significant path through which principals contribute to improved learning in classrooms. Vision refers to a broad picture of the direction in which the school seeks to move (e.g., educating the whole child). In contrast, goals refer to specific targets that will be achieved on the journey toward that vision.

Vision and goals achieve their impact through three primary means (Hallinger & Heck, 2002). First, they inspire people to contribute, even sacrifice, their effort toward the achievement of a collective goal. The motivational power of vision is highlighted in the theory of transformational leadership (Hallinger & Heck, 2002; Kantabutra & Avery, 2007; Leithwood, 1994). Through joining a collective effort to reach a challenging but *meaningful* goal, people may come to realize new aspirations and achieve higher levels of performance.

Second, goals can also impact performance by limiting staff attention to a more narrow range of desired ends and scope of activities. Clearly defined goals provide a basis for making decisions on staffing, resource allocation, and program adoption. They help to clarify what we will do and what we will not do.

Third, they act as connectors between the many and varied facets of school life and operation. Thus, with respect to Fig. 36.1, goals actually connect the three paths (i.e., culture, work processes, and people). As such, they serve to align the work of schools in a more coherent, meaningful manner (Hallinger, 1996; Walker, 2011).

In order to elaborate on these distinctions, we refer back to early research on effective schools which identified a "clear academic vision and mission" as a hallmark of these schools (Edmonds, 1979; Purkey & Smith, 1983). Subsequent research, however, found important differences across effective schools that appeared to be related to their social context. For example, Hallinger and Murphy found that effective schools in high-SES contexts with a history of success appeared to operate with a clear academic vision and mission, but without clearly defined goals (Hallinger & Murphy, 1986). In contrast, low-SES effective schools that had more recently "turned around" had both a clear academic vision and mission as well as clearly defined goals. The researchers proposed that in schools with a history of success, the vision was strongly embedded in the school's culture and provided implicit guidance in maintaining the school's direction. The low-SES effective schools had used goals as a means of developing a shared vision and direction for improvement.

A notable finding that emerged over the years with respect to the use of vision and goals in school improvement concerns the conceptualization of these constructs by scholars studying instructional leadership and transformational leadership. The instructional leadership literature asserted that goal-related constructs (e.g., vision, mission, goals) must contain an academic focus (e.g., Hallinger & Heck, 1996; Robinson et al., 2008). In contrast, the application of transformational leadership to education (e.g., Leithwood, 1994) left open the "terminal value" question as to the focus of the school's vision and goals. Recent research findings that compare these two different treatments of goals in research on leadership for learning appear to favor the instructional leadership approach (e.g., Robinson et al.).

Thus, for the purposes of school improvement, the school vision and goals *should* be learning focused. This highlights the critical role that principals play in sustaining a focus on learning in the school. We note that this finding is supported by research on successful implementation of school-based management as well as school improvement and applies even in contexts where there is strong collaborative leadership (Barth, 1990; Leithwood & Menzies, 1998).

Conclusion

We began this chapter by acknowledging two great leaders – leaders who led "with their values." In order to locate the importance of values in school, we outlined a number of perspectives on school leadership and on the importance of leaders melding vision and goals around improved student learning. We pull our argument together by reinforcing the importance leadership values in contributing to school success.

Both awareness of and the ability to clarify and articulate personal values and beliefs represent foundational competencies for leaders in any sector. Values guide decision making and approaches to problem solving, either implicitly or explicitly; explicit articulation is the preferred mode. Learning to use one's values, beliefs, and expectations in concert with the values of the school is a requirement for leadership for learning.

The ability to articulate a learning-focused vision that is shared by others and to set clear goals creates a base for all other leadership strategies and actions. The principal's vision and goals should interact with the core values of the school's leadership team and the school community more broadly. Visions written on paper only come to life through the routines and actions that are enacted on a daily basis. This was the message from research conducted by Dwyer (1985) 25 years ago. Leadership for learning is not the dramatic flourish or grand announcement of a new innovation. Rather, it is the sustained focus on improving the conditions for learning and creating coherence in values and actions across classrooms day in and day out in the school (Barth, 1980, 1990).

Throughout his distinguished career, Phil Hughes talked and wrote about values as essential for curriculum design, as pathways to equity, and as drivers for change. We all listened, and heard, but what really distinguished him as a leader was what he did – his actions – or the way he lived his values. He applied his leadership values consistently and with remarkable fidelity across all of the many and varied contexts within which he worked and lived. Paraphrasing from Mahatma Gandhi, as a leader, Phil Hughes lived the change that he wanted to see in the world around him.

References

Barth, R. (1980). *Run school run*. Cambridge, MA: Harvard University Press.
Barth, R. (1990). *Improving schools from within*. San Francisco: Jossey-Bass.

Beare, H. (2007). From centralized imperialism to dispersed management: The contribution of Phillip Hughes to the development of educational administration in Australia. In R. Maclean (Ed.), *Learning and teaching for the twenty-first century* (pp. 3–16). New York: Springer.

Deal, T., & Peterson, K. (1999). *Shaping school culture: The heart of leadership*. San Francisco: Jossey Bass.

Dwyer, D. (1985). Understanding the principal's contribution to instruction. *Peabody Journal of Education, 63*(1), 3–18.

Edmonds, R. (1979). Effective schools for the urban poor. *Educational Leadership, 37*, 15–24.

Fien, J. (2007). Care and compassion: Values commitment and attitude clarification in education. In R. Maclean (Ed.), *Learning and teaching for the twenty-first century* (pp. 187–212). New York: Springer.

Hall, G., & Hord, S. (2002). *Implementing change: Patterns, principles, and potholes*. Boston: Allyn & Bacon.

Hallinger, P. (1996). Challenging and changing Primrose. *Prime Focus, 2*(4), 20–29.

Hallinger, P., & Heck, R. (1996). Reassessing the principal's role in school effectiveness: A review of the empirical research, 1980–1995. *Educational Administration Quarterly, 32*(1), 5–44.

Hallinger, P., & Heck, R. H. (2002). What do you call people with visions? The role of vision, mission and goals in school leadership and improvement. In K. Leithwood, P. Hallinger, & Colleagues (Eds.), *The second international handbook of educational leadership and administration* (pp. 9–40). Dordrecht, The Netherlands: Kluwer.

Hallinger, P., & Murphy, J. (1986). The social context of effective schools. *American Journal of Education, 94*(3), 328–355.

Hughes, P. (2004). *How do teachers influence people? A study of the effects of teachers on some prominent Australians* (Australian College of Education. Refereed Paper No. 33). Canberra, Australia.

Kantabutra, S., & Avery, G. (2007). Vision effects in customer and staff satisfaction: An empirical investigation. *Leadership & Organization Development Journal, 28*(3), 209–229.

Kouzes, J., & Posner, B. (2007). *The leadership challenge*. San Francisco: Jossey Bass.

Leithwood, K. (1994). Leadership for school restructuring. *Educational Administration Quarterly, 30*(4), 498–518.

Leithwood, K., & Menzies, T. (1998). Forms and effects of school based management: A review. *Educational Policy, 12*(3), 325–346.

Leithwood, K., & Stager, M. (1989). Expertise in principal problem solving. *Educational Administration Quarterly, 25*(2), 126–61.

McCrimmon, M. (2004). *Kouzes and Posner on leadership – A critique*. Self-renewal group. http://www.google.com/url?sa=t&source=web&ct=res&cd=8&ved=0CCEQFjAH&url=http%3A%2F%2Fwww.cnn.com%2F2010%2FWORLD%2Fasiapcf%2F03%2F12%2Fthailand.protests%2Findex.html&ei=mQedS77OKMqHkAXYxPjYAQ&usg=AFQjCNF4HywZ29AJFOCnWzb5utZJ2abhvQ&sig2=2lc6r6YMrULKvqqZclz0RA. Accessed 24 May 2011.

Purkey, S., & Smith, M. (1983). Effective schools: A review. *The Elementary School Journal, 83*(4), 427–52.

Robinson, V., Lloyd, C., & Rowe, K. (2008). The impact of leadership on student outcomes: An analysis of the differential effects of leadership types. *Educational Administration Quarterly, 44*(5), 635–674.

Saphier, J., & King, M. (1985). Good seeds grow in strong cultures. *Educational Leadership, 42*(6), 67–74.

Stuart, J. (1949). *The thread that runs so true*. New York: Scribner.

Stuart, J. (1987). *To teach, to love*. Ashland, KY: Jesse Stuart Foundation.

Walker, A. (2011). *School leadership as connective activity*. Sydney, Australia: Australian Council for Educational Leaders.

Wolk, R. (2000). *Aspiring principals program* (video). Big Picture Productions.

Chapter 37
Education for Some or Education for All?

Confronting a Persistent Injustice in the Modern World

Rupert Maclean

Worldwide, several major challenges are currently being faced which threaten achieving sustainable development, peace building and poverty reduction. These include turmoil in the global financial markets and an uncertain outlook for the world economy; worldwide, a rapid rise in food prices by an average of more than 40% per year over the past 4 years, with the greatest rises being in developing countries; the trend of rising oil prices and a dependence on petroleum for producing consumer goods, food and transport, which increases pressure on the need to develop and utilize renewable forms of energy; various forms of national, regional and global terrorism and other forms of armed conflict; and climate-related problems such as global warming and desertification.

These problems are particularly marked in the Asia-Pacific region, which is home to almost two-thirds of the world's population of seven billion and most of the world's poor. Many developing countries in this region are experiencing rising social, economic and political tensions as a result of such difficulties.

To effectively address such challenges, what role can education and schooling play in contributing to a more just, equitable and peaceful world, where there is sustainable economic and social development for all, and an end to poverty? Although current international programmes to achieve lifelong Education for All (EFA) and Education for Sustainable Development (ESD), and the United Nations Millennium Development Goals (MDGs), provide a useful foundation for action, this is not sufficient. It is also important to give greater attention to devising concrete, action-orientated ways of promoting social justice and peace building, through means such as lifelong learning, values/ethics education, and skills development for employability, in the light of political realities.

R. Maclean (✉)
Chair Professor of International Education,
D3-2/F-02, The Hong Kong Institute of Education, The Hong Kong Institute
of Education (HKIEd), 10 Lo Ping Road, Tai Po, New Territories, Hong Kong
e-mail: maclean@ied.edu.hk

P. Hughes (ed.), *Achieving Quality Education for All*, Education in the Asia-Pacific
Region: Issues, Concerns and Prospects 20, DOI 10.1007/978-94-007-5294-8_37,
© Springer Science+Business Media Dordrecht 2013

Adopted more than 60 years ago, the United Nations Universal Declaration of Human Rights states that 'everyone has a right to education' (UNESCO, 1948). Yet there are millions of children, youths and adults throughout the world who have never set foot in a place called school. Others have briefly attended school but have dropped out early because the education provided has been of poor quality and not relevant to their needs and those of their family and community.

As the United Nations Educational, Scientific and Cultural Organisation (UNESCO) notes, 'Development and economic prosperity depend on the ability of countries to educate all members of their societies and offer them lifelong learning. An innovative society prepares its people not only to embrace and adapt to change but also to manage and influence it. Education enriches cultures, and creates mutual understanding that underpins peaceful societies. UNESCO is guided by upholding education as a human right and as an essential element for the full development of human potential'.[1]

Worldwide, and particularly in the Asia-Pacific region, the current education provision in many countries remains seriously deficient. The situation is so serious that many governments and members of the international development and aid communities believe that more decisive and better coordinated action must be taken if education and schooling are to be made relevant, to improve qualitatively and to be universally available to all.

I understand the importance of education and lifelong learning from both personal and professional experience. At the personal level, I am the eldest son of parents who migrated to Australia from India after the end of the Second World War in search of a better life for themselves and their children. I know from my own experience just how important it has been for my life chances and those of my family to have had the opportunity to receive a high-quality, relevant education.

Lifelong learning was important for my father, who migrated to Australia with secondary school qualifications but then went on to complete a Bachelor of Economics/Commerce degree through distance education correspondence courses at the University of Queensland. He and my mother viewed education as the key to success in their newly adopted country and so made every effort to ensure that all their children (two boys and a girl) had an opportunity to do well at school and go on to complete tertiary studies.

After first landing by ship in Perth, my family moved to various parts of Australia – Sydney, Brisbane, Elizabeth, Moana Beach in Adelaide and Woomera in South Australia – to improve their employment situation and opportunities in life. They eventually settled in Melbourne where I commenced secondary school at Ashwood High School, later going on to Trinity Grammar School. In all, I went to 4 different primary schools over 6 years of primary education and then 2 secondary schools.

In terms of my own education, my success at school mainly occurred because of the excellent teachers I was fortunate enough to meet and whose classes I attended:

---

[1] UNESCO Medium Term Strategy, 2008–2013, paragraph 32.

Miss Doran when I was attending Woomera Central School in South Australia, Mr. Everett when I was at Ashwood High School in Melbourne and Mr. MacFarlane at Trinity Grammar School, Melbourne. These teachers made all the difference to my education in that they interested and motivated me to study, to read, to do my homework and to want to succeed.

When my father first arrived in Australia, he worked in factories, but through hard work and part-time study, he was successful in improving his education qualifications and was able to move from factory manual work into clerical positions and then on to high-level professional positions within the Commonwealth Public Service.

It is because of my own schooling experience and the education experiences of my family that I have an enduring interest in educational disadvantage, and with what lifelong learning and excellent teachers can do to liberate (as the Delors Report puts it) 'through learning, the treasure within' each of us. As a beginning teacher, I worked at Dandenong High School in Melbourne with lower socio-economic disadvantaged students many of whom were the children of migrants from Europe working in the local car factories. In my Master's thesis at the University of Bristol, I was particularly interested in undertaking research on gender issues in education concerning the educational disadvantages often suffered by girls and women, and when I was a lecturer at the University of Tasmania, my major research areas concerned the characteristics of successful teachers and educational disadvantage. I was also a member of the Commonwealth Government's Disadvantaged Schools Committee which was responsible for administering special funds and resources for disadvantaged schools in Tasmania. It is because of this interest in educational disadvantage that I decided to join UNESCO, where I was particularly involved in helping devise innovative ways of strengthening and upgrading education in developing countries through educational innovation for development.

Professionally, I worked within the Education Sector in UNESCO[2] for almost two decades with postings in Yangon, Bangkok, Paris and Bonn.

Much of my work focused on assisting countries in the vast and diverse Asia-Pacific region, where countries and their populations face some of the most pressing education problems facing human kind.[3] The region of Asia-Pacific is outstanding for the vast range of diversities that encompass almost all aspects of life, whether geographical, socio-economic, cultural, political or developmental. In this region, there are countries of vast landmasses (China, India and Australia) and also island countries lying in expansive ocean areas (the Maldives, and the Pacific island countries) and large multi-island states such as Indonesia and the Philippines. Countries with the largest populations (China – 1.4 billion; India – 1.2 billion) and the most rapidly

---

[2] http://www.unesco.org

[3] These statistics about education in the Asia-Pacific region come from UNESCO Global Monitoring Reports (various from 2002). *Global Monitoring Reports: Education for All.* UNESCO Publishing: Paris.

growing megacities are to be found in the region, as are countries with relatively small populations (Bhutan, 697,000; Niue in the Pacific, with some 2,300 inhabitants). The levels of economic development also vary widely, with some of the richest countries (such as Japan and Australia) and some of the poorest countries (such as Bangladesh and Burma) on earth.

The enormous disparities between rich and poor are brought home graphically when one considers that it is estimated that 60% of those living in the region have never used a telephone, whilst at the same time millions of others can afford access to the latest computers and communications technologies in their own homes.

Asia contains the largest number of poor of any region in the world, and in overall terms, the number is increasing. The incidence of those living below the poverty line remains in excess of 40% in some developing economies in the Asia-Pacific region. Such widespread poverty is a destabilizing factor adversely affecting health, social and educational services and levels of educational attainment. It also intensifies gender disparities.

Most of the major education problems currently facing humankind are evident in the Asia-Pacific region. Despite a commitment in 1990 by most countries, international aid organizations and the broad donor community to achieving Education for All by the year 2000, the Asia-Pacific region continues to contain the largest proportion of the world's illiterates. At present there are estimated to be 625 million illiterates in the Asia-Pacific region: 71% of the world's total, of whom 64% are women and girls.

Some of the disparities that exist between subregions in Asia-Pacific are particularly disturbing. For example, for countries in South Asia, the average literacy rate is currently 42% compared with 72% in East and Southeast Asia; in South Asia, life expectancy is 10 years lower than for those living in East and Southeast Asia.

These statistics are daunting. In Asia-Pacific, 56% of the school-age population (6–11 years old) are not enrolled in primary education. Of those who do enroll, at least one-third dropped out of school before completing the primary cycle. The reasons are compelling and well known: poverty, social exclusion, socio-economic gaps, urban–rural disparities, rampant mismanagement and a lack of adequate and relevant educational programmes. Moreover, gender disparities make the picture bleaker: of the out-of-school children in the region, 62% are girls, concentrated especially in South Asia.

In spite of such challenges and diversity, there is a common, positive thread in that all countries in Asia and the Pacific believe that in order to achieve poverty eradication, sustainable human development, justice and equity in all respects, there is a need to make greater efforts to improve the quality, effectiveness and relevance of education and schooling, with particular reference to lifelong learning. The reform and re-engineering of education and schooling is receiving increasing attention from governments in the region, especially in the less developed countries, with particular reference to achieving universal literacy, lifelong learning and education for all.

The reality is that we already largely know in specific terms what needs to be done to promote sustainable development; peace and poverty alleviation, through the reform; strengthening of education and schooling; and lifelong learning. The question that needs to be answered is 'do we have the courage and commitment to take the necessary action?' This is a moral issue rather than a technical one.

In my view, there is a need to reassess our priorities and in so doing to invest more resources in 'weapons for peace' (such as lifelong education for all, universal health care and clean water and sanitation) rather than weapons of war (military expenditure and armaments of various types). There are some countries in the Asia-Pacific region where the percentage of gross domestic product spent on military expenditure is currently equal to, or greater than, their level of public expenditure on education.

Education is the key to making peace, poverty alleviation and sustainability both a reality and a success. It is through education that a healthy and respectful attitude towards our planet can be promoted, encouraging the safeguarding of environmental resources for a sustainable world for generations to come. In addition, education is a major contributor to eliminating conflict and achieving peace. This is because education addresses the root causes of conflict by preparing people for jobs whilst simultaneously playing a vital role in changing perceptions of conflict within a specific country, through (for example) questioning the stereotypes on which various forms of discrimination, such as racism, are based, through the promotion of values and the encouragement of dialogue between ethnic and racial groups.

These matters are very much currently front of mind for me because in Hong Kong, I have been working on several policy-orientated research projects concerned with documenting and explaining various dimensions of educational disadvantage, the lack of high-quality lifelong education for all and education for sustainable development. These projects concern the transition of students at the end of secondary schooling in Hong Kong into further academic study, vocational education and employment to document and explain their destinations in terms of their socio-economic, ethnic-racial and other characteristics: 'Children on the Move', a study of the education careers of young people who are moving within and between countries as migrants in various parts of the world; a UNICEF and UNESCO project on out-of-school children in 25 developing and/or transition countries in Asia, Africa, Latin America and Eastern Europe; and a study of the greening of the Hong Kong economy through skills development for employability to achieve sustainable development.

Let me conclude by referring to the words of my friend and mentor Professor Phillip Hughes, Emeritus Professor of Education at the University of Tasmania, Hobart,[4] who says

> The future is not something that happens but something which is constructed – constructed on our choices, or our failure to choose …. The nature of the major problems which face us shows us clearly the nature of those choices. They are not technical but moral choices. They are a statement of what we believe a good society should be.

---

[4] Phillip Hughes, *Australia 2000: A Shared Challenge, a Shared Response.*

I strongly believe we have it within our power to construct a better future and a better world through lifelong education for all, and education for sustainable development, in support of poverty alleviation and peace building. The challenge is to make the choices which, as Phil Hughes reminds us, are more moral than technical in nature and then to commit the necessary resources to bring these to fruition.

We already know the range of problems and stumbling blocks that confront us and need to be addressed, both at the regional and global levels, if we are to be successful in peace building and achieving sustainable social and economic development. These are well researched and documented. We also largely know from the evidence available what needs to be done to address these problems to promote lifelong learning for sustainable development, peace building and poverty alleviation. But do we as a community have the courage and commitment, and do our political leaders have the political will, to take the necessary action?

There are no lack of attempts to reform educational systems to address the types of changes referred to in this chapter. Some reform efforts, however, are based largely on improving existing practice, on efficiency rather than effectiveness, and are aimed at modifying or improving the existing situation, rather than coming up with a new paradigm. Thus, for example, some curriculum reform focuses on how to improve and sequence the teaching of specific subject matter blocks, rather than on questioning whether to teach particular subjects at all or replace them with new learning content. Another example of an inadequate approach would be proposals to expand access to an existing educational system without questioning whether the system itself is truly designed to reach the unreached. Reforms in university education frequently look to alternative financing mechanisms and equitable cost recovery measures without questioning whether expansion ultimately leads to an emphasis on credentialing rather than competence and on an eventual devaluation of such credentials.

Rather than 'tinkering with the system', there is a need to 're-engineer education for change', that is, to examine the fundamental, often taken for granted and unexamined values and practices upon which current systems are built and to rebuild these from their foundations upwards.

Reference

UNESCO (1948). *Universal declaration of human rights*. Paris: UNESCO Publishing.

About the Contributors

Joan Abbott-Chapman holds a research appointment at the Menzies Research Institute, University of Tasmania, after retiring as professor of education at the University at the end of 2010. Joan worked with Phil Hughes over a number of years as deputy director of the Youth Education Studies Centre, when Phil was director, later succeeding him as director. Her research reflects a life-long passion to improve the post-compulsory participation of disadvantaged students. This arises from childhood experiences as a working class girl growing up in the North of England, encouraged by parents who were keen for her and her sister to enter university, the first in the family to do so, and teachers who inspired her to reach this goal.

Don Aitkin was a vice chancellor and president of the University of Canberra and before that the foundation chairman of the Australian Research Council. He counts himself as fortunate in never having had a poor teacher and hopes he was never one himself.

Don Anderson taught science in private schools before switching to arts and later a PhD in social psychology at the University of Melbourne. After posts in psychology and education research at Melbourne, he moved to the Australian National University to establish the multidisciplinary Education Research Unit in the Research School of Social Sciences. A central interest is socialisation or what institutions do to people, and, from this perspective, he has studied various professions, the family, schools, colleges and universities. He has conducted education inquiries for Australian governments, OECD and UNESCO. He is emeritus professor and visiting fellow at the ANU.

Geoff W. Beeson has worked as an education consultant to universities and school systems in Australia and Asia for the past several years. Before that, he was provice chancellor and professor at Deakin University in Melbourne, Australia. He started his career teaching science and mathematics in Victorian (Australia) high schools, and subsequently maintained his contact with schools through involvement in teacher education and a variety of school-based projects. He grew up in Reservoir, a working-class suburb of Melbourne, and was one of the first students from that suburb to attend university.

P. Hughes (ed.), *Achieving Quality Education for All*, Education in the Asia-Pacific Region: Issues, Concerns and Prospects 20, DOI 10.1007/978-94-007-5294-8, © Springer Science+Business Media Dordrecht 2013

Raj Bhowon has had a productive career in his own country of Mauritius and also with the World Bank, the International Financial Corporation and with UNESCO in Paris. His graduate work began at the University of Leeds and continued with his Ph D in education at the University of Tasmania. He added further to his experience by working overseas on approaches to educational reform. He returned home to Mauritius to help in the reorganisation of education in that country. On his return to Mauritius, he has continued to play a major role in education and public life. He has been the Director of Education and also Minister for Rural Development and is currently a Member of Parliament in that country.

Professor Denise Bradley AC began her career as an untrained secondary teacher in a public school in South Australia. A product of catholic convents, she has spent her entire career in education in public schools, colleges and universities. Various state and national responsibilities over the last three decades have seen her involved in many aspects of policy development and implementation in schools, Vocational education and training (VET) and higher education. She has been particularly concerned with equity in education and has published in the fields of the nonsexist curriculum, access to higher education and opportunities for women in education.

Dr Paul Brock is the director of Learning and Development Research, New South Wales Department of Education and Training and an adjunct professor in the Faculty of Education and Social Work, The University of Sydney. Dr Brock is also an honorary research fellow within the University of New England; an honorary associate in the Centre for Values Ethics and Law in Medicine within the Faculty of Medicine, The University of Sydney; and a vice patron of the Motor Neurone Disease Association, NSW.

In 1996, he was diagnosed with motor neurone disease. In 2006, Dr Brock was awarded the Order of Australia 'for service to public education, particularly as an adviser and author in the areas of strategic policy development, to maintaining high standards of teaching and professionalism, and to people with motor neurone disease'. In 2009, he was selected by the Sydney Morning Herald as one of the five most influential people in NSW education within that newspaper's list of Sydney's 100 'most influential people' for that year.

Françoise Caillods played a major role in the Institute of Educational Planning in Paris (IIEP), where she worked for over four decades. She began her international career at IIEP in 1969 and has been part of its broadening of emphasis from the post-war theme of education and manpower, through to its more active role in educational planning and its links with the current more comprehensive themes of education, employment and work. She has contributed to the institute's role with the programme in Paris to train educational planners but is even more widely known for her extensive writing on the needs in that area. In her work, she has travelled to most parts of the world both as consultant and teacher.

Brian J. Caldwell is Managing Director and Principal Consultant at Educational Transformations and Professorial Fellow at the University of Melbourne where he served as Dean of Education at the University from 1998 to 2004.

Margaret Clark is currently the CEO of the Australian College of Educators and immediately prior to this spent nearly 4 years working in the Northern Territory (NT), initially with the Commonwealth Office of Indigenous Policy Coordination as deputy state director and later transferring to the NT Department of Education and Training as a director of school improvement. Margaret went to a local socially mixed public school and developed a passion for social justice as a young teenager which has continued and hopefully matured. Her church and family were ideal breeding grounds for this. When younger Margaret sought to distance herself from her well-known, highly respected father (Phil Hughes), he remained and a source of great pride and inspiration. Her particular passion is improving the policy and research engagement around effective service delivery policy frameworks and overcoming disadvantage in remote Indigenous communities.

Helen Connell has worked independently in educational research in several countries and has collaborated on many projects with Malcolm Skilbeck.

Lyndsay Connors developed an interest in education when she was a parent of young children, through her participation in their Canberra preschool community. She is very conscious of the debt she owes to those who fought for a strong public education system, of which her family continues to be the direct beneficiaries. Her interest led to her enrolling in a Diploma of Education at the then Canberra College of Advanced Education and to a career involving schools policy formulation and implementation. As a feminist, she has contributed to policies designed to broaden educational opportunities for women and girls. She is currently the national president of the Australian College of Educators.

Patrick Daunt Phil and Patrick were in the same college at Oxford in the 1940s just after the war, a time of weak beer and strong opinions, bad food and good friendships.

After a time in Australia, he taught classics at Christ's Hospital, happily enough but without being sure why he was doing what he was doing. These doubts ended with the coming of comprehensive schools; Patrick became head of one (Thomas Bennett School, Crawley, known for radical principles and practices) and then chairman of the national campaign for comprehensive education. Britain's accession to the European Community in 1973 offered Patrick something else he could also believe in. So Patrick to Brussels, where he worked in the education department of the European Commission, and then headed the first European action programme for disabled people. Since retiring, Patrick has been chairman of the Association for Spina Bifida and Hydrocephalus in England and Wales and UNESCO's consultant to the Ministry of Education in Bucharest for the review of the Romanian system of special education. He is now an Anglican churchwarden in a small village in Cambridgeshire.

Christine Deer began her professional career as a teacher in NSW schools, moving into university teaching at Macquarie University in 1969. She moved to the University of Technology, Sydney, in 1990 as head of teacher education, working there for the next decade. Her interests in education are wide, with a deep commitment to equity and social justice. Christine has had a major role working with community organisations and in professional associations at both state and national levels. She was awarded the Sir Harold Wyndham Medal by the NSW Chapter Australian College of Educators in 1999.

Neil Dempster is a professor in educational leadership at Griffith University and former dean of its Faculty of Education. His research interests are in leadership for learning, school governance, school improvement and professional development. Neil is a fellow of the Australian College of Educators where he was the national president in 2006–2007. Recent publications include two edited books, one *The Treasure Within: Leadership and Succession Planning (2007)* and the other, *Connecting Leadership and Learning: Principles for Practice*, Routledge (2009). Neil has written widely on leadership and ethics in leadership. Currently, he is engaged in the Australian Primary Principals' led National Project and is the chief investigator on an Australian Research Council funded Discovery Project on adolescent leadership. He is an Australasian regional editor for the Springer International Handbook on Leadership and Learning.

Alexandra Draxler joined UNESCO as an education specialist in 1971 after working for Cornell University and then the Deutsches Institute fur Fernstudien of the University of Tubingen. From 1993 to 1996, she served as secretary of the International Commission on Education for the twenty-first century, chaired by Jacques Delors. Their report, 'Learning the Treasure Within', was delivered to UNESCO and has been published in 22 languages. Alexa later worked for UNESCO in a number of key areas including the major programme on HIV-AIDS. She is currently working in Paris as an education consultant and is the vice-president of the Association for the Promotion of Education.

John Fien is professor of Sustainability in the Innovation Leadership programme of RMIT University, where he is responsible for supporting research on social, environmental and economic sustainability across the Business and Design and Social Context Portfolios. An interdisciplinary background in education and training, natural resource management, public participation and sustainable consumption equip him to work across this broad sustainability agenda and to develop partnerships of university research teams, business and industry, government, NGOs, schools and communities.

His research focuses on social change processes for advancing sustainable development, including education and training for sustainability, organisational learning and change for sustainability, citizen science approaches to natural resource management, especially within integrated catchment management and coastal management, and public participation in local planning.

Michael Fullan is currently chief education adviser to the Premier of Ontario. He has served as Dean of Education at the Faculty of Education at University of Toronto and Dean of Ontario Institute for Studies in Education, University of Toronto. He credits his grandfather and parents for not allowing him to drop out of school at age 16 and instead continuing on eventually to earn a Ph.D. in sociology at the University of Toronto. He works with a small group of colleagues on the improvement of education systems around the world.

John Grant was advised early in his career by a very senior public servant not to confine himself 'only to education'. He is delighted to have ignored that advice. He taught in schools in NSW and Northern Territory (NT) and as a university lecturer. He was appointed director of curriculum in the NT and then in the Australian Capital Territory. He then moved into tertiary education as an assistant commissioner of the Commonwealth Tertiary Education Commission and then deputy vice chancellor of the University of Canberra. Subsequently, he moved to the ANU as a visiting fellow and a member of its emeritus faculty. John cites his time as a teacher at Maningrida, a remote indigenous community in the Northern Territory, in the 1960s as the most influential period for him, both personally and professionally.

Philip Hallinger is a Chair Professor at the Hong Kong Institute of Education. Following a successful academic career in the USA, he has worked in Asia for more than 20 years, largely in Thailand and now in Hong Kong. Philip has published widely in leader development, cross cultural studies, and strategic leadership as well as in quality in education and educational reform.

Ian Hill has been deputy director general of the International Baccalaureate (IB) organisation in Geneva since 2000 and joined the organisation in 1993 as the director for Africa, Europe and the Middle East. Prior to that, Ian was head of a bilingual (English/French) IB school in the South of France, and before leaving Tasmania late in 1989, he was senior private secretary to the Minister for Education in that state. Ian has published and spoken widely on international education. Phil Hughes supervised Ian's PhD at the University of Tasmania.

Michael Jones is a founding member and inaugural managing director of the Wadjularbinna Foundation, a community based, not-for-profit foundation which facilitates educational opportunities for Aboriginal students in Queensland's Gulf Country. He recently graduated from the Australian National University with a Bachelor of Arts (Hons) and Bachelor of Laws (Hons). In September 2011, he commenced studying an MPhil in Politics at the University of Oxford on a Rhodes Scholarship.

Don Jordan is an experienced educator, having taught in range of primary and secondary schools in Tasmania. His perspective has been enriched by his work with disaffected students in the United Kingdom, with Bachelor of Education students in the Gaza Strip and with curriculum developers and teachers on behalf of UNICEF in the Maldives. In March 2011, Don was invited by the Mechai Viravaidya Foundation, to evaluate the leadership, curriculum, resources and teacher training and experience, at the Mechai Pattana Secondary School in northeastern Thailand, in preparation for it to become a demonstration school for the proposed Teacher Training Institute. Don has a particular interest in the philosophical and theoretical place of computers in primary classrooms in Tasmania and their effect on students' learning, behaviour and social development.

Kerry J. Kennedy is currently Chair Professor of Curriculum Studies at The Hong Kong Institute of Education where he has worked for the past 10 years. He was educated at government schools in Sydney's western suburbs where he returned to teach shortly after graduating. He benefited from a visionary school Principal during his secondary education and teachers who went out of their way to support him. He is grateful for his graduate studies at Stanford University and the critical spirit he learnt as the key element of systematic inquiry. Currently his work includes investigating civic and citizenship education in the Asia Pacific region, exploring classrooms in Hong Kong to identify how they can better support ethnic minority students and supervising doctoral students. He is the Series Editor for the *Routledge Series on Schools and Schooling in Asia.*

Joanna Le Métais is an independent consultant, drawing on her experience in teaching, education administration and nearly 20 years as head of International Project Development at the National Foundation for Educational Research in England and Wales, where she devised and led the INCA electronic resource on international curricula and assessment (www.inca.org.uk). Joanna's work includes writing, speaking and advising on curriculum review, reform and development internationally, most recently as part of a UNICEF-funded team in the Republic of the Maldives. She was educated in the Netherlands, Australia, England and France. One teacher who left an indelible mark was Mrs Hancock, the primary school teacher in Modbury, South Australia, who took Joanna's arrival as a Dutch speaker in her mixed age class of 30 pupils in her stride and, by the end of 6 months, had developed Joanna's English language skills to the extent that she came equal second in a class of 9. Thank you, Mrs Hancock!

Mal Lee is an educational consultant and author specializing in the evolution of teaching and schooling from the traditional paper-based mode to one that is digital, and in turn networked, and the impact of the technology on that evolution. Mal's is a macro focus examining all the elements associated with the development, leadership and operation of schools within a digital and increasingly as networked school communities. Mal is a former director of schools, secondary college principal, technology company director and a member of the Mayer Committee that identified the key competencies for Australia's schools. A fellow of Australian Council for Educational Administration, Mal has been closely associated with the use of digital technology in schooling, particularly by the school leadership for the past two decades.

Rupert Maclean is currently a Chair Professor of International Education, UNESCO Chair in Skills Development for Employability (TVET) and Director of the Centre for Lifelong Learning Research for Development at the Hong Kong Institute of Education. Prior to joining HKIEd in 2009, he worked for the Education Sector in the United Nations Educational, Science and Cultural Organisation (UNESCO) for almost 20 years. Rupert commenced his career as a secondary school teacher of economics and history at Dandenong High School in Victoria, before undertaking postgraduate studies at the University of Bristol, and then moving into teacher education at the Berkshire College of Education in the UK and in the Faculty of Education at the University of Tasmania. In the Queen's Birthday Honours List for Australia announced on 13 June 2011, he was appointed an Officer in the General Division of the Order of Australia (AO) 'for distinguished service of a high degree to humanity at large through his work as an international academic and professional working to improve education in developing countries'.

Geoff N. Masters has been CEO of the Australian Council for Educational Research (ACER) since 1998. Educated in government schools in a Western Australia coal mining town, he considers himself fortunate to have had teachers who encouraged his love of learning and held him to high expectations. He includes among these influential teachers his father, timber worker and lay preacher Norm Masters; his mother, primary teacher Lola; and his University of Chicago PhD supervisor Ben Wright. Geoff's current work includes advice to education systems on strategies for enhancing teaching and learning and raising expectations and outcomes for all learners. He is an adjunct professor in the Queensland Brain Institute.

Barry McGaw is a vice chancellor's fellow at the University of Melbourne and chair of the Australian curriculum, assessment and reporting authority. He was previously director for education at the Organisation for Economic Co-operation and Development (OECD) and executive director of the Australian Council for Educational Research. He first met Phil Hughes in 1970 when both were members of the executive of the Australian Association for Research in Education, an organisation in which he succeeded Phil as President in 1976. There were many personal and professional contacts over the following years but none richer than in extended periods in Paris between 1998 and 2005 when Barry was at OECD and Phil was working at UNESCO. Phil was always an inspiration, showing how much could be done and for how long it could be done.

Deborah Meier has been involved in public education in the USA for over 50 years—first as a parent and then as a teacher, principal, reformer, advocate, and writer. She began her career as a prekindergarten and kindergarten teacher. She won a MacArthur for her work—the first educator to do so—in 1987, has written many books starting with The Power of Their Ideas in 1992, and founded a network of small public schools in East Harlem and later in Boston. The schools she has helped create serve predominantly low-income African-American and Latino students and include a typical range of students in terms of academic skills, special needs, etc. There are no entrance requirements. These schools are considered exemplars of reform nationally and affiliates of the national Coalition of Essential Schools founded by Dr. Ted Sizer. Deborah W. Meier is currently at New York University's Steinhardt School of Education, as senior scholar as well as board member and director of New Ventures at Mission Hill, director and advisor to Forum for Democracy and Education, and on the Board of the Coalition of Essential Schools.

Carol Nicoll was chief executive officer at the Australian Learning and Teaching Council from February 2010 until its closure in late 2011. She has a range of experiences in the education sector, including as a secondary school teacher, university academic and senior public servant in a number of iterations of the Australian federal department of education. In all of these roles, she has proudly claimed her identity as a teacher.

Susan Pascoe AM has shared Phillip Hughes' passion for education in her professional, civic and personal life. She has worked as a teacher, researcher, administrator, advocate and leader. Prior to taking on her role as commissioner in Victoria's State Services Authority, she was chief executive of the Victorian

Curriculum and Assessment Authority and chair and chief executive of the Catholic Education Commission of Victoria. She chaired the Australian National Commission for UNESCO and was president of the Australian College of Educators. She remains convinced of the transformative power of education, especially in the lives of the underprivileged.

Colin Power began his career as a science teacher in Queensland schools, moving to the department's research and curriculum section. Moving to the University of Queensland, he continued his research interests in curriculum and then accepted an invitation to be foundation professor of education at Flinders University, South Australia. He was invited to join the education section of UNESCO in Paris and had a distinguished career there for 12 years, first as assistant director-general and then deputy director-general, the highest post for an Australian at UNESCO. Colin is a strong advocate of education for all and for quality education directed to the full development of the human personality as a global public good.

Sylvia Schmelkes is a sociologist, with an MA in educational research from Universidad Iberoamericana in Mexico City and 33 years in educational research, in adult education, quality of basic education, values education, and intercultural education. She has published more than 150 books, book chapters, and articles. She was academic director of the Centro de Estudios Educativos. Sylvia founded and was named coordinator general of Bilingual and Intercultural Education in the Secretariat of Education between 2001 and 2007. She now directs the Institute for Research on the Development of Education in the Universidad Iberoamericana in Mexico City. She chaired the Governing Board of the Centre for Educational Research and Innovation of OECD between 2002 and 2004. She was awarded the Comenius Medal by the Czech Republic and UNESCO for contributions to educational research in 2008.

Nancy Faust Sizer formed a powerful partnership in American education, through programs such as the Coalition for Effective Schools, and also at the school level as co-principals of two charter schools. Nancy continues her interest in teaching at both university and school level.

Malcolm Skilbeck has had a varied and extensive career in education as a teacher, university academic and administrator, working in several national systems and in and for international organisations. His current educational interests are in teaching as a moral and intellectual profession, lifelong learning and the origins and development of nature study within the school curriculum.

Paris Strom is an associate professor of Educational Foundations, Leadership and Technology, Auburn University, Auburn, Alabama, USA. Educated in Australia and Arizona, he has published widely in the field of educational psychology. A groundbreaking book in partnership with Robert Strom was Parents of Young Children, exploring the more complicated challenges and opportunities faced by the current generation of parents than did prior generations. Robert and Paris Strom co-authored a number of books on education including Adolescents in the Internet Age.

Robert Strom is a professor of Educational Leadership and Innovation in the Mary Lou Fulton College of Education at Arizona State University. He is a graduate of Macalester College (B.S.), University of Minnesota (M.A.), University of Michigan (Ph.D.), and postdoctoral fellowship from Cambridge University. Bob's goals are to support the improvement of education at all age levels by designing instruments to evaluate achievement, detect learning needs, and assess the effects of intervention; and preparing curriculum to improve performance of students, teachers, and parents. He has published widely. His most recent work has been with preparing senior citizens to play a useful role in schools. At Arizona State, Bob has been recipient of the Outstanding Mentor Award from the Graduate College and the Outstanding Research Award from the Alumni Foundation.

Edna Tait is currently the Education Advisor on the New Zealand National Commission for UNESCO. She was a principal of a New Zealand state, co-educational secondary school for 13 years and then Director of the UNESCO Office for Pacific Member States for 10 years. She continues to provide assistance with UNESCO projects in the Pacific and Asia. Edna grew up in a remote New Zealand bush community that had six families and a primary school of 12 children. She was taught to question everything by her bushman father David Tait and her mother Edith who had been a waitress but dreamed that their children might work in offices. Schools supported Edna's parents' emphasis on questioning and extended her awareness of the importance of thinking skills. Her doctoral thesis on international work for education was guided by professors who accepted only a vigorous challenge of all information gathered. She has been awarded the New Zealand medal for services to education and made a Companion of the Queens Service Order for services to the Pacific.

Allan Walker is a Joseph Lau Chair Professor and Director of Asia Pacific Centre for Leadership and Change at The Hong Kong Institute of Education. Beginning as a teacher and principal in Australia, he completed graduate studies in the United States. He worked in universities in Singapore, Hong Kong, and Darwin. Allan's research interests include principal preparation and leader learning, leader recruitment and selection, cultural influences on school leadership, leadership ethics, and the principalship in and across Chinese societies. He has completed a number of large-scale funded research projects.

Max Walsh was a mathematics and science teacher, then science consultant in the Tasmanian government education system before joining the University of Tasmania Faculty of Education in Hobart in the same year (1981) that Phillip Hughes became professor of education of the faculty. A short-term assignment in the Philippines in 1997 on a development aid project for AusAID resulted in a career-changing decision to work full time as a freelance educational consultant in SE Asia, providing support for developing countries' educational reforms. His work is dedicated to the memory of his parents, Ron and Sarah Walsh, who unselfishly ensured that Max and his three brothers would get the best education possible through tough economic times.

Index

A
ACARA. *See* Australian Curriculum,
     Assessment and Reporting
     Authority (ACARA)
Agrarian Age, 168
American Educational Research Association
     (AERA), 94
Australia
     Australian education (*see* Australian
        education)
     Australian school (*see* Australian school)
     public and private school (*see* Public and
        private school)
Australian Capital Territory (ACT), 33, 126
Australian Curriculum, Assessment and
     Reporting Authority (ACARA), 59
Australian education
     childhood education, 154–155
     curriculum, 155–156
     government funds, 156
     school finance, 156
     teacher, centrality of, 153–154
Australian Institute for Teaching and School
     Leadership (AITSL), 57
Australian school
     educational arrangements, 10
     educational opportunities, 10
     hidden curriculum, 10–11
     holistic planning, 10
     laissez-faire approach, 12
     leadership, 11
     school atmosphere, 12
     school environment, 9
     school systems, 10
     social and economic circumstances, 9
     student performance, 12
     teacher and parent support, 12
     universal compulsory education, 9
     wider school community, 11

B
Balanced schooling
     collaboration, 181
     digital and networking technology, 179
     facilitation, 181–182
     formal and informal, 178
     function and purpose, 178
     holistic education, 179
     lack of professional advice, 178
     learning, 179
     literacy and numeracy, 179
     nature, 177
     Networked School Community,
        180–181
     organizational structure, 179
     primary schooling, 179
     school performance table, 179
Belief
     achievement gaps, 6
     achievement levels, 6
     educational achievement, 5
     grade inflation, 5
     human intelligence, 4
     international studies, 5
     learning areas, 7
     learning opportunities, 5
     PISA, 5
     scarce resource, 4
     self-efficacy, 4
     student learning, 7
     TIMSS, 5
     visualise success, 3
Bureaucratic Age, 168

Printed by Printforce, the Netherlands